THE BOWLING
CHRONICLES

THE BOWLING CHRONICLES
Collected Writings of Dr. Jake

J.R. Schmidt

McFarland & Company, Inc., Publishers
Jefferson, North Carolina

All photographs are from the *Bowlers Journal International* archive unless otherwise noted.

LIBRARY OF CONGRESS CATALOGUING-IN-PUBLICATION DATA

Names: Schmidt, J. R., 1947– author.
Title: The Bowling Chronicles : Collected Writings of Dr. Jake / J.R. Schmidt.
Description: Jefferson, North Carolina : McFarland & Company, Inc., Publishers, 2017. | Includes index.
Identifiers: LCCN 2016055171 | ISBN 9781476667751 (softcover : acid free paper) ∞
Subjects: LCSH: Bowling—United States—History—Anecdotes. | Bowlers—United States—Biography—Anecdotes.
Classification: LCC GV904 S34 2017 | DDC 794.6—dc23
LC record available at https://lccn.loc.gov/2016055171

BRITISH LIBRARY CATALOGUING DATA ARE AVAILABLE

ISBN (print) 978-1-4766-6775-1
ISBN (ebook) 978-1-4766-2806-6

© 2017 J. R. Schmidt. All rights reserved

No part of this book may be reproduced or transmitted in any form or by any means, electronic or mechanical, including photocopying or recording, or by any information storage and retrieval system, without permission in writing from the publisher.

Front cover: photograph of the stylish Joe Kristof (*Bowlers Journal International* archive)

Printed in the United States of America

McFarland & Company, Inc., Publishers
 Box 611, Jefferson, North Carolina 28640
  www.mcfarlandpub.com

To Terri
Not because I'm supposed to,
but because she deserves it

Table of Contents

Acknowledgments	xi
Preface	1
A (Very) Short History of Bowling	3
Mort the Moose	5
Long John Koster	6
El Zunko	8
Magnificent Marino	10
The Perfect Game	12
Eddie Kawolics and Me	15
The Old Sarge	17
Uncanonized Saint	19
An Interview with Jimmy Blouin	21
The Prince of Bowlers	29
Professor Krumske	33
The Legend of Junie McMahon	34
Seven Days to 300	38
The Flying Falstaffs	40
Bowling's *Cinéma Vérité*	43
That's Shaul, Folks!	45
Nobody's Buddy	46
Things I Learned While Looking Up Other Things	49
Belle of the Ball	50
The Joker Is Wild	53
The Patriotic Bowling Tournament	55
The Greatest Team Match	57

Bowling's Landmark Tour	59
Don Carter: An Appreciation	63
A Dream in Detroit	66
The Original Perfect Man	68
One Soldier's Story	70
Famous Nicknames	72
The Infamous 5–7–10	75
Fabulous Faetz-Niesen	77
How Jimmy Smith Became Champ	79
The Big Three Bowlers Tour	81
Where Have You Gone, Morrie Oppenheim?	83
How We Learned to Love the 10-Pin	88
Weighty Bowlers	90
More Things I Learned While Looking Up Other Things	92
The First ABC Tournament	94
Joe Norris, R.I.P.	96
Style and Substance	98
Brunswick or AMF?	103
Billy G.	104
Jerry Lewis Goes Bowling	106
Church Alleys	109
The Stuff of *Dreamer*	110
Beware the Count!	113
The Buds Shoot 3858	116
Gibby's Big Jackpot	120
Bowling's Defining Moment	124
Time for a Bowling Postage Stamp?	130
I Remember Billy Welu	132
The First National Tournament	133
Strange Inventions	138
Dick Weber, R.I.P.	139
Candy Mac	141

Table of Contents

The Baseball-Bowling Connection	144
The Buzzer	147
Unusual Injuries	150
The Quiet Man	151
Pioneer Don Scott	154
The Hitchhikers	156
The Greatest Action Match	157
The Fred Wolf Story	159
Big Steve	161
Johnny Small's Magic Ball	163
Two Secure Records	164
Movie Star Bowler	166
A Christmas Story	169
Who Was Ned Day?	170
Ed Lubanski's Double 300	174
Andy Varipapa Stories	176
Earl Breaks Through	178
The Petersen Classic Turns 100	181
All Hail, Lady L!	184
The Bowling Ball That Went Around the World	189
Even More Things I Learned While Looking Up Other Things	191
In Search of Johnny King	193
A Different Path	196
Uncle Joe	198
Bowler's Symphony	199
Chief Halftown	201
The Schalk Team Tournament	203
Billy Hardwick, R.I.P.	204
The Longest Longshots	206
The Man in the Picture	208
Allie and Orf and Allison and Some Others	210

The National Bowling League	212
Billy Durant's Bowling Fling	219
The Shanghai Bowling Congress	221
The Pleasure of His Company	222
Undefeated Champion	225
Index	227

Acknowledgments

My first thank you goes to Mort Luby, Jr. As publisher of *Bowlers Journal*, he bought my first series of articles, and later hired me as a regular monthly contributor. Though he's been officially retired for some time now, Mort still writes the occasional piece for the magazine and has continued on with his second career as an artist. Every time I look at his painting of the Chicago skyline in my living room, I'm reminded of how much I owe him.

Keith Hamilton and Mike Panozzo, owners of the magazine for the past twenty-odd years, have carried on in grand fashion the tradition built by three generations of the Luby family. Recognizing the worldwide appeal of American-style tenpins, their flagship publication is now known as *Bowlers Journal International*. My thanks to Keith and Mike for continuing to publish my articles, for their enthusiastic support for this book, and for their kind permission to use photos from the *BJI* archives.

I have been fortunate to work with three fine editors in my years at the magazine—Jim Dressel, Bob Johnson, and now Gianmarc Manzione. Each of them is an accomplished writer in his own right, and I've benefitted enormously from their advice and examples. Thanks, guys.

Thanks also to the staffs at two research archives—to Jerry Baltz, John Dalzell, Travis Boley, and Jim Baltz at the International Bowling Museum (then in St. Louis), and to Mark Miller at the American Bowling Congress (then in Greendale, Wisconsin). On the local level, thank you to the staffs at the Chicago Public Library, the Chicago History Museum, and the Regenstein Library at the University of Chicago. And a special thank-you to Mark Tatara at Luby Publishing for his help with the photographs.

I've interviewed dozens of people in all parts of the bowling industry in the past quarter-century, and the list is too long to print here. I trust that they will understand that this omission doesn't mean I'm ungrateful for their help. At the same time, I will single out a great bowling historian and a great friend, the late Bruce Pluckhahn.

In closing, I salute my children Nicholas Schmidt and Tracy Samantha Schmidt, who grew up listening to my stories, and still managed to develop successful professional careers. As for my wife, Terri Schmidt, the dedication of this book expresses only imperfectly what I owe her.

A.M.D.G.

Preface

I became a bowling historian by chance and by good luck. In 1990 I had just published my doctoral dissertation—about one of Chicago's rare reform mayors—and I was looking for something for light-hearted to write about. The Bowling Hall of Fame was getting ready for its golden anniversary, so I pitched *Bowlers Journal* an idea for thirteen articles profiling the Hall's thirteen charter members. Publisher Mort Luby, Jr., gave me the green light. After the series was over, Mort asked for more historical articles, and I eventually got my own monthly column.

Bowling history had been recorded haphazardly. Bruce Pluckhahn, by then curator of the Bowling Museum, recalled his days as publicist for the American Bowling Congress. A noted bowler had just died, and Bruce told his boss that the press release had the bowler's birth year wrong. "So what!" the boss said. "We got him dead, didn't we?"

With that in mind, I resolved to delve into whatever contemporary sources I could find. The bulk of my research was carried out in the bound volumes of *Bowlers Journal* in the magazine's office. The daily newspapers in Chicago and other cities were helpful, as was the American Bowling Congress files in Greendale, Wisconsin. Each year I made a trip to St. Louis and spent a few days digging through the materials at the Bowling Museum.

Sometimes the facts I found contradicted the traditional narrative. Still, most of my work confirmed what had been reported, and often I was able to pin down specific dates. When I couldn't find documentation for a story, I decided that I had to accept it, until someone or something proved the story wrong.

My research also involved interviewing veteran bowling stars. This usually meant a phone call and a few specific questions. But after Joe Norris died in 2001, I realized that there was a need to systematically record the memories of these tenpin giants while they were still around to share them. The result was a series of oral histories I conducted for the Bowling Museum between 2002 and 2006. Those recordings are now at the USBC Bowling Campus in Arlington, Texas.

Preface

I have written close to 400 *Bowlers Journal* pieces over the course of twenty-six years. Besides my regular column, there have been a number of feature articles. And whenever the magazine celebrated a milestone, the special anniversary issue would have a more historical flavor, and more of my contributions.

This book represents a cross-section of bowling history. In a few places, the text has been edited for clarity—for example, to make multipart stories read more smoothly. However, most of the articles are reprinted as originally published.

A (Very) Short History of Bowling

Why bowling? On the surface, it is a simple game—as one cynic put it, you roll the ball and either you knock down the pins, or you don't. But then, all sports are simple in their basics. You knock a small ball into a hole in the ground, or throw a large ball through a hoop, or hit an in-between-size ball with a stick. Or maybe you just try to beat the hell out of another person.

Ball-and-pin games date back to ancient Egypt. Dutch settlers introduced ninepins to America in the 1600s, but only in 1840 were the first indoor alleys built, in New York City. Many of these early two- or three-alley venues became hangouts for unsavory characters, and ninepins was outlawed in some cities. Modern bowling began when one crafty proprietor got around the law by adding a tenth pin to the setup. At least, that's the legend.

By the 1890s bowling was flourishing in Eastern and Midwestern cities, particularly where there was a large German population. In 1895 a number of clubs joined together to form the American Bowling Congress, with the idea of standardizing playing rules and equipment specifications. Female bowlers organized the separate Women's International Bowling Congress in 1916.

Bowling grew steadily through the first half of the twentieth century, moving into all parts of the United States and Canada. There were also periodic attempts to introduce American-style tenpins to other parts of the world. Bowling was recognized as an athletic activity. Most metropolitan newspapers covered it on their sports pages. A few even had a designated bowling editor.

The 1950s brought the invention of the automatic pinsetter machine, ushering in bowling's golden age. Now it was marketed as a family pastime. Bigger and better bowling centers sprouted up in cities and suburbs, and the sport was all over television. One out of every seventeen adult Americans bowled in organized leagues. A Professional

Bowlers Association tour, based on the model of pro golf, became a success. In 1964 bowler Don Carter became the first athlete to sign a contract for a guaranteed $1,000,000.

In more recent decades, bowling has seen significant changes. The gender-separate ABC and WIBC have merged into the United States Bowling Congress. Though more people than ever venture out onto the lanes, the number of organized leagues continues to drop. This fact was used as a metaphor for the ongoing transformation of interpersonal relationships by political scientist Robert D. Putnam in his book *Bowling Alone: America's Declining Social Capital.* Today, once again, bowling is in the process of remaking itself.

And yet, over the past hundred years, there has been one constant in the bowling world. In November 1913, a Chicago shoe salesman named Dave Luby launched an eight-page weekly newspaper named *Bowlers Journal.* In time Luby's little paper evolved into a monthly magazine. Today *Bowlers Journal International* is recognized as America's oldest continually published sports periodical.

Mort the Moose

(June 1990)

If Mort Lindsey were bowling today, he'd drive the image-makers crazy. Bowlers want to be thought of as athletes, and Mort looked nothing like an athlete. He was short and fat, long-nosed and thick-lipped, with a magnificent pair of flapping ears that earned him the nickname "Moose." His bowling style was pure Fred Flintstone—a mad charge to the line, a mighty heave of the ball, and arm-whirling body English.

Mort was a character. He looked like one and he bowled like one. Yet his skills were hardly comic. In the first half of the century, he was one of the best.

Mortimer Joel Lindsey was born in Newark in 1888. Soon afterward the family moved to Manhattan. The Lindseys were wealthy, and young Mort found time to dabble in all sorts of amateur sports while preparing for a career in the insurance business. He boxed and skated, played baseball, basketball, and tennis. At fourteen he got around to bowling.

Mort was a natural. Within two years of picking up his first bowling ball, he had won his first tournament. By 1911 he'd decided to commit himself to the sport. He quit his job writing insurance policies to buy part-interest in a New Haven bowling alley.

During the 1910s Lindsey established himself as one of the country's top bowlers. He won three American Bowling Congress championships, sharing Team titles in 1912 and 1914, and taking the All Events in 1919. At the 1912 National Bowling Association Tournament—an event rivaling the ABC in prestige—his All Events score of 2031 set a national record.

Naturally Lindsey rated an invitation to the 1922 World Classic, the bowling Super Bowl of its day. He finished third in the tournament proper, then lost a close match to Jimmy Blouin in the roll-offs that followed. As a money bowler, Lindsey developed quite a reputation. Rich enough to provide his own backing, he took on all the giants of his era in free-lance matches, and usually came out ahead. He added to his bankroll with a victory in the 1934 Petersen Classic and bowling's biggest paycheck—$1,000—in the depths of the Depression.

In 1941 Lindsey was one of eleven charter members elected to the Bowling Hall of Fame. And now he finally began to slow down. He qualified for the finals of the 1943 All-Star Tournament, but had to withdraw because of injury. His wife died and he sold off the last of his bowling centers. He began living the life of a retired squire, wintering in Miami, then trekking north with the spring thaws to his residence at the Roger Smith Hotel in Stamford, Connecticut.

Lindsey continued to be a familiar face—and voice—at the ABC, the Petersen Classic, and other gatherings of the bowling fraternity. Long into the night he could be found holding court, sharing a laugh and a nip while telling the old familiar stories which seemed to get only better with age.

He could still bowl, too. In 1952 Lindsey arrived in Milwaukee for the ABC Tournament. He shot 645 in the Team event, then followed with a 615 in the special Hall of Fame exhibition match. Before he left town, he rolled a five-game set of 1093 to take fourth place in the *Bowlers Journal* singles. All this when he was sixty-three, with a single hard-rubber ball, against solid wooden pins, on gutter-to-gutter oil.

Mort Lindsey died on May 16, 1959. A few days later, the Professional Bowlers Association staged its first tournament. It is unfortunate that Mort didn't stay around long enough to bowl on Tour. He might have given the youngsters some real competition. He certainly would have made things a lot more colorful. The old Moose was like that.

Long John Koster

(December 1990)
The picture is arresting. Glancing through a portrait gallery of bowling's Hall of Famers, you can't miss him. The dude with the handlebar mustache. Looks more like one of Wyatt Earp's Dodge City deputies, or perhaps that forgotten ancestor peering out from the dusty picture frame in Grandma's attic. This guy was a bowler?

Meet John Koster. Charter member of the Bowling Hall of Fame. Mentor to Mort Lindsey, Barney Spinella, and other legendary stars.

And through the first fifty ABC Tournaments, the only man to win four championships.

He was a native of Germany, born in Bremen in 1872. Tenpin bowling was considered a German sport in those days, but Koster never touched a ball until he was nineteen years old. By then he was living in Brooklyn, making deliveries for a delicatessen. One day he made a stop at a Manhattan bowling alley and fell in love with the game.

It was just as well he was a big man. Physical strength was vital to successful bowling a century ago. The alleys were pockmarked and badly lit, the pins as rugged as tree stumps. The bowling balls didn't have finger holes. Koster towered over his friends on the lanes. They nicknamed him Long John.

Within a few years he was counted among the best bowlers in the East. Koster won the Greater New York Individual Tournament and was

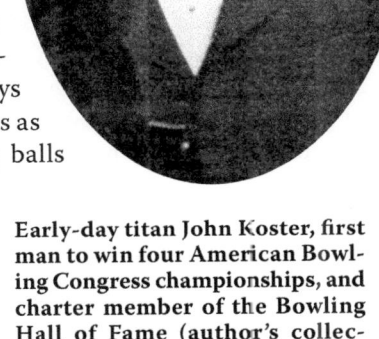

Early-day titan John Koster, first man to win four American Bowling Congress championships, and charter member of the Bowling Hall of Fame (author's collection).

presented a special gold medal by the *Police Gazette*. This prize carried great prestige, since that paper also provided the challenge belt held by boxing's heavyweight champ. At the first ABC Tournament in 1901, Koster ran second in both Singles and All Events. The next year his 247 game—high in the tournament—helped the Fidelias win the Team championship, and his 1841 set took the All Events. If there'd been a Bowler of the Year award in 1902, Koster would likely have been named.

These were prosperous times for Long John. He left behind the deli delivery carts and moved to the fashionable Bronx, buying half-interest in a bowling center. Koster's Bronx Central Recreation became one of the city's best-known houses. In 1912 he was back in the ABC championship circle, as captain of the Brunswick All-Stars. The following year he won his final ABC title in the Doubles with Peter Schultz.

That made four ABC titles for Long John, a feat unmatched until Joe Wilman bagged his fourth in 1954. Though the fields were smaller in Koster's day, it should also be noted that Long John missed at least a half-dozen tournaments because of New York's ongoing feud with the ABC. Possibly he would have won even more championships.

The four eagles are merely the highlight of Koster's resume. He once estimated he'd won thirty-five medals in major competition. Eventually he sold his interest in Bronx Central and moved up the Hudson to Nyack. Long John's last tournament victory came in 1928, when his Nyack Roofing team captured the New York State championship.

By now the handlebar mustache was gone. Koster had become somewhat gaunt, and Long John had begun to resemble Honest Abe. From time to time he showed flashes of his old form, posting a high finish in the Petersen Classic, and rolling a 673 in the ABC Singles when he was past sixty. Arthritis finally forced him to stop bowling in 1941.

Koster died on August 14, 1945. This happened to be the same day the fighting ended in World War II. Peace news held everyone's attention for days thereafter. Long John was already buried before most of the bowling world heard he had gone.

John Koster. Yeah—that guy was a bowler, all right.

El Zunko

(January 1991)
When the Bowling Hall of Fame held its first election in 1941, three men dominated the voting. They were Hank Marino, Jimmy Smith, and Gil Zunker.

Gil Zunker? The first two names are at least vaguely familiar to someone knowing a bit of bowling history. To find anything about Zunker, you must delve deeply into the record books. He died young in 1938.

Perhaps the fact that Zunker was freshly dead influenced those first Hall of Fame voters—that and the man's own charisma. Zunker was one of those larger-than-life personalities who are hard to capture in cold print. Yet even a half-century later, anyone reading the accounts of his short life is struck by his jaunty spirit, and by the warmth his contemporaries felt for him. Here is the kind of guy you'd want on your team, whether or not he could bowl. And make no mistake, Gillie could bowl.

Zunker was born in Milwaukee in 1901 and grew up among his

fellow German-Americans along Teutonia Avenue. When and how he learned to bowl is lost to history. We first find him making his mark in local leagues during the mid–1920s.

For many years he worked as a beer salesman. This is appropriate, since Gillie was built along the lines of a beer keg. He stood 5'10", weighed well over 200 pounds, and was known for his appreciation of good food. A natural extrovert, Zunker couldn't keep still on the lanes. He entertained both teammates and opponents with his noisy exuberance. They called him "El Zunko," and he often referred to himself by that name.

Gillie's sunny approach to life is best illustrated in a story from the 1933 ABC Tournament. Before leaving Milwaukee, he bet several friends malteds and sundaes that he'd shoot at least one 600 series. At the tournament he managed only 598 in the Team event, but then followed with 750 in Doubles and 712 in Singles. He won the Doubles with Frank Benkovic, and his 2060 set a new All Events record. Gillie returned home and paid off his bets anyway. After all, he explained, he hadn't really shot a 600 series—just a "5" and two "7"s.

Zunker was not a fancy bowler. He took four quick steps and rolled a short hook with plenty of speed. He didn't mind if he looked sloppy going to the line. "Smoothness is fine," he said, "but above all, heave that ball out onto the alley." He never tried to spot bowl because he considered it unnatural.

The Depression years were good to Zunker. He bowled with the Heil Products, a Milwaukee-based team that then rivaled the Green Bay Packers in statewide popularity. The Heils held the Bowling Proprietors Association of America's match game title for four years, and won the International Tournament championship at Berlin in 1936. Gillie continued his strong shooting at the ABC, taking over leadership of the Ten Year Average List in 1938.

That December the Heils lost their match game title. Gillie was not at his best in the match, but came back strong two days later with a 742 in league. The next morning he awoke with a headache and blurred vision. He took it easy for a few days and seemed to be recovering. Then he was stricken again over dinner.

Zunker was rushed to the hospital. He was a victim of Landry's Paralysis, a rare condition which was then untreatable. Shortly after midnight on December 19 he died, just thirty-seven years old.

The bowling world was stunned. Memorial tributes poured in to Heil Products, to ABC offices, to *Bowlers Journal*, to anywhere that the sense of loss could be shared. Zunker's teammate, journalist Billy Sixty, wrote a farewell poem which began—

> A vacant seat upon the bowler's bench—
> Strange silence, emptiness, and gloom
> Where once a raucous shout had echoed clear...

Bowling moves on, records fall, new competitors take their places. Not many people in our rough-and-ready sport have inspired poetry, though. Gillie Zunker had to be something special.

Magnificent Marino

(April 1991)
What was it about Hank Marino? He impressed our bowling forebears so much. Top vote-getter in the first Hall of Fame election. Bowler of the Half Century. First place on the pre–1950 *Bowling* magazine all-star team. In the *Bowlers Journal* files, there are more feature articles about Marino than all the other charter Hall of Famers combined. Without much dissent, Marino was the dominant figure of the shellac-and-pinboy era, Bowling B.C. (Before Carter). Was he really that good?

The record book gives only a tantalizing hint. What's most striking is the variety of his accomplishments. Other bowlers seem to have specialized in the ABC Tournament, or match games, or local tournaments, or league play. Marino was not supreme in any one category. He was simply near the top in everything, and for a long time.

He won only one ABC championship (1916 Doubles), but.... He also led the ABC Ten Year average list once—twenty-three years later, and.... He was the individual match game champion for three years, and.... He won bowling's richest prize, the Petersen Classic, and.... He simultaneously held the record for most sanctioned 300 games and 800 series, and.... He was the first man to post six tournament All Events scores over 2000, and.... You get the picture.

He lived the American Dream. Born Enrico Salvano Marino in Sicily in 1889, he came to Chicago at eleven. When he was sixteen some friends talked him into going bowling. He found he had some skill, and kept at it until he mastered the sport. Then came the fame, the wealth, the friendships with movie stars and presidents, and finally, the golden

Bowler of the Half Century Hank Marino, center, with fellow Italian American stars Andy Varipapa (left) and Joe Falcaro. Though rivals on the lanes, all three shared an appreciation of fine cuisine.

years as a revered elder statesman, with a peaceful death—heavy in honors and years—in 1976. It would have been corny, except it was all true.

Hank Marino was a small, slender man of mild disposition. Those who knew him never had a bad word to say about him. What they did talk about was his bowling. Many of the stories seem like something out of Paul Bunyan.

Take the 1937 ABC Tournament at New York City. As the reigning match game king, Marino's appearance drew a large crowd. But when he opened his Doubles with 154, there were boos from the tough Manhattan gallery. Now Marino started striking. He strung 10-in-a-row for 277. Not good enough? He closed with 278. They remembered Marino in New York after that.

Then there was the time in 1944 when Marino was in a slump. On the way out of the house for a league session, he spied an old ball and decided to use it. That night, he shot 300–232–300 for 832—the highest series in the nation that year, and only the fourth time that two perfect games had been rolled in a single series. Marino was then fifty-four years old.

My favorite Marino story is about an exhibition match, when he managed to pick up the 7–9–10 split. Afterward, conversation kept turning to that conversion. The fans wanted to see him make it again.

Marino couldn't convince them the shot was nearly impossible. *Nobody* could convert the 7–9–10 at will. But Hank finally agreed to give it another try. He stepped onto the approach, sighted over the top of the ball, and went into his delivery. The ball spun out toward the right gutter, hung on, then curved back just enough to shave the 9-pin into the 7-pin for another conversion.

Paul Bunyan in bowling shoes. Perhaps Marino was even better than he himself knew.

So how good was he, then? I'm afraid we'll never really know. We are left with only the few statistics to savor, and the stories to cherish and pass on. And yes, we are left with a bit of envy as well—envy for those who saw Hank Marino bowl.

The Perfect Game

(June 1991)

A perfect game. Every competitive bowler's goal. The sport's ultimate achievement.

There have been many more perfect games in recent years, and some claim the mystique of the 300 is fading. Maybe. But taking a trip into bowling's history is worthwhile. Many remarkable things have happened when a bowler started bunching strikes and closing in on the magic number.

Back at the turn of the twentieth century, 300 games were rare events. Whole years would go by without anybody in the entire country shooting one. When the American Bowling Congress first decided to offer three annual awards for the highest individual games, 298 was the top score submitted.

Then, in 1908, two men shot 300 games. ABC officials weren't about to let that scoring explosion force them into giving two gold medals. Therefore, they decreed that the tie would have to be settled by a roll-off. So A.C. Jellison and Homer Sanders, both of St. Louis, had to journey to Pittsburgh and bowl a three-game match at the ABC Tournament to determine who would get the high-game medal. Mr. Jellison won the match and the gold medal. Mr. Sanders had to be content with the silver. With that, ABC reversed itself and decided to provide a gold medal for every sanctioned 300—no roll-off necessary.

Knocking down the pins was hard enough for most early day bowlers. Bill Heerman's problem was keeping them down. In 1920 Heerman was competing in a tournament in South Bend, Indiana. He started a game with the first eleven strikes. Then, on his twelfth shot, a solid pocket hit sent all ten pins crashing into the pit for 300—except that one pin jumped back onto the pindeck near the 9-pin spot. The rulebook confirmed that it had to be scored as a standing pin. And the unfortunate Heerman thus received credit for a 299 game with twelve "strikes."

As close as Bill Heerman came to perfection, James T. Blackstone of Seattle came even closer. One day in 1905, Blackstone also started a game with the first eleven strikes. On his twelfth ball, he swept over nine pins and broke the top of the 10-pin off at the neck. The bottom of the pin remained standing, though, so Blackstone's teammates immediately claimed he had rolled a "299½ game." The story was picked up by the newspapers, and eventually found its way into the "Ripley's Believe It Or Not" cartoon series. It's a definite disappointment that the rules makers would allow Blackstone only a 299.

Something of a companion piece to the Blackstone 299½ is the McDowell 301. Marion McDowell was one of the bowling superstars of the 1920s. In 1928 he registered the first eleven strikes during a pot game in Cleveland. One of the spectators then offered McDowell a side bet that he couldn't shoot "301." So Marion called time, walked down to the pit, and told the pinboy to set up an extra pin next to the 7-pin. He then returned to his place and proceeded to sweep all eleven pins from the deck with his final shot—for 301 and the side bet. Whether Marion ever used this trick to avoid being stuck in the beer frame is not recorded.

At least two famous old-timers rolled perfect games without seeing the pins. Hall of Famer Billy Knox shot 300 with a screen hanging at the foul line, while Count Gengler did it with the lights turned off. Then there are the ambidextrous 300 shooters. The *ABC Yearbook* reveals that six bowlers have recorded both left-handed and right-handed perfect games during their careers.

However, the king of 300 switch-hitters has to be Sid Sherman of Toledo. Once upon a time in 1921, Sid was having difficulty arranging a match. His prospect insisted on receiving a spot. To liven things up, right-handed Sid offered to bowl lefty on alternate shots. Twelve balls later, our hero had rolled a 300 game, symmetrically balancing six right-handed strikes with six from the portside.

We can assume that Sid's opponent asked for a different sort of spot after that.

Then there was an incident involving the great Buzz Fazio, when he appeared on the live *Championship Bowling* show in Chicago on New Year's Eve, December 31, 1955. After two indifferent games, Buzz started the last game with the first eight strikes. Now the wheels were turning in the producer's head—why not have Buzz become the first bowler to shoot a 300 spread out over two calendar years?

Fazio thought it was a great idea. The show was stopped and everyone sat around for ten minutes, counting down. Then, at 12:01 a.m., Buzz stepped to the line and rolled his first ball of 1956—and left the 7-pin. That he then struck out to win his match by two pins was something of an anticlimax.

Those 300 games were darned hard to get, as Buzz Fazio demonstrated. So what are we to make of his contemporary, Buddy Bomar? During the 1950s, Bomar probably held the world's record for unsanctioned 300s. Whenever he appeared on a television bowling show, the announcer was sure to mention that Bomar had rolled 85 perfect games, or 93, or 108—the number kept changing like the number of burgers sold on the old McDonald's signs.

The more cynical fans around Chicago had a theory about Buddy's total. They said he would claim a 300 anytime he happened to roll twelve strikes in succession—over two games, over two matches, during warm-ups, whenever. This led to a nasty local phenomenon. When a Windy City bowler would string the first seven or eight strikes and be stopped, he might go back and find that he had ended the previous game with a five-bagger. Then he could smirk: "At least I got a Buddy Bomar 300."

Whether or not Bomar really padded his 300 count can't be determined. But in fairness to Buddy, it should be noted that a few other cities had the same urban legend—except there they called such twelve-baggers "Andy Varipapa 300s" or "Ned Day 300s."

At the opposite end of the spectrum is the bowler who performed perhaps the most remarkable feat of all. That would be Chuck Collier,

Hall of Famer and captain of the famed Brunswick Mineralites. All Chuck did was roll twenty-seven strikes in succession—without recording a 300 game.

A number of versions of when, where, and why Chuck worked his wonder have been kicking around for years. The most likely scenario takes place in Kansas City in 1928. The story goes that the Mineralites were supposed to roll an exhibition against a local team, but because of a mix-up, only Collier arrived on time for the match. Not wanting to disappoint the fans, Chuck said he would take on the other team by himself.

Chess masters like to show off their skill by playing many different opponents at the same time—they call it a "simultaneous exhibition." Any bowling masters attempting the same stunt would have to go a long way to match Chuck Collier. Bowling straight through in all five lineup positions, he struck and struck and kept on striking for five frames—five five-baggers. He added two more strikes in the sixth frame to reach twenty-seven in a row.

What happened next is unclear. Either the rest of the Mineralites showed up, or Chuck finally missed a strike, or maybe he just collapsed. By then, he deserved a rest.

Eddie Kawolics and Me

(December 1991)

Eddie Kawolics was the first television star I ever saw in person. Kawolics was one of the mainstays of early televised bowling, and by the time I was ten, he was as familiar to me as Howdy Doody. One Saturday morning in 1958, while I was bowling in my junior league, I paused to take a quick comfort break. When I finished, I happened to notice the man standing at the facility next to me.

It was Eddie Kawolics! I suppose the thing that struck me at the time was that he was not black-and-white, but in color.

Eddie was a crony of our proprietor, Rudy Habetler, and would occasionally show up to shoot three-cushion billiards with Rudy. As time went on, Eddie showed up more often. By then his bowling career was in decline.

That career had been long and successful. Born in 1907, Kawolics began to make a name as a bowler around Cleveland in the 1930s. A colorful performer, he made exhibition tours for Ebonite billed as "The Mad Russian from Findlay, Ohio." Actually, he was Hungarian.

World War II interrupted this pleasant life in 1942. Kawolics spent four years in the army, was wounded, and earned a chest full of medals. When the war ended, he moved to Chicago. It was the era of the great teams, and Eddie was on a lot of them. Tavern Pale, Meister Brau, King Louie, Hamm's Beer—his teams dominated the Chicago Classic League and cleaned up in tournaments. Eddie himself won enough titles to be named an All American three times.

Kawolics was not physically impressive. Short and wide, he was built like two men sitting down. As he aged he took on the appearance of a grumpy Buddha—definitely grumpy. Eddie did not suffer fools gladly. To his admirers, this suggested he was direct and honest. Other people simply thought he was a grouch.

His bowling style was unadorned, a measured waddle of four short steps, with little backswing and a stiff-arm pitch onto the lane. Long after it had gone out of fashion, Kawolics was one of the last star bowlers still using a two-hole ball.

Eddie's biggest moment came at the 1963 ABC Tournament. He was now bowling with up-and-comers Jim Stefanich and Les Zikes for Old Fitzgerald. Though Kawolics didn't score well, the rest of the team got hot and carried home the title. After thirty-one years, Eddie at last had an ABC eagle.

But most of the glory was over. His advisory staff contract ran out, television appearances grew rare, and Eddie took a night job at an insurance company. Now we would see him every Saturday morning when he wheeled his ancient Mercury into the parking lot at Habetler Bowl. If a PBA telecast were scheduled, he would stay on at the bar to watch and criticize the bowlers, loudly and often.

We kids in the junior league had grown older along with Eddie. As teenagers, we no longer held him in awe, but tolerated him with amusement. We smiled at his ranting against the current pros, and snickered at his complaints against lane condition—"I've got a better alley out back of my house" was one of his milder comments. Eddie was not to be taken seriously.

He showed us one time, though. The Classic League made its annual trip to Habetler's one winter night in the mid-'60s, and we were all on hand to see what the old man could do. And darned if Eddie didn't start the first game with seven straight strikes! Yet he never once looked back at the cheering section of convinced adolescents gathered behind his bench. He didn't need to—he knew his work.

I don't remember what Eddie finally shot that night. Probably I could look it up somewhere, but it's not important. The memory of that hammered-down little hulk bouncing around the approaches and happily cussing out the pins is still fresh and green.

Eddie Kawolics died in 1976.

The Old Sarge

(February 1992)
Anyone promoting senior bowling would do well to sell the example of Sarge Easter. He was likely the best older bowler the sport has ever known.

Easter burst on the bowling world in 1943, winning both the Marino Open and the rich Dom DeVito Classic as a 61-year-old unknown. He didn't remain anonymous for long. For the next fifteen years he roamed the country's informal tournament circuit, following the cry of the wild dollar from coast to coast while burning up four Chryslers in pursuit. Along the way he built up a reputation as a deadly match game competitor.

Eber Darnell Easter—"Ed" to his friends—was a preacher's son from the Blue Ridge Mountains. The date of his birth is uncertain, though 1882 is the year usually cited. He was called "Sarge" because he spent much of his adult life in the army, twenty-six years in all. Between hitches he lived a bachelor's life of roaming. He played minor league baseball, hustled pool, worked in mines and on construction, and ran a country fiddlers convention. And he bowled a little.

How bowling came to bewitch the crusty old mountain man is illustrated by a story from his first ABC Tournament. Around the time one of his enlistments was up in 1938, Easter had a hankering to compete in the big event. The army brass refused to grant him leave. So the Sarge formally retired from the army and went off to Chicago to bowl—badly, as it turned out. He then re-enlisted as a private.

By the early 1940s Easter was assigned as a marksmanship instructor with the University of Wisconsin ROTC. He spent his off-duty hours at the famous Schwoegler Lanes in Madison. The Schwoeglers took

Easter in hand, converted his backup into a hook, and refined his game. What they finally got was an awkward, somewhat stumbling style delivering a ball so slow it seemed ready to stop on the lane. It wasn't pretty, but it would prove effective.

Easter himself added the finishing touch. His friend Connie Schwoegler was the first big-time bowler to use a fingertip grip. The Sarge came up with a variation in which the middle finger had a fingertip span, while the ring finger was conventional. For years that "Easter Grip" would enjoy some popularity.

At the end of World War II Easter quit the army for good and took up bowling full time. He lived a few years in Detroit, a few years in St. Louis, and a few years in Burbank, California. These were only the places where he picked up his mail. He spent most of his time on the road.

The tales of his travels are legendary. The old gent once drove forty-four straight hours over pre-interstate highways from California to Detroit to appear at the grand opening of a friend's bowling lanes. On another occasion, while living in St. Louis, he read about a high-paying sweeper in Florida. He immediately jumped in his car and took off, only to arrive and find the event had been cancelled. "Nice weather you got here," was his only comment as he turned his car back north.

Then there was the time the fast-moving Sarge outran so many Tennessee state troopers they had to stop him with a roadblock. Charged with going 120 miles per hour—which was double the speed limit—he escaped with a $16 fine. The judge, it happened, was a bowling fan.

Easter reached his peak during the 1949–50 season. He made the finals of the 100-game All-Star Tournament, finishing thirteenth. Then he led Pepsi-Cola of Detroit to the ABC Team title. Then he won the BPAA Match Game Doubles with 21-year-old Ed Lubanski, who was young enough to be his grandson. The Sarge was named an All American and finished second in the Bowler of the Year balloting. He was then sixty-seven years old.

He put one more record on the books in 1955, becoming at seventy-two the oldest man to roll a 300 game. He was briefly in the news again in 1958, when he was discovered teaming in a fast California doubles league with a boy young enough to be his *great*-grandson. And here Easter proved to be a shrewd judge of bowling talent—eleven-year-old Barry Asher eventually grew up to be a PBA star.

His last years were not happy. Easter's bowling earnings were long gone, and he lived on an army pension in a brother's small cottage in North Carolina. Progressive emphysema made his days and nights miserable. He told a friend that he only wanted to stay alive long enough to see himself voted into the Hall of Fame. That election finally came in 1963—a little more than a year after Sarge Easter's death.

Uncanonized Saint

(June 1992)
You'd see it in the Help Wanted section of your newspaper. There would be a picture of a smiling gent or lady who'd just joined the ranks of the happily employed. The caption would read something like, "I got my job through the *New York Times*." Jim St. John was a great bowler who always said he got his career through *Bowlers Journal*.

Back in 1960, St. John was just another guy with a 200 average. He went to Toledo to bowl in the ABC Tournament that year, and a teammate suggested they hit the "BJ" events. Jim didn't want to—there were no openings until 4 a.m., and he was tired. Finally, he was talked into it. And sure enough, he proceeded to win the Singles and the $5,000 first prize. "That changed my life." St. John later said. "It gave me the big boost I needed. It gave me confidence in myself."

Born in 1930, James Raymond St. John learned bowling growing up in Montana. He joined the navy after high school and became a radioman. Halfway to his pension, he quit the service to concentrate on bowling. He was only a couple of years back into civilian life when he made his "BJ" breakthrough.

Big-time bowling was in transition then. Over the next several years, St. John did a bit of everything. He won some money on television bowling shows, then spent a season traveling with the Twin City Skippers of the National Bowling League. After the NBL folded, he hooked up with Hamm's Beer of the Chicago Classic League while competing on the PBA Tour full-time. During the hectic 1962–63 season, St. John managed to pace the Chicago Classic in individual average while winning three PBA tournaments.

He became a bowling immortal in the 1963 World's Invitational Tournament. That 100-game marathon was bowling's toughest test, and St. John started slowly. Going nowhere with conventional tactics, he switched to a radical outside line near the first arrow, a shot seldom seen in the days of lacquer-finished lanes and hard rubber balls. The

Jim St. John poses for photographers after winning the 1963 World's Invitational Tournament, a scene that would be repeated the following year.

result was devastating. St. John ran away from the field, averaging 233 in the finals, a full 14 pins better than the average of the nearest man. The "gutter shot" had rocked the bowling world.

St. John's road now took him to St. Louis and a contract with the Falstaff Beer team. He must have done something to spark the crew—Falstaff went on a rampage, winning both the BPAA Match Game and ABC Classic Team titles within a matter of months. Meanwhile, St. John enjoyed another year among the PBA's leading money winners. And when the World's Invitational rolled around, he won that again, too.

The little man with the silver hair and hawk nose remained a familiar figure on the lanes into the 1970s. Watching him play a line that wasn't near the first arrow always seemed strange, however—it was like turning on the television and seeing Joe Montana place-kick. St. John won a total of six PBA titles and was named an All American four times. He never won another World's Invitational, but only because the tournament went out of business after his second victory.

St. John ran a pro shop and managed a liquor store after his bowling career wound down. He eventually settled in rural Oregon with a job at an army depot. He died in 1987, only fifty-six years old. A few years later, the PBA elected him to the Veterans section of its Hall of Fame.

The Bowling Hall of Fame has not chosen to honor St. John. For a long time I couldn't understand this, since Jim was an honorable man and had a better record than a dozen other bowlers who are already in the Hall. However, the recent election of Pete Tountas convinces me that St. John's plaque will soon hang in St. Louis.

It goes back to the 1964 Waukegan Open—which, by coincidence, was the first PBA tournament I attended. St. John was leading the field as the event moved toward its climax. There was no stepladder finals at Waukegan that year, so the title came down to Jim's fill ball in the last game. Needing nine pins to win, St. John steered his shot high, left the memorable 3-6-7-8-10, and dropped all the way down to third place. The winner of the tournament, for his first PBA title, was Pete Tountas. Therefore, because St. John threw one bad ball and blew the tournament to Tountas, he has had to wait for election to the Bowling Hall of Fame until after Tountas got in.

Perhaps that theory doesn't make sense. But then, it's never made sense that Jim St. John is not in the Bowling Hall of Fame.

An Interview with Jimmy Blouin

(December 1992)

Every so often, Bowlers Journal *would publish a special Nostalgia Issue. For 1992, I was asked to put together an imaginary interview with some figure from bowling's past. I picked Jimmy Blouin.*

You captured many major bowling titles in your career, but you were best known as a money bowler. How did you get into that?

I started out by bowling challenge matches for money before I did anything else. My buddy Crook Smith and I had jobs setting pins at a place in Blue Island [Illinois] called Lichthemeyer & Green's. We were about thirteen or fourteen. Anyway, there was this doctor who used to come in and roll a few games on Sunday afternoons. He was pretty good, so when the two of us started teasing him a little, he thought he'd bowl us and teach the two punks a lesson. Well, I'd bowl him one week while Crook set pins, and the next week Crook would bowl while I set. And we kept beating him, taking him for a dollar or a dollar-and-a-half every week. That was a lot of money for a couple of snotty kids back then. But it didn't last. We were setting up thirteen pins for him when he shot, and he finally caught on.

Sounds like you learned early how to make a good match. From there, you moved on to bigger things?

Not right away. I enrolled in St. Viator's College, near Kankakee. I did a lot of bowling there. During my second year, I got a job carrying the mail back and forth between the campus and the post office in town. They gave me a bike to use. One day I stopped at the local bowling alley to roll a few games when I was supposed to be delivering the mail. One of the professors saw my bike outside, and I lost the job. A little later, I quit college. That's when I really got involved in bowling.

Your father, Ed Blouin, was the man who developed your game.

Right. Pop was quite a bowler himself. By the time I left college, he owned a four-alley place in Blue Island. That's where I put it all together. Pop taught me a lot.

Is that when you became associated with Nick Bruck?

Nick Bruck—you can't forget Nick. What a nice guy, really jolly fellow. He was my manager—my match-maker—all through my career. And, yes, I started making money with Nick about when I left college—1904, 1905. Nick had lost a $100 match against Billy Metcalf, a guy they called "The Pride of the Stock Yards." Nick had seen me bowl, so he set up a return match between Metcalf and the kid—me. I made $400 on that one.

Was that your first big money match?

That's right. And that was very good money then. When I quit school I got an office job with a clothing manufacturer. That $400 was like three or four weeks' salary.

That's when you started to make a career as a match bowler.

Right again. After I cleaned up most of the guys around Chicago, Nick started writing letters to other cities, trying to scare up matches. We'd put together a team and go. We'd bowl team, doubles, singles, whatever. Frank Brill, who won the first ABC Singles, used to make a lot of those trips with us. He was like a second father to me.

Didn't those bowling trips interfere with your job?

Not really. If there was any trouble with the boss, I'd just quit. The country was growing and prosperous—you could pick up another job easily. I used to bowl doubles with Phil Wolf. Same thing—he had dozens of jobs. I think he worked in every bowling alley on the [Chicago] South Side, and in most of the pool rooms, too. And if you think about it, it wasn't much different for us from the PBA Tour today.

"Blue Island Blouin": Jimmy Blouin, bowling's first official match game champion, strikes a confident pose in 1924 (author's collection).

How is that?

A pro in the 1990s goes around to different cities and bowls for money in tournaments. That's his job, right? And if he doesn't make money, he has to quit and take a 9-to-5 job somewhere. Well, we did basically the same thing. The difference was, it wasn't centrally organized. We had to make our own arrangements, our own matches. But the result was the same. If we made money, we could keep bowling. If we ran out, we had to take a "real" job.

You didn't have many tournaments then.

All we had was the ABC Tournament and a few minor things. And in 1921, the Petersen Classic came along—that was big. But the main thing we had were the money matches.

Your ABC Tournament record was notable—the All Events championship in 1909, and the Singles two years later. Are you saying that wasn't important?

That's not what I'm saying at all. Of course it was important, since it was just about all we had for tournaments. What I am saying is that—for me—the money matches were more lucrative. Especially on those ABC Tournament trips.

Do you mean there was gambling at the ABC Tournament?

Oh, no. Abe Langtry and the officials were very strict about no gambling. Anything we bet at the tournament was under the table. The real action was at the local alleys in the tournament city. See, with travel so expensive and slow, most guys would come to the city, bowl the ABC, then hang around for a couple of weeks. That's all the tournament lasted, anyway. It didn't go for months and months like it does today—it didn't have the entries. The year I won the All Events, I stayed in Pittsburgh a month and made $5,000 from matches. The only guy who beat me was Mort Lindsey.

That was quite a bit of money. What did you do with it?

I blew most of it. One thing I did was throw a big party after the tournament, and most of the guys I clipped came. But I was just a kid then. Kids don't save.

Did getting married slow down your match bowling?

(*laughs*) Well, I was more careful with money after I got married. But no, I still bowled the big matches. That was my job, and my wife understood.

Yet you did give up bowling completely for a few years.

That was when my second daughter was born. My family needed me at home, not on the road. Then the war [World War I] came along. I was rejected by the army, so I would up doing defense work at a steel mill. There wasn't much time left for bowling.

How did you get back into the game?

Well, by that time, I had beaten everybody two or three times over. Jimmy Smith was supposed to be the world champion then—this is after the war, 1919, 1920. He'd been champ for ten or fifteen years. But it was all unofficial. Everyone just *knew* that Smith was the top dog because he'd shoot you anywhere and beat you. But word was out that he was starting to slip. So in '21 Dave Luby from *Bowlers Journal* arranged a match for us. Home-and-home, forty games, $1,000 a side. And was I rusty when I went out to practice the week before! But when it was over, I beat Smith by 300 pins.

Yet after you defeated Smith, it took another year for you to be recognized as the match game champion. Why was that?

I sure couldn't figure it out! Probably because Smith had been number-one for so long, his fans just couldn't believe he could lose. They thought I must have cheated somehow. And of course, my fans considered me the champ. Then Smith dropped a few more matches, and it got really confused.

So the result was the famous World Classic Tournament in 1922.

Right. Louie Petersen decided to hold one big tournament in Chicago to settle the title, once and for all. It was about time!

The World Classic was probably the high point of your bowling career. What memories do you have of the tournament?

The biggest impression is that it was classy. There had never been anything like it in bowling. Louie got Brunswick and the Chicago proprietors to kick in, and they rented the Coliseum. That was where the political conventions used to meet to nominate the candidates for president—it was a better spot than the ABC had when they came to town. So then Louie and his committee invited the twenty-four best bowlers in the world—Smith, Marino, Mort Lindsey, my old doubles partner Phil Wolf, Otto Stein from St. Louis—the whole crew. You bowled each of the other guys a five-game match. That made 115 games. The whole thing lasted a week and a half. It was really something.

I've heard it said that you almost missed the tournament.

That's true. I was a hot-head then. I figured that I'd already beaten Smith and everybody else, so what did I have to prove? But Nick Bruck and Pete Howley talked me into it. First prize was going to be $1,200. A lot of money. So I bowled.

And so you won the tournament and became the first official world's champion match game bowler.

Not quite. That's what most people think when they look it up in the record book. Okay, let me explain this, because it gets complicated. We bowled the matches, 115 games. We bowled with Louie's Petersen Points—so many points for winning a match, so many for your total pins—and at the end of 115 games, J. Blouin of Blue Island had the most points and got the $1,200 top prize. But now, to be *recognized* as the official champion, I had to go back and beat the next three guys in the standings in separate 60-game matches.

Why do that? That's weird.

No, that's promotion—though I would have agreed with you then that it was weird. But look at it from the promoter's angle. Here you get three more title matches—and it's sudden death. I lose, and I'm out. No world championship. Great for the gate. We drew some good crowds for those follow-up matches.

But suppose you lost one of those matches. **Then** *who was the champ?*

Nobody. Noooooo-body. That's why it was such a great promotion. Louie thought that nobody could win a 115-game tournament, and then turn around and win three straight matches. He figured he could string it out for years. People would have talked about it all over the country—"Is this the year that somebody finally becomes the bowling champion?" Every bowler would be thinking about that vacant title sitting there.

I guess you spoiled Petersen's plans.

[*Laughs*] I guess I did. But not right away. We bowled the Classic in February. Then we let the publicity build up for those three roll-off matches. So in the fall, I bowled my buddy Phil Wolf, who'd come in second, and I beat him. Then the third-place man, Mort Lindsey, came back from New York, and I beat him, too. By then, people were really getting interested in this. I'd bowled 235 games over eight months trying to become the world's champ, and I still wasn't done. I had to beat the fourth-place man from the Classic. And guess who that was?

Jimmy Smith.

You've got it! It finally came down to a straight man-on-man match, sixty games at Randolph Recreation in downtown Chicago. And that was a big deal. Every night, we filled the place up with 400 seats and we had to turn away a couple of thousand more. People were standing out on the street, and people were yelling out the windows to them, telling them what was happening. If we could've gotten the Coliseum again, we could've filled that. The newspapers were headlining it like it was the World Series. People were going crazy betting on the match—heck, they were betting on every block, on every game.

Do you remember much of the match itself?

I remember every ball. Smith was tough. Don't think he wasn't because I put the knock on him. I just knew that he was over the hill, and I was better than he was.

So it wasn't a runaway.

[*Laughs*] Hardly. I never saw a man hit the pocket like that. It was monotonous. I don't think he crossed over Brooklyn more than twice. Of course, I was on, too. I blew only one spare in the last thirty games. It was so close—do you know that we were *dead even* after fifty-seven games? But then I pulled away and beat him.

I've heard it said that the pinboys bet heavily on you, so they sabotaged Smith's thumbhole.

Smith told that story so many times he probably started believing it himself! Look, we bowled sixty games—and remember, we only used two-hole balls then. Smith used to fire the ball with that big backswing, and I'd just sort of push mine down the alley. *Of course* his thumb gave out! What did he *expect*?

Once you were the official world's champion, how did things change for you?

Well, for one thing, there was never another World Classic. Without the vacant-title angle, there was no reason to continue it. So the proprietors fixed me up with some exhibition tours. My wife and I went all over the country and into Canada. I got paid $125 an exhibition. Good money.

Were there any challenges for your title?

A few. I made them put up at least $1,000 on deposit. That was to make sure they were serious. I finally wound up defending five times, though it should only have been four. I was ready to retire by the middle on 1926.

After all the bother you went to getting the title?

That was pride more than anything else. I knew I was the best bowler in the world—I just wanted everybody else to know it. But when you're forty years old and have a family, you don't feel like doing all that traveling for matches or exhibitions. I had enough money. I had my own bowling alley, and made more by running that than by bowling. And I *would* have quit sooner, but pride got me to defend one more time.

How did that come about?

I announced that I was retiring. But as a favor to Nick Bruck, I went to Detroit to bowl in the Central States Tournament. Well, all the Detroit bowlers got on my case, saying I was a "cheese champion," that I came to their town to bowl but was afraid to take on their local boy,

Joe Scribner. So I got angry and said I'd bowl him, eighty games for $1,000 and the title. They wanted me to bowl the whole match at Scribner's place, but I said home-and-home. I was angry, but I wasn't stupid.

And you defeated Scribner.

I cleaned his clock good. Beat him by exactly 1119 pins. Then Frankie Kartheiser challenged me. Well, by now I was like one of those old gunfighters, with all the young punks challenging me to shoot it out. I knew Frankie well—he was a Chicago boy. So when I said that I was retired, he didn't make a big deal about taunting me into a match. I just quit, and he became champ, and that was that.

After that, you never came back. You stuck to league play and an occasional ABC Tournament. How do you find bowling has changed between your glory days and now?

Pinboys and women. We didn't have the automatic machines then. As for women, if a woman wanted to bowl in my day, most people would think she was a ... well, that she was immoral.

What about changes in the game itself?

The equipment is much better today. Just getting a ball that fits right is a big improvement. We didn't have anything like precision drilling, we didn't have all the scientific knowledge—ball balance, the different surface materials, all that business. And bowling shoes—those are so much better today. All we had were glorified street shoes.

Have lane conditions improved as much?

It may surprise you—but no, not really. We knew how to fix alleys to bring the scores up or keep them down. The difference was that we used shellac on the alleys, and that demanded a shot with more topspin. And I guess there was another difference, too—we saved the blocking monkey-business for the money matches. In leagues and tournaments, you just tried to put out a fair shot for the bowlers. Not like today, where every bowler in the house wants the alleys to make him look good without any effort on his part.

What's your assessment of the top pro bowlers today?

There's no question that the top bowlers on Tour today would slaughter Smith and Marino and the best bowlers from my era. But that's because of the better equipment, and mainly because the guys today bowl so many games a week. Even when one of our guys worked in a bowling alley, he did just that—he worked. He didn't spend the day shooting practice games. For one thing, he couldn't bowl unless he hired a pinboy. So today's bowlers are better. But if the old timers had the same situation as the pros today, they would have been just as good. Maybe better.

What about Jimmy Blouin? Where do you fit in?
I was the best. And I'd do all right today. I could probably average 200.

That's not really so high.
Well, don't forget—I'd be 106 years old!

The Prince of Bowlers

(December 1992)
I first heard about Frank Kafora when I was twelve years old. We had an instructor named Bill Wernicke at our bowling lanes then. Bill the Spider was an old-time star, and he delighted in spinning tales about his youth.

One of the stories had Kafora bowling a match in 1920, when a guy in the audience started heckling him. This went on for a while, until Kafora decided he'd had enough. Kafora was brawny and muscled, so when he strolled over to where the heckler was sitting, many in the crowd feared mayhem. But instead, Kafora merely bowed graciously to the heckler, then turned around—and farted in the man's face.

For a twelve-year-old, that was a great story. There were other tales told, and Frank Kafora became something of a black-sheep hero to me. Yet there was nothing about him in the bowling guides or Who's Who books. Were Bill the Spider and the other old-timers making this fellow up?

The truth was pretty prosaic. Kafora had died young in 1923. Ancient bowling records being what they are, he was known only to his contemporaries. And their numbers were dwindling every year.

They are all gone now. But from bits and pieces of oral history and yellowed newspaper clippings, we can reconstruct the short, sweet career of Frank Kafora.

His parents came from Poland, and his actual name was Franciszek Jacob Kafora. He was born in Chicago in 1889. Growing up with the other Polish kids along Milwaukee Avenue, he set pins for some extra money, while dreaming of becoming a big league baseball player.

In his teens he caught on with one of the fast semi-pro teams at Polonia Park. Kafora was a catcher, and a loud one. He shouted a continuous stream of encouragement to his pitcher, urging him to "put the old tomato in the big mitt." Soon the kid was known around the league as "Tomatoes." Among his own Polish teammates, though, he was called *Grubas*—"Fatty."

Kafora made the jump to pro ball in 1912, signing with Butte, Montana, of the Union Association. He put in two seasons with Butte and was among the league's batting leaders when the Pittsburgh Pirates drafted him at the tail end of the 1913 season. As it happened, Kafora couldn't hit a major league curveball. His National League career consisted of twenty-two games spread over two years, with a batting average of .125. After two more seasons back in the minors, his pro baseball days were over.

Athlete that he was, Kafora excelled in other sports. He played some football and did some wrestling. He was an accomplished billiards player, good enough to give exhibitions with the famed Cowboy Weston. But as the baseball dream flickered out, bowling became Kafora's passion.

He had a natural talent for the game. Not long after he started setting pins, Kafora was taking his turn at the other end of the lane and posting scores over 200. That attracted the attention of C.J.B. Wronski.

Wronski, a neat, spade-bearded little man, might be described as a sports entrepreneur. He had his finger in all sorts of athletic activities in the Polish community. He himself had been one of the first Chicago bowlers to roll a 300 game, and among his properties was one of the city's largest pin plants, Universal Recreation. So while Kafora was struggling to break into baseball, Wronski was helping him become established as a bowler. Kafora took a winter job managing Universal. He began competing in the better leagues.

The larger bowling world first heard of Kafora at the 1915 ABC Tournament. After an anemic start in the Team event, Frank caught fire in the Doubles with a 687 series. Though his partner could manage only 550, the pair still landed in fourth place.

That autumn, Kafora turned the Chicago Bowling Association Tournament into a one-man show. He began by leading the Nienstadts to the Team title. Then he returned to win the Singles with a 711 set, only one pin short of the tournament record. Meanwhile, his 1895 total took the All Events. Nobody had ever won three championships in a single tournament, let alone in a major like the CBA. Some observers ranked Kafora's feat second only to Billy Knox's perfect game at the 1913 ABC. *Bowlers Journal* featured Kafora on its front cover. And over at Universal Recreation, Wronski began billing his protégé as the "Universal Expert" and the "Prince of Bowlers."

Kafora had arrived. Over the next few years, he consolidated his position as one of Chicago's finest bowlers. One of his favorite doubles partners was Sykes Thoma, a future Hall of Famer. The pair won a number of tournaments in the Midwest. Kafora also joined two other immortals, Hank Marino and Jimmy Blouin, on the first all-star team sponsored *by Bowlers Journal.*

He still climbed into his catcher's gear on occasion. But after he passed thirty, Kafora was content to simply manage a baseball team. By then he owned a pair of bowling alleys. Depending on what night it was, he could be found greeting customers at either Armitage Recreation or Avondale Arcade.

Kafora was noted for his wicked sense of humor. Nowhere is this better illustrated than in a story involving his good friend Nick Bruck. The large, beloved Bruck (later the first president of the BPAA) was known to enjoy a good, strong drink—or sometimes, six or seven good, strong drinks. One day Kafora found Bruck peacefully passed out at a table of a tavern they frequented. There was a ventilation pipe next to Bruck that led up to a storage room on the second floor. So Kafora went upstairs and began calling down the pipe in a deep, ghostly voice, "Nick Bruck, your time is nearly up!" Bruck stirred a bit, listening to the disembodied voice proclaiming his doom. Then he charged out of the tavern, vowing to abandon adult beverages.

Kafora said nothing about the incident to anyone. But a few days later, he sidled up to Bruck during a league session and whispered, "Nick Bruck, your time is nearly up!" Other bowlers present could not understand why the good-natured Bruck suddenly started chasing a wildly laughing Kafora around the bowling alley.

After his near-miss at the 1915 event, Kafora never again seriously challenged for an ABC title. His lifetime average in the big tournament was 188, one of the better marks of his era. Just one ABC eagle, and Kafora might now have his own plaque in the Bowling Hall of Fame. He certainly would if he'd had better luck in the World Classic.

That 1922 event was the first real national match game tournament. Kafora was among a select field of twenty-four men bowling 115 games for the largest single prize ever offered, $1,200. Along with the big check went a diamond-studded gold medal and recognition as the world's top bowler. The *Chicago Tribune* called the Classic "the World Series of Bowling."

And Kafora grabbed the opening lead. He swept through early matches against Otto Stein and Hank Marino with little bother. For a while he was the only man averaging over 200. By the end of twenty-five games he was pulling away from the field.

Then he ran into trouble. Louis Levine and Jimmy Blouin took him in back-to-back sets. Soon after that, during a match against Dom DeVito, Kafora's thumb split open. Blood gushing on every shot, he rolled a 150 and a 169. Friends urged him to drop out. Kafora hung on.

As late as the sixtieth game, he was still in second place. But the rest of the bowlers were finding the lanes by now, and Kafora could not keep up with the quickening pace. One by one, they passed him in the standings. (Among those edging by was none other than Spider Bill Wernicke.) When all the bowling was over, Jimmy Blouin was on top, with Kafora in seventeenth place.

The World Classic was staged only once, so Kafora never had a chance to show what he could do with a healthy thumb. But in 1923, his Bowlers Journal team won the important International Bowling Association championship in St. Paul. And over the next several seasons, Kafora continued to win his share of minor medals.

Life was wonderful. Kafora had gotten married and was now living in an elegant new apartment on the so-called "Polish Gold Coast." He bought another bowling center. In 1927 the *Chicago Herald-Examiner* hired Kafora to run its women's bowling tournament. The event was the largest of its kind, and added to his prestige in the tenpin world.

Then he got sick. Tuberculosis was spoken about in hushed tones in Kafora's day. How long he had the disease is uncertain. The reports that have come down to us merely cite his "lengthy illness" or his "recurring throat problem." At the end, there was also bronchial pneumonia. Kafora died on March 23, 1928.

"Frank Kafora Goes to the Great Beyond" read the headline in *Bowlers Journal*. The news also made the front page of Chicago's Polish language newspapers. And of Frank's funeral, it can be said that he would have enjoyed it. St. Wenceslaus Church was packed with floral tributes of both bowling and baseball motifs. Old friends gathered to submerge their sorrow with shared stories about Frank/Tomatoes/Fatty. Elmer Baumgarten of the ABC was amazed by "the outpouring of men of every nationality." The funeral Mass itself was delayed two hours, so that a team returning from the ABC Tournament at Kansas City could make it to the service.

Kafora is buried at St. Adalbert's Cemetery, just outside Chicago. That's about ten minutes from my home. Most of my own Polish ancestors are out there too, and the next time I visit them, I will look for Frank's grave. He seems like a member of the family.

Professor Krumske

(July 1993)
When bowling was big and Chicago was the bowling capital of the world, Paul Krumske was the best bowler in Chicago. And there is one story about Paul Krumske they always tell.

During a close match, Krumske suddenly keels over on the lane, grabbing his chest and gasping for breath. The match stops. Medical help is summoned, and Krumske is revived. He gamely declares that he will go on. By now the opposition is totally unnerved—especially when Krumske strings the next half-dozen strikes.

This incident happened during the famous match Krumske bowled against Ned Day ... or in a team match in the Chicago Classic League ... or in a tournament in Detroit ... or was it in a late-night pot game at Marigold? Perhaps he faked heart attacks on all those occasions. After the first few times, though, you'd think the other bowlers would get wise, and just step over Paul as they bowled.

The point of the story, of course, is Krumske's competitiveness, which didn't fit his looks. With his wispy physique, thick glasses, and prissy hair style, he reminded you of the nerdy kid who hung out in the school science lab. When Krumske had a television show in Chicago, it was even called *Bowl the Professor*. Yet from the time he broke in the Chicago Classic League in 1933 as a 21-year-old graduate of a church league, Krumske was a killer on the lanes. He was one of the rare breed who actually improved his performance under pressure. *Bowlers Journal* once took a poll to identify the greatest clutch bowlers of all time. Krumske was rated the best of his era.

His career stretched over forty years. Usually he was captain of a high-powered team, usually sponsored by Meister Brau Beer. Krumske teams won eighteen Classic League championships. He personally led the league in high average seven times.

He came close, but never won an ABC eagle. The BPAA events, with their match game format, were more to his liking. In 1945 Krumske won the Doubles title with Joe Sinke. His Meister Braus held the Team championship in 1946–47, and almost won it back (as King Louie) in 1952. That was the year the championship match ended in a flat-out tie. E&B Beer later won the roll-off and kept the title. But who do you think rolled the clutch strike that tied the first match?

His finest moment was his 80-game match against Ned Day in 1944. The year before Day had won the All-Star Tournament, and with it the individual match game championship. Krumske had finished second, earning the right to challenge Day for the title. Trouble was, Krumske couldn't come up with the $1000 deposit to seal the match. Day was considered unbeatable, and for once Krumske wasn't sure he could win. Finally, after eleven months, he scraped together the money, and they bowled.

Krumske handled the match the right way—he blew Day away in the Chicago half, then hung on through the champion's counter-attack in Milwaukee. In the end Krumske won and got to be match game champ for a month, until the next All-Star. It was the first time Day was ever defeated in a home-and-home match.

But then Paul always had a way of shining through. He was named an All American seven times and was elected to the Bowling Hall of Fame. In 1951 a newspaper poll selected him as Chicago's Bowler of the Half Century. Considering all the great stars who had come out of the Windy City, it was a singular honor.

Time finally caught up with him in the 1970s. The Meister Brau brewery closed, taking with it his longtime promotional job. Krumske's game was just about gone by then, as well. He did some instructing and ran a few tournaments. Early in 1979 he decided to make a fresh start and moved to Florida. That same summer, Paul Krumske died in his new Boca Raton home ... from a heart attack.

The Legend of Junie McMahon

(November 1993)
Junie McMahon! His name still sends a thrill through the hearts of an older generation. For a decade or so after World War II, he was the

"So smooth going to the line he could balance a tray of drinks on his head": Junie McMahon in 1946, shortly after his move to Chicago.

ideal of American tenpins. Many of those who watched Junie McMahon in action remain convinced there has never been a finer bowler.

He had an impressive presence. Tall, erect, and square-shouldered, with a barrel-chest physique tapering to a narrow waist, he seemed to radiate coiled power. On the lanes his style was classic—compact, direct, with no wasted motion. It was said that McMahon was so smooth going up to the line that he could balance a tray of drinks on his head. And of course, there was that devastating hook. In the days of rubber, lacquer, and hardwood, nobody rolled a ball like Junie McMahon. Put him on the modern pro tour, and they might have to stick weights on him, as they do for a race horse.

He was born in Passaic, New Jersey, in 1912. Named James after his father, he was first called Junior—which he hated—and then Junie, which he learned to live with. He was a schoolboy athlete of note, though he did not bowl his first game until he was seventeen. Then Pop McMahon was put in charge of the church's new bowling lanes. Nature took its course, and the kid was hooked.

Much of his career would have a storybook flavor. Take the matter of his first bowling tournament. After four seasons on the lanes, Junie had worked his way up to a 200 average. Some friends talked him into entering the New Jersey State Tournament. So Junie proceeded to walked off with the Singles title, and added the All Events for good measure. He felt so good about the whole business that a week later, he rolled his first 300 game.

He moved up from there. Over the next dozen years he made himself into a deadly match game opponent, knocking off sweepers, and rolling boxcar numbers, until he got too big for the East. Bowling's big time was in the Midwest in 1945. McMahon decided to sell his talent to a major team in either Chicago or Detroit—it didn't matter which, so his wife, Helen, suggested they flip a coin. It came up Chicago.

He joined Joe Wilman's Monarch Beer team. And for the first time, the terror of the East ran into trouble. The tough competition didn't bother him; it never would. What bugged McMahon was the peculiar Chicago habit of waiting for two lanes to clear on either side before you bowled. Accustomed to a swifter tempo, his game suffered. It wasn't until he had a full season under his belt that he felt comfortable.

McMahon's performance at the 1947 ABC Tournament was his first brush with national fame. Rolling in the Singles, he came down to his last eight frames needing eight strikes to pass the leader. He began stringing. As usually happens in such situations, the rest of the squad paused to watch. Just as McMahon went after his sixth strike, a restless pinboy signaled his bowler by banging a kickback. The noise startled Junie. He pulled his shot onto the nose—but all the pins fell anyway. After that, the last two strikes were anticlimactic. McMahon had won the ABC Singles. And just as he had done in New Jersey in his first tournament, he took the All Events as well.

He bowled with the world's best teams, but McMahon is not thought of as a team bowler. Tightly wound and aloof, a man who would never speak a sentence when a single word would do, he never quite fit in with Wilman's easy-going Monarch crew. After two seasons he moved over to Paul Krumske's high-powered Meister Braus. The Braus promptly lost their team match game title. All the people McMahon had alienated over the years had a field day with that one.

Junie did have a more serious problem than the occasional personality conflict. He drank too much. Old-timers still shake their heads about it, remembering him belting down shots of whiskey between matches at the All-Star Tournament. He led that most prestigious event going into the final day in 1946, then abruptly fell to third. Among insiders, it was whispered that alcohol was the reason.

He redeemed himself in 1949, running away with the All-Star by an impressive 11-point margin. According to legend, some of Junie's friends took turns chaperoning him, keeping him well-rested and sober. The enduring image of that tournament, however, is of the new champion sitting at a table, stoically soaking his mangled right thumb in Epsom salts. The annual 100-game destruction of that thumb would become another part of the McMahon legend.

He was named Bowler of the Year a few months later. Then he set an ABC Ten Year Average record—something he always called his proudest accomplishment. A second All-Star title followed in 1951. When *Bowlers Journal* announced its All American team each year, McMahon seemed to have a permanent spot.

As he had outgrown the East, McMahon now outgrew the bonds of conventional bowling. He quit weekly league play to bowl exhibitions. He appeared in films and wrote an instruction book. Stories on "America's top bowler" ran in glossy journals. His income climbed past $30,000, unheard of for someone in his profession.

It was inevitable that McMahon would be elected to the Bowling Hall of Fame in 1955, his first year of eligibility. By then Junie and Helen had returned to New Jersey to open a pro shop. And though he remained the biggest name in bowling, sharp-eyed observers detected signs of deterioration. He no longer challenged in the All-Star. The ABC scores were not so high. Other bowlers were knocking off the tournaments. At an age when Marino, Varipapa, Wilman and many other greats had not yet reached their peak, McMahon was already going downhill.

Early in 1959 he appeared on the premiere of the new television show, *Jackpot Bowling*. The format was strikes only, and Junie showed some of his old fire defeating his opponent, Carmen Salvino. Minutes after the program signed off, McMahon collapsed in the dressing room. He'd had a stroke.

Junie McMahon would never bowl again. At forty-seven he was now partially paralyzed and speech impaired, and would spend the rest of his days at home and in a succession of medical facilities. Every few years a story might appear in one of the bowling magazines about how he was coming along. Always it was worse than the last time. The end finally came in 1974.

The number of people who remember him dwindles each year. Yet you can still find a few of them at bowling tournaments. Let a young hotshot with a slashing hook bunch together some strikes, and for a time the light will shine in their eyes. And you will know what they are thinking. They are hoping to see the magic of another Junie McMahon.

Seven Days to 300

(November 1993)
On the long roll of ABC-sanctioned 300 games, there is one curious entry: "Koralewski, Barney—Buffalo, NY—March 22–29, 1934." It's not a typo. Barney Koralewski's perfect game took a week to bowl.

The tale begins on the first of those Thursday evenings, March 22. Koralewski was a printer at the *Buffalo Evening News* and bowled on a team sponsored by the paper in the Genesee Arcade Major League. After a mediocre opening game, Koralewski started his second game with a strike.

Koralewski had been having tough times on the lanes recently. Tonight he was using a ball borrowed from his team captain, Lorne Robertson. The first strike raised his hopes—perhaps his slump was over. Barney found that all he needed to do was apply a slight wrist turn as he released his shot from the corner of the lane. Then the ball would roll smoothly into the pocket.

Another strike. Three, four, five ... that one was on the Brooklyn. Six, seven, eight. Barney had the first eight in a row. And then everything went black.

The lights had gone out. Blown fuse? Somebody stuck his head out the door and noticed that the entire neighborhood was dark. That meant a power failure at the nearby electrical plant. So the bowlers lit a few candles and sat down to wait.

After forty-five minutes, nothing had changed. The team captains huddled, trying to decide what to do. They were about to suspend play when Lorne Robertson spoke up. Robertson reminded the other captains that his bowler, Barney Koralewski, was working on a string of eight strikes. Perfect games were rare events. Barney should have the opportunity to go for his. The captains agreed to wait a while longer.

Another hour passed. By now it was midnight. With the league little more than halfway through its session and no clue as to when the lights would return, the captains saw no alternative. They reluctantly declared bowling suspended. Koralewski would have to wait until the following week.

The next day's papers carried the story of the printer's *perfectus interruptus*. He took a lot of kidding from the rest of the guys at the *Evening News* and from his friends. Barney's big adventure became the hot topic of conversation at Buffalo's bars and bowling centers. Most people wished him luck. Those with money to wager were less sentimental. Koralewski was rated a longshot.

Thursday the 29th finally came. The electricity had long since been restored, and Genesee Arcade was ready for the continuation of Barney's quest. A large crowd packed the house. The suspended games were to be picked up immediately, before the regular league session.

Five minutes before bowling time, Barney arrived. He seemed surprised to see the crowd. No one talked to him. He changed shoes quickly, grabbed his ball, and walked over to the lanes. The bowlers were not allowed any practice—they were in the middle of a suspended game. So after 165 hours of delay, Barney merely stepped up, rolled his ball, and delivered a perfect strike. Loud applause from the spectators, and then he sat down.

After that first (ninth) strike, the tension was released. Koralewski had not cracked. The crowd was almost serene when play rolled around to him in the tenth frame. And Koralewski himself was matter-of-fact. He stepped up again and rolled strike number ten. Back up once more, and there was number eleven. The final ball was anti-climactic. And then the crowd went wild.

The shouting gradually died down. Now the official business had to be taken care of. Oddly enough, no one had sent notice to the ABC about Barney's unique situation, probably out of fear of jinxing him.

With the 300 safely completed, a telegram was immediately sent to Peoria, where the ABC High Score Committee was meeting during the annual tournament.

In due course, the decision was handed down. Barney had bowled his game in accordance with all ABC rules and regulations. Proper procedures had been followed for the order of bowling, the alternating of lanes, and so on. The long delay in the middle of the game did not affect the legal course of the game. Therefore, the 300 was approved.

Koralewski received his gold medal afterward. As an extra bonus, the Buffalo Bisons baseball team of the International League gave him a season's pass. For a while, Koralewski was the most famous sports figure in western New York. "I don't know what I could have done to make more friends," he said.

Fast-forward to 1967. An episode of television's *Andy Griffith Show*. Mayberry town clerk Howard Sprague is working on a perfect game when the lights go out. After a week's delay, he gets his 300.

Nice going, Howard! But Barney Koralewski did it first. And for real.

The Flying Falstaffs

(November 1993)

The next time you complain how your teammates picked a bowling alley so far from your home, stop and think about our sport's long-distance commuters. There have been some famous ones. Ned Day used to make a 180-mile round-trip between Milwaukee and Chicago to bowl with Buddy Bomar in the Chicago Classic League. Connie Schwoegler traveled 270 miles back and forth from Madison for the same league one season. Frank Clause and George Billick made a weekly auto trip of similar length between Old Forge, Pennsylvania, and New York City.

And then were the champion commuters of all time, the Falstaff Beer team. Each week during the 1956–57 season, the Falstaffs made the 600-mile journey between Chicago and St. Louis—by airplane.

The whole adventure started because of a brewery rivalry. Falstaff and Budweiser were longtime competitors in the St. Louis beer market.

The Flying Falstaffs

The Flying Falstaffs pose with brewery officials and the company plane in Chicago, before the team's first flight to St. Louis. Captain Buddy Bomar is in the light colored sports coat (center). Moving to the right from Bomar are teammates Don Ellis (back row), Stan Gifford, Bill Lillard and Bill Bunetta. The man on the far right is an unidentified brewery official.

In 1954 Budweiser had begun sponsoring a team of big-time bowlers that was soon drawing loads of publicity. Falstaff had responded by signing up Buddy Bomar's team in Chicago. They had enjoyed the first big return on their investment when the Bomar crew won the 1956 ABC Team championship.

But Falstaff wanted to go head-to-head with Budweiser at home in St. Louis. Since they couldn't very well abandon the ABC champs, writer Ray Nelson came up with an idea. Why not fly Bomar and company into St. Louis each Wednesday to bowl in the Budweisers' own league, the St. Louis Masters? It was such an audacious plan that the Falstaff bosses bought it.

Initial plans were to transport the team on the brewery's private plane. That was scrapped when commercial flights proved cheaper.

Some changes were made in the lineup, too. Bomar, Bill Lillard, and Stan Gifford stayed on from the crew that had won the ABC title. Ned Day decided a double-commute from Milwaukee to Chicago to St. Louis was too much, and Earl Johnson was dropped. The new Falstaffs were Bill Bunetta, Don Ellis, and Carl Richard.

The first flight went off on August 22, 1956. Air travel was more casual then, and the plane arrived in St. Louis an hour late. The brewery sent a brass band to meet the team. The captains from the other seven teams in the Masters League were also on hand. Newspaper reporters and a television crew covered the short ceremony at the airport. The Flying Falstaffs were already becoming a big sports story.

The St. Louis Masters bowled at Floriss Lanes, a cozy little venue known for its friendly conditions. The Falstaffs didn't burn up the lanes that first night, though their 2910 set was good enough to take two out of three games from the tough Pulaski Savings team. Lillard's 633 series set the pace.

The Wednesday flights settled into a routine. Meanwhile, on Tuesdays and Thursdays, the Falstaffs were still bowling in the Chicago Classic League. That fact was nearly forgotten as the bowling world watched the doings in St. Louis.

Six weeks into the season, the Falstaffs and the Budweisers finally met. Scores were high, and Dick Weber even tossed a perfect game for the Buds. Falstaff won two out of three in that first encounter. Yet as the year progressed, they remained behind their rivals in the league standings.

An unusual situation developed in midseason, when Budweiser and Falstaff ran 1–2 in the BPAA Team Match Game qualifying. The format called for a home-and-home title match between the teams. But since the Falstaffs were already familiar with Floriss, the Buds found another home. Falstaff wouldn't use Floriss either, and they had to settle for their third choice when their favorite Chicago center was unavailable. When the match was finally bowled, Budweiser won easily.

That was symbolic of the Falstaff season in St. Louis. Despite the high hopes and the publicity, they couldn't quite catch the Buds. Bill Lillard made the best adjustment; his 223 average ranked second in the league. The rest of the team had less success—and considering the circumstances, that's not a criticism. Falstaff finished third in the St. Louis Masters, behind the Buds and Pulaski Savings. Adding to its disappointment, the team also placed down the list in the Chicago Classic League.

Still, Falstaff was pleased. Having a topflight team on the lanes in St. Louis was wonderful advertising. For the next season, the brewery decided to save the $6,000 airline fees and base the team locally. Bomar refused to leave Chicago, so a new team was formed around Buzz Fazio. Only Carl Richard remained from the flying squad.

The great airlift was over. But the Falstaff/Budweiser wars had begun. Over the next several years, they would become a highlight of the Great Team Era.

Bowling's *Cinéma Vérité*

(November 1993)
They say that life imitates art. One of the more colorful cases of this maxim has a bowling angle.

The original *Scarface* was one of the movie hits of 1932. Starring Paul Muni as a thinly disguised version of Al Capone, it chronicles the rise and fall of a brutal bootlegger in Prohibition-era Chicago. Onetime city-beat reporter Ben Hecht wrote the screenplay, so the film carries the stamp of authenticity.

About halfway through the story, Muni decides to eliminate rival mobster Boris Karloff. Karloff learns of the plot and disappears. But he can't stay put. One night he goes bowling.

Muni is at the theater when word comes that Karloff has been spotted. So our scarfaced hero and some henchmen head for the bowling alley. And they don't take their bowling equipment with them.

Out on the lanes, Karloff is happily spilling pins. Muni and crew enter unseen. "Now watch this one," Karloff tells the guy next to him.

Into his delivery goes Karloff. Just as he reaches the foul line gunshots ring out, and he crumples to the floor. The camera, however, follows the ball down the lane. The ball hits the pocket. Pins scatter—all except the 10-pin, which spins crazily in circles a few times before finally toppling over.

Film critics loved the bowling scene. They praised director Howard Hawks and his use of the slowly toppling pin as a symbol of Karloff dying off-screen. In fact, the whole idea of killing a character in a bowling alley was brilliantly original. That had never been done.

Gangland applauded the film, too. Members of the Capone mob

were tickled to see their exploits portrayed on the giant screen in glorious black-and-white. One of those mobsters was Machine Gun Jack McGurn.

A trusted Capone lieutenant, McGurn was reputedly the lead gunman in the notorious St. Valentine's Day Massacre. Yet he didn't fit the public image of a gangster. McGurn dressed in conservatively cut charcoal gray suits, and charmed those he met with his gracious manners. He could discuss history and literature insightfully. Disdaining the wicked city where he made his livelihood, he owned a bungalow in sedate, suburban Oak Park.

McGurn was also a sportsman. As a golfer he was good enough to qualify for the 1933 Western Open and play the first six holes in one-under-par, until some spoilsport cops turned up to arrest him. In winter he was a regular 200-shooter at Avenue Recreation on Chicago's Northwest Side.

On St. Valentine's evening in 1936, McGurn decided to roll a few lines. Along with two friends he journeyed into the city, arriving at Avenue about midnight. McGurn and his pals removed their outer clothing and prepared to bowl. Suddenly, three men rushed in, brandishing pistols and announcing a stickup.

Reports of what happened next are confused. Most of the patrons dove for cover. So did McGurn's companions. The intruders ran up to where McGurn was standing and shot him three times before he could draw his own gun. Machine Gun Jack died on Alley Two with a house ball in his hands.

Within hours the papers were on the streets with extra editions. McGurn's death was bigger news that FDR, Hitler, or the turmoil in Spain. One homey touch was the unsigned Valentine left on his body—

> "You've lost your job,
> You've lost your dough,
> Your car and your fine houses.
> But things could be worse, you know—
> You haven't lost your trousers."

The murder was never solved, credited to the usual "Person or Persons Unknown." What's unmistakable is the eerie echo of Karloff's death in *Scarface*. Someone had seen the movie, been impressed by the staging, and decided to copy it.

A few observers claim that bowling's image problem dates from the McGurn slaying. By extension that puts the blame on screenwriter Hecht and director Hawks. Certainly their *Scarface* scenes put bowling in a sinister light. But they might have done worse. They might have given us *Dreamer*.

That's Shaul, Folks!

(November 1993)
The poster told the story. Bill Shaul was coming!

There was a picture of a balding, middle-aged gent in glasses, with a cheery grin on his face. The text went on, in that breathless style of the 1940s, to notify all present that Bill Shaul would appear in this very bowling establishment! He would be available to give instruction, to fit bowling balls, to explain the Shaul Method of Spare-Making—for one week only! His engagement was being sponsored by Ebonite, as the company's "contribution to better bowling."

For over two decades, Bill Shaul roamed America with his one-man bowling medicine show. He was a promoter and a pioneer. In the long history of tenpins, he was the first truly professional instructor.

Born in Brooklyn in 1883, Shaul learned bowling as a pinboy. His first ambition was to be an opera singer. After touring with some traveling companies, he landed a baritone spot at the Boston Opera. Then he took a few years out to study for the ministry, followed by a stint running the music program at a Vermont school.

Always there was bowling. In 1923 he finally settled in Syracuse and opened his own establishment. A good but not great bowler, he finished as high as third in the ABC Singles and competed in the 1929 International Tournament in Sweden. Meanwhile, to lure more patrons to his center, Shaul began giving bowling lessons. His success convinced him he could make a living as a full-time traveling instructor.

Teaching bowling was something new. Jimmy Smith, Floretta McCutcheon, Joe Falcaro, and a few others were already touring, rolling exhibition matches, doing trick shots, and giving a few pointers. But as star performers, they concentrated on showing off their skills, with any instruction an afterthought. A novice who came to Smith for a lesson might spend the whole time watching Jimmy demonstrate how it was done, without getting to roll a shot himself.

Shaul shifted the emphasis. He didn't care whether he impressed his students, only that they learn something useful. When he ran a clinic he was not selling Bill Shaul; he was selling the game.

Ebonite signed him in 1936 and his tours went nationwide. Besides bowling centers, Shaul appeared in theatres, school auditoriums, department stores, and military bases. In Cleveland he gave demonstrations for 24,000 high school students. He taught blind veterans to roll the ball straight ahead by having them mimic the military salute. He appeared on the first-ever bowling telecast.

His shows were always entertaining. Shaul traveled with the latest high-tech graphic devices—which meant a chalkboard, flip charts, and colored bowling pins. At the start of each session, he distributed copies of his booklet *Better Bowling: How It's Done*. During his first year with Ebonite, he ran through 1.2 million of them.

His theories were the simple, meat-and-potatoes of bowling that would nourish generations of new players—squared shoulders, natural speed, pendulum arm swing, uniform delivery. His spare-making method was basically aiming cross-alley and turning your body toward the target. All standard stuff today. But that's because Shaul spread his message so widely.

He died in 1955, on the eve of the great bowling boom he'd helped usher in. Of all the million-plus people he had worked with, the gentle Shaul had mostly fond memories. However, he did relish telling the story of a heckler who'd confronted him in Columbus, Ohio.

He was moving through his presentation when a guy in the front row piped up, "I can do that!" This happened several times—Shaul would make a point, and the loudmouth would shout, "I can do that!"

Finally Shaul stopped and told the audience he had just been reminded of something from his opera days. With that he opened his mouth wide and emitted an ear-piercing yodel, a 30-second, three-octave, virtuoso performance. Then he turned to the heckler, smiled sweetly and asked, "Can you do that?"

Nobody's Buddy

(June 1994)
Buddy Bomar's nickname never fit him. Herbert was his given name, but he shouldn't have been saddled with something that made him sound like a chirpy cartoon squirrel. Tex would have been better, or maybe Bull, or Duke. Because Buddy Bomar was John Wayne on the lanes.

He was a handsome, hard-bitten guy, a Texan in everything but his 1916 Oklahoma birth, and his speech never did lose the twang of the prairies. When he bowled, his style was almost a parody of John Wayne's famous walk. Bomar ambled to the line pigeon-toed, one foot in front of the other, hips and arms swinging loose. And then there was that glare of iron concentration. Had he left a 10-pin on a crucial shot, you wouldn't have been surprised to see him whip out a six-shooter and blast it down.

Competition was Bomar's lifeblood. Once he got himself in a pot game with some ordinary bowlers. As a spot, he was permitted only one ball per frame—which meant he'd automatically miss each spare. All he did was roll a 300.

He came to bowling literally by accident. A cement mixer chewed off the index finger of his left hand when he was a youngster. His baseball playing suffered, so a coach suggested he try bowling to build up his good arm. Bomar turned out to be a natural, and forgot about baseball.

A group of Texas oilmen became his backers. Bomar won two state All Events titles before he was old enough to vote, and beat the great Andy Varipapa in an exhibition match. Varipapa was not very impressed with the kid's game, and said so—which probably destroyed Bomar's self-confidence for a good fifteen minutes. A few years later Bomar went up to Chicago for the All-Star Tournament, rolled some big numbers, and was signed by Bill Flesch's Monarch Beer team.

Wherever he was, Bomar was going to be the boss. Nothing against Flesch or the Monarchs; that's just the way it had to be. Inevitably, he wanted his own team. After he won the 1944 All-Star and was elected Bowler of the Year, he began looking for a sponsor. Bomar finally settled on cosmetics tycoon Harry Daumit, and allowed Daumit to put up a whopping $12,000 stake for the Kathryn Products team.

Bomar's crew would later be called Tavern Pale, then Jockey Cooper, then Falstaff, then Munsingwear—he could always find a sweeter deal than the one that came before. He liked to recruit bowlers from other cities, the same way Flesch had recruited him. Among those he brought to Chicago were Ned Day, Eddie Kawolics, Joe Kristof, Bill Lillard, Ray Bluth, Don Ellis, Earl Johnson, and Bill Bunetta. And that's just the Hall of Famers.

Bowling on a Bomar team was an intense experience. The story is often told of how he froze his home lanes and had his players practice in sweaters. Another time, the BPAA suspended him from a championship match for rules violations. Opponents found themselves subjected to exquisite needling. His own men endured sarcastic snarls, or threats to be bounced from the team. After hours and away from the lanes, Bomar could be a good ol' boy, all charm, cheer, and courtesy. But dammit, work was work!

Despite all the bloody sweat, the Bomars never dominated the Great Team Era. The record shows two years as match game champions and a single ABC Team title in 1956. There was always some team just a little better. Even when Bomar's Falstaffs made their highly publicized weekly flights into St. Louis, they finished third in the league.

For his part, Bomar came close to being the best of his day. He was named an All American nine times between 1943 and 1956. In 1947 he was again elected Bowler of the Year, one of the few times the honor didn't go to the All-Star champ. Bomar merely captured both ends of the Petersen Classic and raked in more prize money in one season than any bowler in history, $17,400. He won so many individual events that "Who's Who in Bowling" eventually stopped listing them.

When his skills began to desert him, he didn't hang around. Bomar was a longtime member of the Brunswick advisory staff, and at one time owned four bowling supply stores. But after his election to the Hall of Fame in 1966, he quit the game and became a stockbroker. He didn't touch a bowling ball for a dozen years, not until the inaugural Great and Greatest Tournament. Then he took to the lanes one last time, the scores maybe not so high, but the form unmistakable.

Buddy Bomar died in 1989. One veteran summed him up memorably: "If I had a match for my house, my car, and everything I owned, I'd want Buddy Bomar to bowl it. He knew how to win." And you'd better believe that, Pilgrim.

Advertisement for the 1945–46 All-Star Tournament, featuring defending champion Buddy Bomar.

Things I Learned While Looking Up Other Things

(September 1994)

It took me nine years to finish my PhD. One reason was that I'd get sidetracked during my research. I might be looking for information on Illinois election law changes in a 1907 newspaper. I would wind up reading about a juicy murder story, or checking out the merchandise and prices at Marshall Field's, or maybe stumbling across a picture of my neighborhood when it was farmland.

I haven't improved any. Every time I delve into the *Bowlers Journal* archives for a story, I emerge with a dozen chunks of unrelated trivia. I've been showering the staff with this stuff for years. They suggested it was time I share the wealth with others.

The title is obvious. I got that from the late, great syndicated newspaper columnist, Sydney J. Harris.

- Don't be too quick to label a PBA star who loses a tournament on a bad count "the worst choke artist in history." In 1940 Charley Lausche was rolling against Lowell Jackson to decide who'd challenge match game champ Ned Day. Lausche came to his final frame needing only a seven-count on his first ball, and nine pins in all. He left the 4–6–7–9–10 split, missed it, and handed the match to Jackson.
- Smoking controversies are nothing new in bowling. In a 1939 column, Mort Luby, Sr., suggested that ABC Tournament smoking policy should be altered—to *allow* smoking on the lanes.
- Health care reform is also an old issue in the bowling world. In 1935 Indianapolis proprietor Jess Pritchett outlined a plan "whereby the sick and disabled bowler can be taken care of by hospitalization."
- Rolling the ceremonial first ball of the 1941 ABC at St. Paul wasn't enough for Minnesota governor Harold Stassen; he competed in the tournament as an official entrant. After a rocky start of 101 and 159, the gov wowed his constituents with a 208 finale.
- Bowlers were conscious of physical fitness as early as 1916. Advertisements for the Bensinger chain in Chicago declared their bowling centers were "actual health factories." Regular

- bowling was proclaimed to be a sure cure for kidney disease, paralysis, heart trouble, and cancer.
- Political candidates also advertised in *Bowlers Journal*. Running for Cook County State's Attorney in 1928, Judge William J. Lindsey billed himself as "The Bowler's Friend." He lost the election by 150,000 votes.
- A.J. Cermak was a more successful politician. He also ran campaign ads in *BJ*. Between elections he sponsored individual teams and an entire league. In 1931 Cermak was elected Mayor of Chicago, and the next year fielded a powerhouse team in the city's Classic League. Though he was never named to any bowling hall of fame, today one of Chicago's major streets is called Cermak Road.
- Many star bowlers have also been excellent golfers. But Steve Nagy topped them all. Playing in the Ohio Amateur Tournament during the early 1950s, Nagy defeated none other than Arnold Palmer.
- When the U.S. government forced Japanese-Americans into relocation camps during World War II, some bowling proprietors came up with an alternative plan. They proposed hiring the Nisei as pinboys to solve the wartime shortage.
- The next time you plunk down some cash for a "thirty-clean" pot, reflect on the skill of Howard Glover. In a 1944 league session in San Francisco, he became the first bowler ever to roll an all-spare three game series.
- During the 1913–14 season, *Bowlers Journal* awarded a prize for the highest game rolled each week in Chicago—a pair of bowling shoes.
- When Hall of Famer Joe Wilman died in 1969, his widow arranged to have his favorite bowling ball placed in the casket. The interesting part of the story is that Joe was not buried, he was cremated. Think about that for awhile.

Belle of the Ball

(March 1995)
"Why don't you ever write about women bowlers?" the Oldest Bowler

asked me. It was a reasonable question. I knew that I didn't have a reasonable answer. I also knew that he must have someone in mind.

"Val Mikiel," he said firmly, as if the matter were settled. "You should write about her."

I recognized the name—the first female Bowler of the Year. But the Oldest Bowler had already been launched.

"Velma Allison. That was her original name. She was born in Texas in 1915. Played a lot of tennis down there. Track star, too. Yet she didn't bowl right away. That came after high school. The way Val told it, she had a job as a singer with a traveling band. They got to Chicago, and some of the guys took her bowling—in high heels, no less. But she did okay, and she liked it, so she started working at it. The next thing you knew, she was a bowling instructor in Houston."

I remarked that the story sounded almost like a fairy tale.

"People suspected that Val was pulling their leg a lot of the time," the Oldest Bowler said. "For instance, she had a habit of fainting in competition. Pass out right on the approach. It really shook everybody up. But a teammate swore that one time when Val was lying down there, Val slipped her a big wink."

The Oldest Bowler chuckled. "Maybe she learned that routine in Chicago—from Paul Krumske. Anyway, Val started getting known as a bowler during World War II, the early '40s. She used to bowl in the men's tournaments and did pretty good. That's how she met her husband, Vince Mikiel. He was one of Detroit's big bowlers. They got married before Vince went into the service. After the war, they both got instructor's jobs in Detroit."

My bowling almanac told me that Val won the WIBC Singles in 1946. The Oldest Bowler remembered that, too.

"Kansas City. The whole business actually started in the second game of the Doubles. Val shot 264. But she couldn't do anything the other games, and then started the Singles with 182. She turned to her teammate, a lady named Eddie Coy, and said, 'I could sure use that 264 now.'

"Well, Eddie asked Val if she'd settle for a couple of 230s. That sounded good, so Val rolled 232. Now Val was really pumped. She started stringing strikes, and practically jumping on the ball return—she was always good for body English. Val got 268 the last game. That 682 was the second-highest series anybody had ever rolled in the WIBC Singles. And Val got her eagle—or whatever they give them at the WIBC."

Scores were lower then, it seemed.

The Oldest Bowler agreed. "Val was one of the top women bowlers in the country, yet she only averaged in the 190s. But when she was on her game, she could be awesome.

"Take what happened at Wurm's Recreation in Detroit that same year. Labor Day. Val and her friend Gladys Dempsey got into a friendly

The 1948–49 Bowlers of the Year, Val Mikiel (left) and Connie Schwoegler, comparing notes.

match against a couple of guys. First game, Val left a 10-pin, picked it up, and struck out for 290. She came back with 234. When she started her third game with a few strikes, word got around that she had a shot at 800. Well, she did just that—shot 278 the last game for 802. Only one ball out of the pocket the whole way."

The Oldest Bowler chuckled again. "Val always claimed she should have had 803. On her last ball, the 10-pin was falling and the pinboy grabbed it, so she only counted nine pins."

I reminded the Oldest Bowler that the 800 series would not have been sanctioned.

"Of course not!" he snapped. "But it was still such a big deal. The only other woman to bowl 800 ever was Mrs. Mac, Floretta McCutcheon. Heck, 800s were so rare then, the ABC used to list every one of them in their yearbook."

The Oldest Bowler paused. "That 800 is probably what got her elected Bowler of the Year. Val won a lot of informal home-and-home matches. But women just didn't have many events in those days, didn't get much publicity. So when the writers started electing a woman Bowler of the Year in 1948, they remembered the lady with the 800. And they elected her again in 1949. Then the women's All-Star began, and everybody could see that Marion Ladewig was the best.

"That was about it for Val. She made the finals of the All-Star and the World's Invitational a few times during the '50s, but was never really in the running to win. Along the way her marriage broke up. She moved back to Texas and died there in 1969."

The Oldest Bowler smiled at his memories. "I don't know how good Val Mikiel would be today. But you can bet on one sure thing— she sure would be fun to watch." And then he slipped me a big wink.

The Joker Is Wild

(June 1995)
Someone once asked George Frederick Calder if he claimed to be the greatest bowler in the world. "Naw, I don't claim that," Calder replied. "I admit it."

He was an accomplished performer during the 1940s and '50s, though his record never did measure up to his bravado. Calder was best known for his flamboyant personality. He probably collected more nicknames than tournament titles.

People generally called him Ace. He was also known as Bowling's Dizzy Dean, The Gorgeous George of the Alleys, The Clown Prince of Bowling, or simply The Great Calder. You could say he made an impression. Thirty years after his death, old-timers around Chicago still trade Ace Calder stories.

He was born in the city in 1911, and grew up wanting to be a baseball player. He had the talent. After graduating high school, Calder signed with the St. Louis Cardinals. He was working his way through their farm system when he injured his arm.

If you read the biographies of PBA stars, you'll be struck by how many were aspiring baseball players who started bowling "to build up their arm." Calder was one of these. He was twenty-five years old and had never bowled in his life. Yet within a year he had rolled a 300 game in one of Chicago's toughest leagues. He never went back to the Cardinals.

Calder's bowling style hardly had the grace of a professional athlete. He scuttled up to the line on dips and lurches, like a puppet with its strings tangled. The large cigar clasped between his teeth might have been there to keep him from tipping over. His release was the overturned spinner common in the days of shellac. It produced a shot that was unremarkable—unless it found a friendly track.

Calder found that track on Lanes Seven and Eight at Kaadland Recreation. He became captain of a team in the North End Traveling League sponsored by Keeley's Half-and-Half, a dreadful brew that combined the worst features of beer and malt liquor. The North End was a home-and-home league. As such, teams were expected to doctor their home alleys to suit their games. Nobody did that better than Calder and his Keeleys.

In 1946 the team won the ABC award for the country's highest three-game series, 3629. The following year the Keeleys became the first team to take the award back-to-back with 3577. Calder himself rolled a 796 set in 1948, the best in Illinois that season. When the Keeleys didn't crack 3300 at home they considered it a bad night.

You did not beat Calder or the Keeleys at Kaadland. During those glory years, Calder rolled a series of eight-game charity matches on his favorite pair. He knocked off Andy Varipapa, Connie Schwoegler, Joe Kristof, and a whole roster of other stars. The only invader to defeat him was Joe Norris—and Norris had to shoot 300 the last game to do that.

On the lanes, Calder appeared to genuinely enjoy his bowling. He ran out strikes, he yelled at the pins, he kidded the spectators, he mimicked the styles of his opponents. Critics said he might do better if he would only get serious. They claimed he could bowl well only at Kaadland, where he didn't have to think.

But life was more fun Ace's way. Sometimes he'd bet every horse in a single race so he would come up with a winner. Returning to Chicago after a tournament, he might check into a suite at a Loop hotel and throw a party—and then send the bill to Keeley. The team bowled exhibitions around the Midwest. On the day of one of these matches, the Keeley front office received a telegram from its captain which read: "Am in South Bend. Where should I be?"

Another tale concerns the young hotshot who lost a $100 match to Calder and couldn't pay. The debt dragged on for weeks. When the kid finally decided to settle, he tried to carry it off with a flourish, appearing at Kaadland before a packed house and ceremoniously presenting Calder with a $100 bill. Calder accepted the money without comment. Then he struck a match, ignited the $100 bill, and lit his cigar with it.

A fatal stroke ended the good times in 1965. But something of The Great Calder has survived. In 1954 he appeared against Buddy Bomar on the *Championship Bowling* television show. Calder goes through his whole routine and has the match locked up until he chops a spare in the final frame. With that, he picks up Bomar's ball and nearly flings it down the lane.

It's worth getting the tape of that match, even though the result is known. Everyone, at least once, should see Ace Calder in action.

The Patriotic Bowling Tournament

(October 1995)
In the spring of 1917, the United States entered World War I. Among the unforeseen results was the largest bowling tournament the world had ever seen.

Germany was the enemy, and anti–German hysteria was sweeping the country. Schools dropped German language courses. Opera houses cancelled Wagner programs. Restaurants changed sauerkraut to "liberty cabbage." Some resident Germans were tar-and-feathered.

Because bowling was still close to its German roots, some super-patriots talked of outlawing the game. With many proprietors and tenpin officials sporting German names—Bensinger, Baumgarten, Bruck, Schuenemann, Mueller, and so on—the major players sounded like a roll call of the Kaiser's General Staff.

It happened that many army recruits from Chicago were taking their basic training at Camp Grant, near Rockford. Word reached home that the recreational facilities at the camp were limited. The boys didn't even have a bowling alley.

ABC treasurer Frank Pasdeloup announced the solution in *Bowlers Journal* in February 1918. The city and state bowling associations, along with the local proprietors, were going to build bowling facilities at Camp Grant. To raise money, they planned a Patriotic Bowling Tournament. Now all the doubters would know that bowling was truly an All-American game.

Over the next few months, the tournament committee rounded out the details. They decided to make the Patriotic Tournament a full-blown "ABC-style" show, with Team, Doubles, and Singles events. All male bowlers in Illinois were eligible. Entry fees were set at a modest $1 per event. Bowlers would be allowed to shoot at the establishment of their choice.

The last proviso set the tone for the tournament. With so many houses involved, scoring conditions couldn't be consistent, so the Patriotic Tournament would forget about competitive standings. Prizes would be awarded through a blind drawing.

Public response was enthusiastic. As Patriotic Tournament Week got closer, entries poured in. Some leagues simply added an extra week to their schedules and bowled as a unit. Churches, fraternal societies, athletic clubs, offices, and factories all organized teams. At the Chicago Stock Yards, rival meatpacking companies engaged in friendly competition to see which one would field the most teams. Armour won, and had to reserve an entire floor of Wabash Recreation to accommodate its bowlers. The largest contingent from a single business was the 104 teams representing the Crane Plumbing Company.

The games began on Saturday, May 25. One bowler at Prima Recreation got into the patriotic spirit by showing up dressed as Uncle Sam. A total of 1,066 teams participated, including 134 from towns outside Chicago. The Doubles entry was 762, while the Singles attracted 1,585. All entry figures were records. In fact, the biggest bowling tournament up to that time had been the 1916 ABC at Toledo, with 756 teams.

The concluding festivities were held at Randolph Recreation on June 22. Former ABC president Judge Howard was master of ceremonies. Medals were presented for the highest scores in each division: Team—Olsens (3223), Doubles—Hank Marino and Bob Rolfe (1336), Singles—Robert Phelps (759). Then the Judge began drawing for the prizes.

The monetary awards were in the form of war certificates and thrift stamps, ranging in denomination from $1 through $20. Various businesses had donated merchandise. Boxes of cigars and subscriptions to *Bowlers Journal* were hot items, though the prize list included socks, straw hats, fountain pens, a new bowling ball, a case of marshmallows, and an "assortment of cookie treats." Everyone who bowled in the tournament received a red-white-and-blue badge.

The Patriotic Bowling Tournament raised $2,646.48, an impressive sum in 1918. Unfortunately, government red tape then began to tangle things. Army officials backed out of their commitment to provide a building for the lanes. Angry words were exchanged, letters were fired off to the Secretary of War. Both the YMCA and the Knights of Columbus were approached to co-sponsor the Camp Grant bowling facility. Neither group was interested.

At last, the Great Lakes Naval Training Camp agreed to accept the gift. Ten new bowling lanes were installed at the base. On December 19, 1918, the facility was formally dedicated. Its work finished, the Patriotic Bowling Tournament committee disbanded. By then the war had been over for a month. But in this case, it was the thought that counted.

The Greatest Team Match

(December 1995)
For a match to be great, a meaningful prize should be at stake. Next, the bowlers should be highly skilled. Finally, the outcome should be in doubt until the last possible moment. The 1952 showdown between E&B Beer and King Louie Bowling Shirts had all of these things. Did it ever.

To be decided was the BPAA's Team Match Game championship. During the 1950s this event carried enormous prestige. Win the title, and your team was considered the best in bowling. The championship this time was to be decided by a challenge match, 24 games home-and-home.

Detroit-based E&B had won the title in 1949, and had successfully defended four times. Captain of the champions was little Louie Sielaff, a former teenage wiz who never won many individual titles, yet always seemed to get the most out of his bowlers. He was backed by an odd-couple doubles partnership—bulky, intense Therm Gibson and slender, laid-back George Young. Anchoring the team was Fred Bujack, whose powerful strike ball had earned him the nickname "The Blonde Bomber." These four had been together for almost a decade. The last spot on the 1952 team was filled by two alternating youngsters, Bill Bunetta and Bill Williams.

The King Louie challengers rolled out of Chicago. They had held the title as Meister Brau Beer in 1946–47. Paul Krumske, captain and anchorman, was a veteran campaigner known for his steely nerves under fire. Leadoff man Ed Brosius had a sunny smile, a picture-book style, and a devastating hook. Eddie Kawolics was hammered down and wide, and had one of the loudest mouths in Chicago. That probably evened out for Harry Lippe, who never said much as he methodically plodded to the line. For the final spot, Krumske brought in a ringer. Two-time All-Star champ Junie McMahon had already quit the King Louies and moved to New Jersey. But you put your strongest team on the lanes for this championship, and McMahon was the best in the game.

They started on March 1 at Uptown Melody Lanes in Chicago. Young sat out for the E&Bs, and the strategy paid off when Williams roared out of the gate with 713 in the opening block. The Detroiters took that one, 3024–2900. Then the King Louies battled back. At the end of the 12-game Chicago set, they led the champions by 73 pins.

The match moved to Detroit's Palm Beach Recreation for the final blocks. Back on familiar lanes, the E&Bs moved out to a 103-pin lead after the fifth block. Once more the King Louies came back, taking the sixth block and moving ahead in the match by 99 pins. In the seventh block they increased their lead to 207 pins. Williams had cooled off, and Young was now rolling for E&B.

A turn-away crowd was on hand at Palm Beach as the final block began on the evening of March 9. Paced by Young's 257, the E&Bs took the first game, 1121–1027, cutting the opposition's lead to 113 pins. They won the second game 999–906. With one game to go, King Louie led the charging E&Bs by a margin of just 20 pins.

The third game was all guts. First the E&Bs moved ahead, then the King Louies were on top, then it was the E&Bs once again. During the last game, the lead changed hands no fewer than twenty-five times. Finally, it all came down to the anchormen.

E&B's Bujack was up first. Five quick steps, a little flick of the wrist, and the ball spins out onto the lane. A sudden left turn—*strike*! Wild cheers from the hometown crowd.

Then up on the other lane for the King Louie's Krumske. Much jockeying of the ball at the stance, the graceful trot to the line, the ball away. In the pocket—but the 4-pin stands.

Back to Bujack. Another strike will win the match. He makes his approach and delivers. The crowd holds its breath. The Blonde Bomber's ball explodes the pocket—*8–10*!

The crowd gasps. Then everybody starts counting on fingers, trying to figure out who needs what. Krumske decides he might as well pick up his spare, and he does. Now word comes back to Bujack—go for the count. Still looking shocked from his first ball, Bujack picks off the 8-pin.

After 2,399 frames of bowling, the King Louies trail the E&Bs by exactly 10 pins. Krumske has exactly 10 pins left to shoot at. He takes his stance, flicks his right thumb against his trouser leg a few million times, inserts his fingers into the ball, jockeys it around some more—and then he's going down the approach. The ball rolls away. It hits the pocket. *Strike*! A tie! The match is a *tie*!

This had never happened in the history of the BPAA team matches. There was nothing for them to do but bowl another four games the next day.

The roll-off was anticlimactic. Gibson got hot and averaged 245, the E&Bs put back-to-back 1100s on the board, and coasted to victory. Their final margin was 275 pins.

Was this the greatest team match ever? It's got my vote.

Bowling's Landmark Tour

(May 1996/January 2000)

As a historian, I have always been disappointed that bowling neglects its historic sites. It's not that way with other sports. You can easily locate the place where Ebbets Field stood, or find the golf courses where Bobby Jones won his Grand Slam, or the arena where Wilt Chamberlain scored 100 points in a basketball game. Try that with a bowling landmark.

I finally decided to assemble my own list of historic sites. Here's the result, originally presented in two separate articles. Sadly, most of these venues are long gone.

Allen's Bowling Alleys, 31 Walnut Street, Lockport, NY. Site of Allie Brandt's 886 series.

Arcade Lanes, 7579 Olive Street Road, St. Louis, MO. The House Above the Hardware Store, famed for high scores in the 1950s and '60s.

Archer-35th Recreation, 2051 West 35th Street, Chicago, IL. Longtime home of the Petersen Classic.

Avenue Recreation, 805 North Milwaukee Avenue, Chicago, IL. Machine-Gun Jack McGurn was rubbed out here while rolling open play in 1936.

Beethoven Hall, 210 East 5th Street, New York, NY. Birthplace of the American Bowling Congress.

Bensinger's Randolph Recreation, 29 West Randolph Street, Chicago, IL. Home of the Randolph League; also site of seven world championship singles matches.

Bowl Haven Lanes, 3003 Humbert Road, Alton, IL. Where the movie *Dreamer* was filmed.

Bowl-O-Drome Recreation, 179 South Gratiot Avenue, Mount Clemens, MI. First center with automatic pinsetters (1951).

Capitol Recreation, 1680 Broadway, New York, NY. The first televised bowling show (1947).

Chicago Coliseum, 1513 South Wabash Avenue, Chicago, IL. Home of the All-Star, the World's Invitational, two ABC tournaments, and the 1922 World Classic.

Chicago Heights Recreation, 1532 Halsted Street, Chicago Heights, IL. The only bowling alley ever owned by Count Gengler, where he rolled his legendary "300 in the dark."

Cleveland Public Auditorium, Lakeside Avenue and East 6th Street, Cleveland, OH. Scene of Count Gengler's Last Stand, against Jimmy Smith (1926).

Crest Lanes, 12707 Fullerton Avenue, Detroit, MI. Where Stroh's Beer rolled a record triplicate in 1950.

Del-Mar Recreation, 5025 Delmar Boulevard, St. Louis, MO. Site of the Hermann Undertakers' 3797 series in 1937.

Denver Bowling Company, 1523 Champa Street, Denver, CO. Where Floretta McCutcheon made headlines defeating Jimmy Smith in a 1927 exhibition.

Detroit Recreation, 212 West Lafayette Boulevard, Detroit, MI. An early mega-center (eighty-eight lanes in 1917); also the first with a "Women Only" floor.

Diamond Café, 519 North Howard Street, Baltimore, MD. Early day establishment operated by baseball Hall of Famers John McGraw and Wilbert Robinson.

Faetz-Niesen Recreation, 5961 North Ridge Avenue, Chicago, IL. Location of various television shows featuring "Whispering Joe" Wilson.

Falcaro Recreation, 1422 St. Nicholas Avenue, New York, NY. Home of the irrepressible Chesty Joe.

Fanatorium, 40 Jefferson Avenue SE, Grand Rapids, MI. Where Marion Ladewig and Therm Gibson learned the game.

Floriss Lanes, 4339 Warne Avenue, St. Louis, MO. Here the Budweisers rolled a record 3858 set in 1958.

Genesee Arcade, 1440 Genesee Street, Buffalo, NY. Site of Barney Koralewski's "week-long" 300 game (1934).

Globe Bowl, 4949 South Aberdeen Street, Chicago, IL. Where the last World's Invitational Tournament was staged (1964).

Hagerty's Interurban, 439 North Superior Street, Toledo, OH. Home base of Midwestern bowling pioneer Jack Hagerty.

Hollywood Star Lanes, 5227 Santa Monica Boulevard, Los Angeles, CA. Where The Dude abided in *The Big Lebowski*.

Hudson Recreation, Broad and Cherry Streets, Philadelphia, PA. First bowling center with more than 100 lanes (105).

Johnson's Alleys, 326 7th Street, Rockford, IL. In 1902 Ernest Fosberg rolled the first 300 game in sanctioned competition here.

LaHabra "300" Bowl, 370 East Whittier Boulevard, La Habra, CA. Site of Glenn Allison's 900 series.

Live Stock Press Building, 836 West Exchange Avenue, Chicago, IL. First office of *Bowlers Journal*.

Llo-Da-Mar Bowl, 507 Wilshire Boulevard, Santa Monica, CA. Bowling-goes-Hollywood center owned by film star Harold Lloyd, in partnership with Ned Day and Hank Marino.

Marino Recreation, 536 West Wisconsin Avenue, Milwaukee, WI. For more than thirty years, the home of the Bowler of the Half Century.

Newark Recreation Center, 6 Elizabeth Avenue, Newark, NJ. Graz Castellano rolled the first televised 300 game here in 1953.

Olympic Alleys, 175 North 2nd Street, Milwaukee, WI. Where Abe Langtry ran the early ABC out of a desk drawer.

Palace Recreation, 6626 Gratiot Avenue, Detroit, MI. The Motor City's leading bowling establishment for four decades.

Palm Beach Recreation, 16920 Meyers Road, Detroit, MI. Where the E&B-King Louie championship match of 1952 ended in a tie.

Paramus Lanes, 200 Route 17, Paramus, NJ. Frank Esposito's famous showplace.

Peoria Auto Parts Recreation, 815 Adams Street SW, Peoria, IL—The bowling alley above the auto parts store, where Nelson Burton, Sr., trimmed Mort Lindsey in a memorable 1934 match of tenpins, duckpins, rubber band duckpins, and candlepins.

Polk City South, 8530 South Cottage Grove Avenue, Chicago, IL. Where bowling was telecast from the window of an appliance store.

Riviera Lanes, 20 South Miller Road, Fairlawn, OH. Longtime home of the PBA's Tournament of Champions.

Schade's Academy, 170 Ontario Street, Albany, NY. Site of the inaugural PBA event, the 1959 Empire State Open.

Schuetzen Park, 3167 Kennedy Boulevard, North Bergen, NJ. The first national bowling event, the 1900 International Bowling Tournament, was held on the grounds of this German-American amusement park.

Stein Brothers Recreation, 3911 Hampton Avenue, St. Louis, MO. First center to feature concourse carpeting, and home of match game champ Otto Stein.

Strike 'n' Spare Lanes, 185 Skokie Boulevard, Northbrook, IL. Site of the legendary Jerry Lewis vs. Paul Krumske exhibition re-match, and of the last All-Star Tournament.

Sullivan Bowl, 645 Missouri Avenue, Sullivan, MO. The lanes where onetime 300/800 king Elvin Mesger rolled most of his big scores.

T-Bowl, 1055 Hamburg Turnpike, Wayne, NJ. Where Junie McMahon suffered a disabling stroke after the premiere telecast of *Jackpot Bowling* in 1959.
Tomasch Recreation, 4125 Lorain Avenue, Cleveland, OH. Here Skang Mercurio averaged 238 during the 1934–35 season.
University Lanes, 2568 West Bancroft Street, Toledo, OH. Site of Ned Day's last great victory, the 1959 *Championship Bowling* television tournament.
Washington Alleys, 716 West Washington Street, St. Louis, MO. Dennis Sweeney's lanes, where the WIBC was born (1916).
Welsbach Building, 141 North Wabash Avenue, Chicago, IL. Site of the first ABC Tournament (1901).
White Elephant Bowling Academy, 1241 Broadway, New York, NY. Uncle Joe Thum's place, the first tenpin palace.
Willow Grove Park Lanes, Moreland and Easton Roads, Willow Grove, PA. America's largest-ever bowling facility (116 lanes).

Don Carter: An Appreciation

(July 1996)
Don Carter turns seventy this month. Can it really be true? So much time could not have passed so quickly. It is still 1960, bowling is booming, and on the lanes there is no one but Carter.

Many people have forgotten. Many who did not live then do not know. And there is that matter of the polls. Once the consensus said that Carter was the greatest bowler of all time, no debate or second thought. Now they say it should be Dick Weber, or Earl Anthony. Perhaps. But did any single bowler ever mean as much to the game as Don Carter?

He possessed a special aura. Joe DiMaggio had it. Ben Hogan, too. Each went about his business with egoless superiority, matter-of-factly lifting his chosen activity to new levels, while quietly defining the quality called "class." Human nature being what it is, DiMaggio or Hogan or Carter might cause envy in those they were surpassing. What they earned was sincere respect. And awe.

In Carter's case, the image called to mind was of a repeating machine, like a punch press endlessly stamping out bottle caps. The crouched, bent-arm style surely enhanced the mechanical metaphor. One story claimed that Carter had to discard his bowling ball after every All-Star Tournament—his release was so consistent that his track would quickly wear a groove in the ball.

For roughly a decade he dominated bowling like no one before or since. Most tournaments then were sweepers of eight games or less, which anyone could win with a hot hand. There was not yet a PBA Tour. The closest things to a modern pro event were the All-Star and (after 1957) the World's Invitational.

In the nine All-Stars between 1952 and 1960, Carter won four times, once withdrew with an injury, and never finished below fourth in the other four years. In two of these latter events, he actually knocked down more pins than the champion. His record in the World's is even more astounding—five titles and one second-place in six years.

It was truly Carter versus The Field. Today, if a pro makes a career Grand Slam in the major tournaments, he is considered a bowling immortal. Carter nearly turned the trick in a single season, when he won the PBA National, World's, and Masters back-to-back-to-back.

That was in 1960–61. By then the Tour was getting established, and it's no exaggeration to say that Don Carter made the PBA. He gave it the stamp of legitimacy. Later, when the National Bowling League failed to sign Carter, it lost public credibility and died.

He was the perfect representative for bowling in the post-war Eisenhower years as the game was expanding to the suburbs and the consciousness of Middle America. Carter was a gentleman. When he wasn't busy spilling pins on the lanes, he could be found puttering around the garden of his split-level ranch home, or hobnobbing with the other successful businessmen at the country club. If such a man were the world's top bowler, then perhaps this was a fit game for Mom and the kids.

He was always doing something a little special, a little better. He was Don Carter. So he bowled a tournament with a white ball. He started using a bowling glove. He took over as sponsor of his old Budweiser team. He signed a million-dollar endorsement contract. Heck, even his wives were the stuff of every male bowler's fantasy.

To be honest, many of us who grew up in the Carter Era became bored with him. He always won. We'd buy the morning paper, scan the standings of the All-Star or the World's, and note with satisfaction

Don Carter (center) receiving yet another trophy, this one from *Bowlers Journal* publisher Mort Luby, Sr., while Joe Norris (left) looks on. A 1999 poll ranked Carter the no. 1 bowler of the twentieth century.

that Fazio or Lillard or Welu was leading the pack, with Carter down the list. But as the week passed, each morning would find the familiar name creeping closer to the top. By the last day, with Carter in first place, all we could do was check his Petersen Point margin and calculate—if Carter suddenly dropped dead, then could the Buzzer catch him?

When he did stop winning, it was as though the natural order of the cosmos had been shattered. Dozens of magazine articles and an entire book were devoted to the mysterious question of what had happened to Don Carter. And the public fascination continues. Twenty years after his last tournament victory, he was the one bowler famous enough to appear in Miller Lite Beer commercials.

So mark your calendars for July 29. If it's not the newest of the official holidays, it is a prime time to celebrate the glory of the grand old game. Happy Birthday, Mr. Bowling.

A Dream in Detroit

(April 1997)

In 1917 Detroit was America's boomtown. The auto industry was moving into mass production. Everybody wanted to buy a car, and every Detroiter from Henry Ford to the rawest rookie on the assembly line seemed to be making money. When it came time to spend that loot on fun, much of it flowed into local bowling alleys.

William Sweeney and Irvin Huston already owned one successful center. Now they acquired a prime parcel of downtown land at the southwest corner of Lafayette Boulevard and Shelby Street. There they planned to build the biggest bowling and billiard palace in the world.

Most bowling took place in the extra room behind the neighborhood saloon. The average layout was four lanes. Plankinton Arcade in Milwaukee had just opened with the amazing total of forty-one. Imagine the bombshell the Detroiters dropped when they announced that their place would have eighty-eight!

A 1917 advertisement for the new Detroit Recreation (author's collection).

Actually, the partners had picked a bad time to start building. The U.S. entered World War I in April, leaving an uncertain future for the nation's businesses. But by then the walls of Detroit Recreation were already going up. In all, the price tag would reach $1.1 million. That was serious money in 1917—Comiskey Park in Chicago, the grand "Baseball Palace," had cost only $750,000.

Billiards would occupy a significant portion of Detroit Recreation. Brunswick was contracted to supply 103 top-of-the-line tables, mahogany with inlaid mother-of-pearl. Fifty-three of the tables were carom, thirty-eight pocket, and twelve snooker. The budget for house cues alone came to $13,000. Balkline champ Ora Moringstar was hired to run the billiards operation.

The Recreation was to be "a working man's private club." As such, the amenities were many and varied. The ground floor was devoted to the lobby and lunchroom. A larger restaurant was located in the basement, along with a 20-chair barber shop and a chiropractor's office. The carom billiards tables were on the second floor, surrounded by a 200-seat balcony. Pool and snooker tables were on the third floor. Floors four through seven housed the bowling lanes, in banks of twenty-two each. Each of the game floors had its own soda fountain and cigar shop, and at the rear of the second floor balcony, there was a small reading room.

Somehow, Sweeney and Huston forgot to include overnight guest rooms and a chapel. Otherwise, it might have been possible for a patron to live out his life without leaving the building.

Detroit Recreation was thrown open with a grand celebration on November 5, 1917. Five thousand visitors passed through the building that first evening. The opening week festivities included nightly bowling and billiards exhibitions, with the tenpin matches featuring Jimmy Smith and Count Gengler.

Detroit bowlers were proud of their new Recreation. "It was a marvelous place," Joe Norris later recalled. "They had the finest facilities and the best of everything." Bowling had emerged from the backroom, moving into a grand palace that seemed to symbolize the exciting future ahead. In their own way, Sweeney and Huston proclaimed that the bowling business had come of age when they advertised their showplace with a single word headline—"Environment."

The Recreation was also in the forefront of sociological change. The entire fourth floor of the building was set aside for women. Ethel Green, a visitor from upstate New York, had gotten the partners interest in women's bowling, and she was put in charge of the program. Her floor staff was all female, including the twenty-two "pingirls." In an era when bowling was considered unladylike, it was a giant step forward.

With the success of Detroit Recreation, megacenters began to rise in other cities. Linsz Recreation in Cleveland opened its own eighty-eight lanes. In Philadelphia, Hudson Recreation topped them all with 105 lanes. Both of these houses fell casualty to World War II. By the end of that war, Detroit Recreation was once again the world's biggest bowling center.

Oddly enough, for such a large and well-regarded venue, the Recreation played only a minor role in competitive bowling. Most of the Motor City's money matches and top-level tournaments were held at other houses, like Chene-Trombly, State Fair, or Palace. One exception was the 1953 WIBC Tournament, which drew a record 5,000 teams to the Recreation.

Detroit Recreation closed in 1959, a victim of changing demographics. But by then, the principle it pioneered had become firmly established—give the public quality, and there are no limits on bowling.

The Original Perfect Man

(May 1997)

Back in the 1960s, when bowlers used hard rubber balls and the ABC gave out gold rings with diamond chips, Elvin Mesger was a legendary figure. Mystery was part of the legend. You never saw him on *Championship Bowling* or the PBA's Saturday afternoon telecast. You never saw him among the leaders at the All-Star, the World's Invitational, or the ABC Tournament.

Yet each fall, when the ABC's yearbook came off the presses, there would be Mesger's name, with a few more 300s or 800s listed after it. At one time he held the record for most 300 games (27) and most 800 series (21). This was in an era when the ABC was particularly diligent about examining high scores—just ask Ray Orf, whose 890 series was rejected. To look at it another way, before Mesger came along, the most 800s anyone had bowled in a career was *five*. So who was this guy, anyway?

Elvin Mesger was a farm boy, born in Rosebud, Missouri, in 1916.

He didn't take up bowling until he was twenty-five and living in St. Louis. Then he wasted a dozen more years throwing a backup ball. He finally got tired of cruising around in the 170s and taught himself to roll a hook.

Though his bowling style would always have a homemade look, Mesger began to steadily build his average, until he passed the 200 mark. By 1958 he was competing against the likes of Don Carter and Dick Weber in St. Louis's fastest leagues. He bowled his first perfect game that year.

Mesger lived a difficult life. His wife and seven children were settled on a small farm near the town of Sullivan, fifty miles west of St. Louis. During the week he worked in a pencil factory in the city and roomed alone in a small apartment. Bowling helped fill the long, lonesome hours.

In 1962 Mesger's 855 won the ABC award for high series of the year. Like his first perfect game, it was bowled at Arcade Lanes in St. Louis. Over the next few years, he added a few more honor scores at Arcade and at Sullivan Bowl in his hometown. The legend was building.

On May 25, 1967, Mesger busted loose. Competing in a doubles tournament at Sullivan Bowl, he rolled a 300 game and 837 series. The following day he "slumped" to 299 but still managed an 834. The tournament rolled on, and so did Mesger. At the end of forty days, he had posted eight 300s, six 800s—and two 299s.

This was too much for some people to believe. Though ABC approved his scores, Elvin Mesger never did get much respect from the national bowling media. He was never in the running for All American or Bowler of the Year awards, and "Who's Who in Bowling" didn't even carry his biography. For his part, Mesger shrugged off the controversy and kept piling up pins, mostly at Sullivan Bowl. He rolled his last honor score, a 300 game, in 1978.

He didn't claim to be a great bowler. Still, the doubts about his accomplishments must have bothered him. As long as there's been bowling, bowlers have had their pet lanes. Yet nobody had ever mastered a set of lanes like Mesger. He couldn't explain why he controlled his nerves so well during a strike run. "I just knew what I had to do, and I did it," he said modestly.

He did think about becoming a touring pro. But by the time the PBA settled in, Mesger was past forty and raising a family. He never got rich from bowling—his honor scores attracted a few minor endorsement deals, and he won a couple of $1,000 checks at the Petersen Classic. His best payoff came during a National Cancer Week fund drive. As one of nine bowlers who happened to roll a 300 that week, Mesger split a $10,000 jackpot, netting $1,111.11.

When the last bowling book is written, Mesger's name might only be a footnote. His most notable tournament victory was in a 1970 event called the Hustlers Tournament in Columbia, Missouri. He will probably never be elected to the Hall of Fame, and that might not be fair—George Billick, who held the 300 record before Mesger, was elected to the Hall with a record comparable to Mesger's.

At age eighty, Elvin Mesger still takes his turn on the lanes at Sullivan Bowl. Last season he managed to put a 279 game on the board, with a string of twelve strikes spread over two games. By the time this story appears in print, perhaps he will have remembered how to put those strikes together in a single game. After all, compared to Joe Norris, the man is still a youngster. We may not have heard the last of Elvin Mesger.

One Soldier's Story

(July 1997)
Joe Wilman, the old Hall of Famer, had a fabulous career on the lanes. As a youngster, he rolled against Charley Daw for the match game championship of the world. At the ABC Tournament he won four eagles, including two All Events titles. He won the All-Star once, and on two other occasions lost the title in the final frame of the final game.

He had a million bowling memories. Yet there was one game—indeed, one shot—that Wilman said meant more to him than all the others. And it happened under singular circumstances at an unlikely place.

In 1944 Wilman was an army private stationed at Fort Lewis, Washington. It was the middle of World War II, and the fort was crowded with men who knew they might never come home alive or in one piece. Gambling was their main recreation. For his part, Private Wilman spent much of his off-duty time bowling pot games with the other soldiers. Eventually, he piled up a sizeable bankroll.

When word of Wilman's winnings reached his superiors, they

decided he was just the man they needed for a bowling match against McChord Air Base. The teams were competing for the championship of the Ninth Service Command. Wilman was recruited to bowl with four high-ranking officers as their anchorman.

The match was scheduled for the fort's bowling facility, a six-lane setup squeezed into a small room above the gymnasium. Just as they were to begin play, in walked the commanding general, followed by his entire staff of sixteen officers. The general, it seemed, was a bowling fan.

There was barely enough space for bowlers, let alone spectators. The general declared that his party would sit in folding chairs along the unused lanes. Wilman was the only enlisted man present and—designated ringer or not—he was sent to fetch the furniture.

Running around a fort in search of folding chairs is not the best way to loosen up for a bowling match. Wilman was noticeably off-form when they finally got underway. The teams split the first two games.

As they moved into the final game, Wilman's skills came back to him. He began striking. By the tenth frame, Fort Lewis had the match wrapped up. Along the way, Wilman had strung the first nine strikes. It was at this point that one of the general's aides sidled up behind him with a message.

"Private Wilman," the officer said, "the general has never seen a perfect game. If you can shoot 300, he promises you a two-week furlough and a round-trip home to Chicago, with all expenses paid."

Fort Lewis was 2,000 miles from Chicago. Wilman had not been home to see his family in more than a year. With such an incentive before him, he took a measure of extra care as he stepped to the line for the final frames. He rolled a perfect strike for the tenth. He rolled another for the eleventh.

Bowlers and spectators edged forward in their seats as Wilman delivered his last ball. It looked good, and he went down on one knee as the ball smashed into the pocket. Pins went flying in all directions. The 10-pin was a little late. One pin hit it, and it began toppling. Then another pin hit it from the other side. Now the 10-pin was spinning crazily on its base while sliding upright across the pindeck.

Suddenly there was a loud crash from the left side of the room. Wilman turned his head sharply at the sound. It was the general. He had gotten so excited by the last shot that he had stretched too far forward and had fallen head-first onto the floor. Then Wilman shot his eyes back at the pindeck. The 10-pin had stopped spinning. It stood defiantly just behind the 5-pin spot. There would be no 300 game today.

Before he left, the general stopped to personally congratulate the Fort Lewis bowlers on their victory. When he got to Wilman, he remarked that this was the first time he had ever seen a 299 game. However, Joe knew better than to hope that the general would reward him anyway for a gallant try. "The army never gives you anything for nothing," the old soldier's lament goes. That one spinning 10-pin had cost him mightily.

Still, there was one souvenir of the incident that Wilman would always treasure, if only for its irony. A few days later he received a note from the general. "Private Joseph Wilman is to be commended," it read. "He is the only soldier in World War II to knock a general flat on his face and not get a court-martial."

Famous Nicknames

(October 1997)
Nicknames are a colorful aspect of sports. Through the years, bowling has been no exception to that rule.

In the early 1900s, Johnny Voorhies was the first man reckoned as bowling's unofficial match game champion. He was also the first bowler famous enough to earn a nickname—"The Little Wizard." Whether he got the name before or after the championship is not known, but it's a good guess that wizard business was worth a few pins a game as intimidation.

From then on, any bowler worth writing about was worth a nickname. Frank Brill reigned as Chicago's top bowler for so many years people started calling him "Pop." John Koster was a tall man, so he became "Long John." And of course there was "The Count," the dapper hustler John Gengler.

Nicknames could come about in many ways. Joe Falcaro had a cocky attitude, so he became "Chesty Joe." "Tango Tony" Karlicek got his name from a peculiar stop-and-dip approach. "Ace" Calder was a poker fanatic. Lou Campi bowled right-handed while finishing on his right foot, so he was "Wrong Foot" Louie. Harold Asplund and Harry Smith were aggressive competitors, so each man became known as "The Tiger."

Of course in those old, unenlightened days, nicknames could get

Famous Nicknames 73

A famous hustler with a famous nickname: John Gengler, "The Count."

pretty raw. Nobody thought about being politically correct. Frank Kafora was a large man, so you called him "Fatty." Johnny Klares was the opposite, so he was "Skinny." Today, Ray Schanen might be termed "vertically challenged." Forty years ago, he was known simply as "The Shrimp."

Physical appearance produced many other nicknames. Mort Lindsey had big ears and a long nose; somebody said he looked like a "Moose," and the name stuck. Hair color gave us "Red" Irwin, "Red" Johnson, "Red" Elkins, and "Whitey" Harris. However, nobody dared to call Rudy Habetler "Baldy"—he was an ex-prizefighter.

A few bowlers became identified with catch phrases. Old bowling yearbooks tell us that Ed Mady was called "Who Hits 'Em Better?" after an expression he used when he got a strike. The same book might also carry an ad featuring Joe "Are You All Right?" Joseph, those four words being Joe's familiar greeting.

Then there was Adolph Carlson. He also had a pet phrase that identified him. Unfortunately, it was an expression he used when he got tapped, and it was not the sort of thing you repeated in print. More than anyone, Carlson needed a nickname; somehow, it didn't seem right for a sports hero to have the same first name as Hitler. Check out Carlson's Hall of Fame bio, and you'll see his approved, G-rated nickname—"Swede."

Some of the brighter stars had elaborate nicknames. Phil Wolf was "The Coney Island Dutchman." Walter Ward was "The Man With the Crooked Cigar." Frank Clause was "The Bowling Schoolmaster." Young Joe Norris was "The Fireball Kid." Johnny Crimmins became "The Masked Marvel" after appearing on the lanes with a hood over his head. He was also called "The General," a name he seems to have made up himself.

A number of bowlers' nicknames became so famous, their birth names were nearly forgotten. Consider Buddy Bomar, Buzz Fazio, Ned Day, Junie McMahon, Skang Mercurio, Lindy Faragalli, and Sarge Easter. You may rate yourself an expert in bowling trivia if you were able to match these bowlers with the following list: Herbert, Basil, Edward, James, Walter, Alfred, and Eber (*Eber?*).

On the other hand, a few tongue-twister last names gave way to new forms. Billy Golembiewski was often listed as "Billy G." Andy Rogoznica's family name was always butchered, so he bowed to the inevitable and named his bowling center "Andy Rock Lanes." Joe Zelinsky even had his name legally changed. When he was not busy blasting bowling pins, Zelinsky played some top-notch pool, and made so many kiss shots that people began calling him "Joe Kissoff." That's the name on his Hall of Fame plaque.

Nicknaming reached its peak around 1960. The Who's Who books of that era are filled with intriguing entries like "Punk" Limmer, "Houdini"

Kaelin, "Bing Bong" Lown, and "Mighty Mouse" Gifford. Then the practice began to fade.

Television was the culprit. When bowling fans followed their favorites through the print media, there was a need to make the stars come alive and be distinctive. That was no longer necessary when bowling was on the tube every week. Now you could see everything about Weber or Anthony or Aulby. Today's PBA champs might have nicknames, but they are not widely reported.

The Infamous 5–7–10

(March 1998)
Your ball is heading for the pins. It hooks smartly into the pocket. Looks like it will be a perfect hit. The pins scatter—and there it is, leering back at you. The nightmare split. The 5, the 7, and the 10. Oh, fudge!

Is there any other leave that will deflate confidence so quickly? Leaving the 5–7–10 is a major embarrassment. There, for everyone to see, is evidence of the weak delivery, the impotent shot. Other leaves may tell a similar tale of defect and deflection—the 8–10, or the 2–4–5–7–8. But somehow, the 5–7–10 is worse, and not just because it is so much more difficult to convert. Part of the reason might be that it is so symmetrical-looking, with one pin on each corner and one smack in the middle. Where did the ball go, anyway?

For members of the male gender, leaving the split can be considered downright un-macho. When I was bowling in my first adult league, we had a guy known as Gismo who gloried in his muscular physique. One night in the tenth frame of the second game, he left the 5–7–10. He immediately hit the sweeper-button and took the seven-count for the frame. Then he changed his shoes and left, without bothering to take his bowling ball. That was the last we ever saw of him.

Nobody knows who first discovered the 5–7–10. Early bowlers did not bother to remember what they had to shoot at when they were forced to roll a second ball. Nor did they mock each other for making a sissy shot. Great-grandpa had enough trouble knocking over any pins, without worrying about what a particular leave said about his skill.

By the 1940s, though, bowlers had recognized that the 5–7–10 was something infamous. A bowlers' dictionary of the period refers to the split as The Lily. No etymology is given. However, since lilies were considered a funeral flower, the implication is clear.

The 5–7–10 was called The Sour Apple by *Cleveland Kegler* publisher Sam Levine. League secretaries would let Levine know when someone left the split, and he would print their names in his weekly paper. Detroiters went Levine one better when they formed a 5–7–10 club in 1943. It was started when two bowlers in the famed Detroit Times Classic left the split on adjoining lanes. From there the idea spread to other leagues. An elaborate initiation ritual was devised, along with a register of all the unfortunates who had left the split. Within three years the club had nearly 500 members. Among the repeaters, Hall of Famer Johnny Crimmins was on the list *seven* times.

Leaving the 5–7–10 is one thing; converting it is another. As early as 1946, the Detroit club credited Larry Loch with picking up the spare. However, the ABC record book states that the first authenticated conversion was by Al Dugay of Toledo in 1956. During the old *Championship Bowling* television series, one of the contestants almost accomplished the feat on film, with the 5-pin sliding into the 7, then bouncing back to rock the 10. Though I might be wrong, I seem to remember the bowler was Ed Lubanski.

Today, many observers believe that the 5–7–10 is becoming rarer. Better equipment and changing conditions are the reasons cited. Modern bowlers roll hooks that break later, with more drive. Twenty years ago, you rarely saw the 2–8–10. Now it pops up almost every night. Meanwhile, the 5–7–10 is slowly disappearing.

And yet, when a bowler does get stung by the 5–7–10, it still causes a commotion. Last year my teammate Jim Pennino left the split after stringing the first nine strikes. Now Jim has rolled 300 games in the past, and nobody paid particular attention to them. But the day after his 5–7–10, when he walked into a pro shop six suburbs away, people he'd never met were ready to "congratulate" him. Such is the mystique of The Lily.

In closing, I should state that I, too, have left the 5–7–10. It happened on Lane Twelve at The Bowlium on February 12, 1964. We were in high school and had the day off for Lincoln's Birthday, so some of us decided to try out a few games at a different house. Somewhere along in my first game I got a shot a little in-between, and the next thing I knew, I had stopped open play for ten lanes in either direction.

Since that day, more than thirty years ago, I have never left another 5–7–10. Whether I'm tempting fate by bringing this up, I do not know. Frankly, I'm not very superstitious.

But if I do leave the damn thing after writing this, I'm going looking for Gismo.

Fabulous Faetz-Niesen

(July 1998)
Throughout bowling history, a few establishments have become legendary. One of them was a little joint on the North Side of Chicago named Faetz-Niesen Recreation.

Matty Faetz was one of the better bowlers around town during the early decades of the century. Over the years he operated a succession of successful centers. In the summer of 1939 he took over an empty dry-cleaning plant at 5961 North Ridge Avenue in the elegant Edgewater district, and began assembling another Faetz Recreation.

The new house would have twelve lanes, the last eight coming from the recently completed ABC Tournament at Cleveland. Faetz opened the doors with an invitational team tournament on September 15. Business was brisk from the start, and grew steadily.

Faetz had a counterman named Chet Niesen, and Chet had a brother named Matt. When Faetz decided to retire he sold a piece of the house to Matt. In 1951 it was renamed Faetz-Niesen.

Matt Niesen had been a bookie. The story goes that he became a bowling proprietor because the mob was muscling in on his original business. Whatever the reason, Niesen was a promoter. Television was just becoming popular. Niesen thought bowling would be an ideal subject for the new medium.

After trying a few different formats, Niesen began broadcasting man-to-man singles matches in the fall of 1953. Then Don Carter rolled 299, and just missed winning the new Pontiac being offered for a perfect game. When the papers headlined Carter's feat as a news story, Niesen knew his program was a winner.

More shows followed. The long-running film series *Championship Bowling* was launched at Faetz-Niesen in 1954, to be followed a few years later by *Bowling Stars*. Meanwhile, Niesen's live broadcasts continued.

Television ratings soared. By 1958 the programs were drawing a bigger audience than any sport except boxing.

The old dry-cleaning plant on Ridge Avenue had become the most famous bowling center in the world, with the highest-scoring pair of lanes. All the greats took their turns on "Fabulous Five and Six." Even today, the numbers they posted were impressive. Eight of the first twelve televised 300 games were rolled on the pair, as well as two 846 series. Lindy Faragalli averaged 247 over 48 games. During one warm-up session, five bowlers put together a three-game set of 3908.

Some critics claimed that the pair was fixed—all the bowler had to do was toss the ball out on the lane somewhere, then rush back to the scorer's table to make sure that the "X" for his strike was marked neatly. Niesen replied that he was putting out a fair shot and allowing unlimited practice, so naturally the scores were high. Lane Six was thought to be the easier of the pair, and most competitors chose to finish on it. If anything, the rest of the house was tough. Whispering Joe Wilson, the announcer for the shows, claimed that "nobody could crack an egg on Seven and Eight."

In 1959 the television bubble burst. Rival networks began broadcasting first-run movies, and suddenly no one was watching bowling. Niesen quietly folded his shows. A few years later, he sold the center.

Now the owner was Gene Schmidt (no relation), a veteran Chicago proprietor. With the Niesen brand of flash gone, the place settled back into being a typical, neighborhood bowling alley. Ridge Bowl was the new name on the marquee. The biggest excitement occurred in 1963, when one of the house teams went to the ABC Tournament and came back with the Booster championship.

Still, some of the old Faetz-Niesen mystique endured. During the late '60s, Whispering Joe returned to broadcast a local show. And each year a certain number of pilgrims made their way to Ridge Avenue to try their skills. Most of them came away satisfied. The average citizen would never play baseball at Yankee Stadium, or golf at Augusta, or hoops at Boston Garden. But for a few bucks he could roll a set on the same planks graced by Carter and Wilman and Bomar and Nagy. That happy thought was probably good for at least a ten pin boost in average.

Eventually business tailed off. Faetz-Niesen Recreation, *aka* Ridge Bowl, closed for good in the mid–1980s. Today the building houses a combination garage and car wash. The whereabouts of Fabulous Five and Six are unknown.

How Jimmy Smith Became Champ

(August 1998)
During the early years of the twentieth century, Jimmy Smith was match game champion of the world. It was all unofficial, but was based on general consensus—everyone just *knew* that Smith was the best bowler around.

But how did he first get the title? There are about a dozen versions of that. The only way to separate truth from legend is to consult contemporary sources. And sure enough, the story is there, in a New York City paper with the arresting name of *The Bowler's Journal.*

Back in bowling's Jurassic Age, most man-to-man matches went eleven games and were decided by games won, not total pins. Smith first popped into the news in November 1902. Still in his teens, he defeated George Fraenkle for the juvenile championship of Greater New York before a crowd of 400 people at Montauk Alleys. Over the next few years, there'd be periodic reports of Smith victories in other matches against other bowlers—and not just juveniles.

Among all New York bowlers, the most feared competitor was Johnny Voorhies. In 1901 he had gone to Chicago for the first ABC Tournament and helped bring back the Doubles championship. Later he toured the country as part of an exhibition troupe known as the All-American Trio. Voorhies made his living managing the Universal Bowling Academy in Brooklyn and knocking off foolhardy challengers in best-of-eleven gamers. Admiring fans called him The Little Wizard.

By the fall of 1905 Voorhies had run out of victims and was taking it easy. Perhaps trying to stir up a little action, New York-*BJ* observed that "since Voorhies has withdrawn from the ranks of Brooklyn's bowling cracks, Smith has been considered the champion of the borough." The jibe seemed to have worked, for within weeks Voorhies had gone back into training. He emerged from retirement in February 1906 to stomp John Koster, 6 games to 2. When Smith challenged the winner, The Little Wizard said he was ready.

Formal match articles were signed. Voorhies and Smith would meet on the evening of March 13 at Superba Recreation in Brooklyn. The contest was the customary best-of-eleven, for a $250-a-side purse. The gate was to be split 60/40 between winner and loser. Lanes Three and Four were to be resurfaced and cross-planed. Neither man would be allowed to practice on the pair.

The Voorhies-Smith showdown was eagerly anticipated and much discussed. Yet when the big night arrived, only about two-thirds of the seats were filled—the hefty $2 charge was probably the reason. Regard-

Jimmy Smith in 1906, at the start of his fabulous career. The first person to make a living as a bowler, he was the consensus match game champion for fifteen years (author's collection).

less, President John J. Clingen of the New York Bowling Association called the proceedings to order promptly at 8 p.m. The combatants were introduced. The match began.

One of my favorite movies is the Errol Flynn classic, *The Adventures of Robin Hood*. Whenever I watch the climactic battle between Robin's bandits and the knights of Prince John, I'm struck with an intriguing thought—if I could go back to the twelfth century with a Sherman tank, I could become King of England.

Looking at the scores of Voorhies-Smith produces a similar reaction. Time-warp me back ninety years with my current equipment, and I might be king of the bowling world. (Game 1) Smith-179, Voorhies-167; (2) Voorhies-172, Smith-156; (3) Smith-226, Voorhies-179; (4) Smith-186, Voorhies-183; (5) Voorhies-197, Smith-170; (6) Smith-190, Voorhies-183; (7) Voorhies-207, Smith-192; (8) Smith-189, Voorhies-161; (9) Smith-203, Voorhies-190. Smith defeats Voorhies, 6 games to 3.

Of course, in the days of shellac, newly resurfaced lanes were difficult to hit. But even by 1906 standards, the scores were puny.

After the match, NY-*BJ* tells us: "Smith announced he was claiming the world championship, and would meet all comers in defense." His manager would be ABC secretary Samuel Karpf. He would begin a tour of Southern states in a few weeks, after the ABC Tournament in Louisville.

And that, boys and girls, is how Jimmy Smith contrived to become bowling's first match game champion.

The Big Three Bowlers Tour

(January 1999)
Exhibition tours are almost as old as organized bowling. One of the earliest—and most publicized—trips was undertaken in the fall of 1902 by a Chicago crew calling itself The Big Three.

Leader of the group was W.V. Thompson, star bowler and Brunswick executive, who convinced the company to bankroll the expedition. The other members of the trio were veteran kegler Fred Worden and reigning ABC Singles champ Fred Strong. As a sub, the Big Three brought along a 21-year-old farm boy who was just starting to make a name for himself, Harry Steers.

They left Chicago by train on September 28. First stop was a three-day engagement in St. Louis. The tour's format called for the traveling trio to roll a three-game match against whatever local talent the home houses could round up. As expected, the Big Three swept the competition. Knowledgeable fans were impressed by the 1832 series the Chicagoans rolled against the Martin Kern Missouri Big Three.

From St. Louis the tour moved west through Texas, with performances at San Antonio and El Paso. Then it was across the high plains and desert to California. Outlaw bands still roamed the wild country—New Mexico and Arizona were not yet states—and the travelers were relieved to reach Los Angeles without incident. There they rolled three matches in three different establishments in a single day. One of the L.A. stops was at Monarch Recreation, which Thompson pronounced the most luxurious bowling center he had ever seen.

At Santa Monica, the audience was two-thirds female. Perhaps it was because Steers was on the lanes that day—the baby-faced young man seems to have been a sort of 1902 version of Leonardo DiCaprio. In any case, the Chicagoans put on a good show. In the seventh frame of the final game, when Steers rolled a strike, Strong tossed him a silver dollar in tribute. Steers struck again in the eighth, and Worden gave him his watch. Another strike in the ninth, and Strong threw in his coat. The kid then proceeded to close with three more strikes, and his colleagues tossed him a "gift" after each ball, Thompson capping off the fun with a $50 bill.

Santa Monica was followed by Santa Barbara, before the tour moved up the coast to San Francisco. The highlight of the three days in the Bay Area was the grand opening of the new Central Alleys, where the Big Three was the headline attraction. The final California exhibition was at Stockton. Then the boys began heading home.

Once more they went into the wilderness, this time through mountains. The 1,000-mile journey took nearly forty hours, and the train was late getting into Denver. The Big Three barely had time to get to their engagement at the Overland Alleys. Stiff and out of practice, they lost badly to the local team. The next day, after getting acclimated, they returned to form and had no further trouble in Denver.

Lincoln, Nebraska, came next, and the Big Three posted their highest single game of the tour, 674. In Iowa they gave performances at Carroll and Boone before arriving at Marshalltown, the boyhood home of baseball star Cap Anson. The old first baseman was now a Chicago proprietor, and Fred Worden was one of his bowling teammates. After the Big Three rolled their match, they were feted in a special banquet, complete with welcoming speeches from Marshalltown politicians.

The last stop was Dubuque. Here the hometown team swept the match with a 1756 series. That was the best score rolled against the Chicagoans on the tour, so Brunswick awarded each of the victors a new bowling ball and leather bag.

The Big Three tour lasted five weeks. During those thirty-five days, they traveled over 5,000 miles and rolled forty-four separate matches. They lost only four. Thompson was the leading scorer among the regulars, averaging a shade under 188 for the trip. Worden stood next at 187, with Strong posting 186. Thompson's 258 was the highest single game.

After the tour, each of the Big Three continued to make news. Strong won the 1903 ABC All Events championship. Worden moved to St. Louis and managed the city's largest bowling resort. Thompson continued his distinguished career as a bowler, writer, and promoter. And little Harry Steers, the sub who'd wowed the ladies of Santa Monica, went on to become a charter member of the Bowling Hall of Fame.

Where Have You Gone, Morrie Oppenheim?

(February 1999)
There were giants in those days. Read off the list of winners in the early Professional Bowlers Association tournaments, and you'll hear a roll call of tenpin immortals. Dick Weber ... Don Carter ... Lou Campi ... Carmen Salvino ... Bill Bunetta ... Earl Johnson ... Tom Hennessey ... and Morrie Oppenheim.

Nine out of the first ten PBA events were won by future Hall of Famers. Oppenheim is the joker in the pack. In the summer of 1960, at the age of twenty-three, he beat out a fast field to capture the Southern California Open, and was hailed as one of bowling's brightest young stars. Barely four years later, he quit the game completely.

To find Morrie Oppenheim today, you must leave behind the cities and suburbs, and journey to the lake country of northern Illinois. For a dozen years he has lived here on a few acres of pasture land, raising horses and repairing saddles while working at his main job selling cars for a local dealership. Before that there was a career in the clothing business. And before that there was bowling.

He was born in Chicago in 1936. Growing up on the city's North Side, Morrie's first ambition was to be a musician, and he bowled only casually. But as he passed his sixteenth birthday, he began to show an aptitude for the game.

"My mother decided I should get some technical expertise in bowling," Morrie remembers. "Somebody said I had a style like Ray Bluth. That was when Bluth was in Chicago bowling with Buddy Bomar. So she signed me up to have weekly lessons with him."

Bluth must have been quite a teacher. The Chicago bowling community soon started hearing about the big, husky kid with the crew cut who handled a bowling ball like it was a tomato. Morrie pushed his average up over 200, and the captains of the better teams came calling. In 1955 he went to Fort Wayne for his first ABC Tournament. He rolled 1930 All Events, good for seventh place.

The 1950s was the age of the great teams. As a young man on the way up, Morrie made it to all the important matches and tournaments. When he wasn't bowling, he was watching—and learning. He became close friends with many established stars, particularly Therm Gibson, who became his new mentor when Bluth returned to St. Louis. The warm attitudes of the veterans made the experience memorable.

"Here I was, a punk kid, and I was hanging around with all these older guys all the time—Bluth, Bomar, Gibson, Bill Bunetta, all of them," says Morrie. "And they treated me like an equal. Everyone was helpful, there was no jealousy, they went out of their way for me. It was fantastic."

Still, there was time for the pleasures of young manhood. Morrie liked to race sports cars and do equestrian riding. Pistol shooting was also fun, until he tried a fast draw and accidentally shot himself in the leg. "Another inch and I would have lost the leg," he says. "As it was, I missed rolling Doubles in the ABC with Ned Day. I was more careful after that."

Paul Krumske signed him to bowl in the Chicago Classic League in 1959. As a rookie in the country's strongest league, Morrie could have been excused for having a dose of stage fright. Instead he led his team to the championship by topping the league in average. Meanwhile, the PBA was just getting off the ground with a limited schedule of tournaments. Morrie became a charter member, bowled a few events, and made some money.

In July 1960 the pros gathered in Los Angeles for the Southern California Open. After the qualifying rounds, the format called for the finalists to roll two six-game blocks, total pins. Morrie jumped out in front with an opening block of 1400, then saw his lead gradually dwindle. With three games to go, Glenn Allison caught him. Then Morrie came back strong with a pair of 230s. When it was all over, Morrie had won—by 10 pins.

Morrie Oppenheim, winner of the 1960 PBA Southern California Open.

Morrie was one of the big boys now. *Bowlers Journal* named him an All American. Buddy Bomar recruited him for the famed Munsingwear team. He joined the AMF staff and rolled exhibitions. He appeared on all the television bowling shows.

Life was good on the informal pro circuit of the early 1960s, full of high-spirited camaraderie. Morrie admits to having a mischievous streak, so the humor and gags suited him. He remembers rolling Johnny King's bowling ball across a patio into a motel swimming pool on a dare. He also recalls one time it was his turn to become the victim.

"We were bowling in Albany, New York," he says with a smile. "I parked my car on the side of a hill and ran into my motel room to get my ball. When I came out, the car was gone. I thought maybe I forgot to put the brake on and it rolled down into the ravine. I'm running around frantic and then I hear the laughing. A few of the guys had simply lifted up my car and carried it around the building."

He was also hearing talk about something called the National Bowling League. Like many of the younger stars, Morrie was intrigued by the idea of an intercity bowling circuit patterned after major sports leagues. The promoters approached him and he listened. In the late summer of 1961, Morrie signed with the Dallas Broncos along with Munsingwear teammates Carmen Salvino and Jack Biondolillo.

Readers with long memories will recall that the NBL started hemorrhaging money almost immediately. Morrie was one of the early casualties. He bowled only occasionally, and not well when he did. When the Broncos cut their squad to save money, Morrie was let go.

"I was devastated," he says today. "But Steve Nagy sat me down to reassure me that it wasn't the end of the world. He told me not to get down on myself. He said there were highs and lows in the game, and this might be a blessing in disguise." Nagy was also ready to find a spot on his own NBL team for Morrie.

It happened that the PBA was about to hold its National Championship in Cleveland. Morrie wired in his entry, flew back to Chicago for a night's rest, then caught a ride to the tournament with another bowler. He arrived with barely $100 in his pocket.

The National Championship was the PBA's richest event. Morrie was a hungry bowler that week in Cleveland. He wanted to prove to himself that he could still perform at the highest levels. He wanted to show the bowling world that the Broncos had made a mistake by releasing him. And since he was short on cash, his hunger was literal.

It would be pleasant to report that Morrie came back from nowhere to win the PBA National. And he gave it a good try. Among the leaders all week, he faced off against front-runner Dave Soutar in a four-game showdown for the title. Morrie won the first two to draw even with two games to go.

"Then I did something I never allowed myself to do," Morrie recalls, shaking his head. "I started thinking how great it would be if I could win this tournament after being fired. Or maybe it was just that invisible necktie—a choke. Well, I punched the nose and left a rail. And Dave had me."

Still, second place was not shabby. Morrie returned to the Tour and rejoined Bomar's team. But as time went by he had less success. He dropped to seventy-second place on the PBA's money list. Finally, in 1964, he quit bowling entirely.

What had happened? Carmen Salvino had one theory. Writing in his autobiography years later, Salvino suggested that his old teammate was too high-strung to continue in competition, and would freeze on the approach.

Morrie himself has a different explanation. "I had been taught how to bowl a certain way," he says, "coming through the ball hard with a power shot. Then lane conditions started to change. I had to weaken my shot, and couldn't do it. I just didn't have the talent to make the adjustment. It's as simple as that."

Morrie went to work as a dress buyer. But he was not quite through with bowling. After a four-year layoff he started practicing again. Then he hooked up with a friend's league team. Then he decided to try a few tournaments,

It was as if he had never left. Morrie won the Chicago Match Game Championship and led the local qualifying for the All-Star Tournament. He rolled an occasional PBA event. His best finish on Tour this time around was sixth place in the Durham Open.

By now Morrie was a family man. He had met his wife, Shirley, through his equestrian riding. There was one child at home and another on the way. The vagabond life of a touring pro was no longer appealing. "I had proved to myself that I could come back, so it really didn't matter whether I kept going," he says. "There were other things that were just as important as being the big professional bowler." In 1972 he quit again, this time for good.

Morrie remained in the clothing trade until the company closed in the late '70s. His next move was a natural. He had worked with cars since he was a teenager. He had always had a gift for conversation, and people told him he'd be a natural in the automobile business. Morrie became a car salesman. He's been doing it ever since.

The equestrian hobby also developed nicely. Morrie and Shirley now own six horses which they display at shows. As a sideline to this sideline, Morrie began repairing equipment for other horse-owners. From there it was only a short hop to custom leather-working, the latest Oppenheim venture.

Family, job, and horses have kept Morrie busy. He did get out to the lanes with his kids a few times while they were growing up, but that was the extent of his tenpin activity. Bowling remained part of a past life, something he had closed the door on long ago. Then, a couple of years ago, he began to feel the old urges.

Nearly a quarter-century had passed since Morrie had bowled seriously. Lane conditions were once again friendly for power-shooters, and the Senior Tour looked inviting. Morrie was about ready to dig out his bowling shoes when he ripped open his hand while working on a saddle. He has had some hip trouble recently, so any new comebacks have been placed on hold.

Whether Morrie ever does return to competition is a moot point by now. Looking back on his career in bowling, he doesn't dwell on the expectations that went unfulfilled. Rather, he sees them as a matter of choices being made. As for regrets, he laughs and admits, "I wish I could rebowl that match against Dave Soutar." But really, there was nothing he would change. His life on the lanes could not have been better.

"What I remember most—and what I miss most—is the personal relationships," he says. "I was a young kid, and I was with these older guys all the time, and they were such beautiful people. I learned so much from them about how to act and about growing up. Bowling helped mature me. It made me into a human being."

How We Learned to Love the 10-Pin

(June 1999)

Eight score or so years ago, some anonymous genius added an extra pin to the old game of ninepins, and modern bowling began. Most bowlers agree that this was a positive development, except for one thing. Now they had to shoot at the 10-pin.

Through the years, bowlers have employed various methods to topple this nasty spare. At first they took the simplest route—they stood directly in front of the pin and tried to roll the ball straight down the boards. *Spalding's Official Bowling Guide 1900*, one of the earliest instruction books, doesn't offer any specific tips on making the 10-pin. But the guide does have a few diagrams of other spares, and down-the-boards seems to be the preferred strategy.

Nobody knows who first moved cross-alley for the spare. Jimmy Smith, the great touring pro of the early twentieth century, originally played all his shots from the right corner, including the 10-pin. By 1929 he had changed. Writing in *Bowlers Journal*, Smith advised bowlers to move away from the 10-pin and use the full width of the alley for the conversion. At about the same time, Bill Shaul launched his famous clinics, which did much to popularize the cross-alley spare shot.

Even with everyone moving left and playing the angles, there were still questions of just how you should deliver the ball. If you rolled a straight shot like Smith, matters were relatively easy. But bowlers were developing bigger and better hooks. Some stars, like Otto Stein and Nelson Burton, Sr., solved the problem by shooting a backup at the 10-pin.

Ned Day saw things differently. He believed a bowler should use the same delivery on all shots, without resorting to backups or other tricks. "I seriously question the advisability of flattening the ball out if you are really interested in making your delivery as automatic as possible," he wrote. "Bowlers should pursue the policy of remaining in the groove at all times."

So Day continued to roll his wide bender at the 10-pin. He did lose a number of tournaments by blowing the spare, including the 1941 Petersen Classic. Still, he compiled one of the most glittering records in bowling history. In Day's case, consistency probably did pay off better than accuracy.

It's impossible to over-emphasize Day's influence on bowling tactics. Starting in 1938 he made nationwide exhibition tours, appeared in movie shorts, and wrote four instruction books. And for four decades, his method of shooting the 10-pin was gospel—move left, turn your shoulders a bit, and try to duplicate your strike shot. Then, in 1975, Mark Roth burst on the scene.

Roth was not a pretty bowler. He stomped down the approach and cranked the ball until it bled. On the 10-pin, he flattened out his shot.

Roth didn't seem to worry about losing his groove; he seemed to improvise each shot as he went along. When Roth became one of the dominant players on the PBA Tour, bowlers began rethinking the conventional wisdom.

Today, in the era of mega-revs, many bowlers are again going after the 10-pin with flattened shots or backups. For the rest of the population, who do not want to mess with a grooved delivery, there is a modern response—switch to a hard-surface ball. Now every topflight bowler has at least one non-hooking rock in his arsenal. And yet, this idea is not really new. During the 1950s, Junie McMahon appeared on the *Championship Bowling* television show with a special 10-pin ball. There's evidence that Tango Tony Karlicek was doing the same thing as long ago as 1914.

Bowlers have come a long way in their war against the 10-pin. You face the enemy today with a century of theory and technology behind you. Have confidence as you approach the line. The shot has become routine.

But as your ball drops into the gutter, or hooks away to the left, take a good look at that single pin standing alone and untouched at the far corner of the lane. And see if it isn't laughing at you.

Weighty Bowlers

(April 2000)

Bowling has long had critics who claim it's not a real sport. Memories of the old "saloon alley" days are surely part of the reason. But more likely, it is the number of famous bowlers who have been unambiguously, unashamedly, and undeniably ... *fat*.

The first large bowlers to make a mark on history were the Kreunz & Quer team of New York City. Not much is remembered about them, except that during the 1901–02 season they established a record by weighing in at a combined total of 1,400 pounds—an average of 280 per man, if you're keeping score.

As bowling grew in popularity, so did the number of stars with extra ballast, including many early Hall of Famers. Match game champ Otto Stein trained on beer and had the physique to prove it. Gil Zunker, another big man, worked as a beer distributor, but his size did not come from his livelihood alone—he was known to wager malted milks and sundaes on his bowling scores. Pioneer woman bowler Floretta McCutcheon outweighed most of the males she trimmed in her exhibition matches.

A few bowlers started thin and expanded. At 6-foot-1, Frank Kafora was a 185-pound catcher with the Pittsburgh Pirates; by the time his bowling career peaked, he was known as "Fatty." Billy Knox, Philadelphia's greatest-ever bowler, demonstrated his patriotism and hometown pride by growing into the shape of the Liberty Bell. When Mort Lindsey captured the 1919 ABC All Events, photographs showed a thin little man with big ears. The ears were still prominent forty years later, but by now our hero had taken on the figure of a Buddha. His Hall of Fame biography explained that Mort was "a lover of good food."

Mort Lindsey, charter Hall of Famer and lover of good food (author's collection).

By the 1950s bowling guides were carrying vital statistics, making it easier to identify the portly pros. Still, there was the matter of human vanity. Jack Benny, the comedian, would never admit to growing old, and always gave his age as thirty-nine. Steve Nagy, the bowler, had a similar hang-up—he would never admit to getting fat, listing his weight as 199. Connie Schwoegler's book-weight stayed at 225, even when he was edging over 300. Therm Gibson's 240 was equally as arbitrary, and equally as suspect.

This was the golden age of the heavy bowler. Besides the men just mentioned, the era included such chunky all-stars as Eddie Kawolics, Joe Joseph, Dick Hoover, Ace Calder, Joe Kissoff, Carl Richard, Ed Lubanski, Junior Powell, Tom Hennessey, Fred Riccilli, and Whitey Harris. And though Graz Castellano never became particularly porky, it wasn't for lack of trying—he listed his hobby as "eating."

With the coming of the Professional Bowlers Association in 1959, bowlers began to get into better shape. Perhaps the PBA's emphasis on public image had something to do with this. I suspect that a more important reason was the emergence of Dick Weber at a svelte 113 pounds.

When the game's dominant player weighed only as much as one of Therm Gibson's legs, other bowlers took notice. Maybe Weber should get a Rip Van Winkle Award for contributing to the good health of his fellow pros.

In researching this article, I decided to track the average height and weight of prominent bowlers over the last four decades. I used ABC's Who's Who in Bowling for 1960, and the PBA Tour Programs for the years thereafter. Remarkably, the height for the men listed has stayed at around 5-foot-10. The weight is another matter:

1960: 175.7 pounds
1970: 166.6 pounds
1980: 167.9 pounds
1990: 169.1 pounds
1997: 176.5 pounds

After dipping during the Age of Weber, pro weights have been steadily rising. And note that the most recent figures available are from 1997. After that year, the PBA quietly dropped physical stats from its programs.

Did they know something? From all the evidence, we're moving into a new era of big-size big-time bowlers. And if our next superstar is built along the lines of a navy blimp, will bowling ever get any respect? I think I'll grab a beer and a hunk of pizza while I ponder that.

More Things I Learned While Looking Up Other Things

(November 2000)

- When the 1941 ABC Tournament was held at St. Paul, one Canadian team used a unique mode of travel. Living in an isolated Manitoba settlement named Flin Flon, they loaded their bowling equipment onto dogsleds, and mushed over a hundred miles to reach the nearest railroad station.
- While he was a lawman in Tombstone, Arizona, Wyatt Earp saved an outlaw known as Johnny-Behind-the-Deuce from a lynch mob by hiding the man in the town bowling alley.

- Billy Sixty wrote about bowling and golf for the *Milwaukee Journal* for over sixty years. On the lanes he won a number of tournaments, including an ABC eagle. But on the links, he could never quite get over the top. Between 1923 and 1936, Sixty reached the finals of the Wisconsin Amateur Golf Championship four times—and lost all four matches. As a post-script, son Billy Sixty, Jr., also reached the final match in the 1951 Wisconsin Amateur, and also lost.
- During the 1932–33 season, Edward Mullen of Schenectady, New York, averaged 192 without rolling a 600 series. His best set was 599.
- How Promotions Have Changed Department: In 1917 Metcalf's Recreation of Chicago ran display ads in *Bowlers Journal*. The ads made sure to emphasize a prominent feature of the establishment—Metcalf's provided Free Shower Baths.
- Like a concert pianist, Ned Day felt his performance depended on keeping his hands in optimum condition. According to a 1947 article in *Sport* magazine, Day bathed his hands in alcohol before each match. After bowling he soaked them in hot water for ten minutes. Why Day found it necessary to treat both his hands is not explained.
- In the early days of bowling, 102 was an unlucky number. If a bowler posted that score—in any frame—he was expected to buy a round of drinks for his team. The custom lasted into the 1940s.
- Retired ABC Secretary Elmer Baumgarten became the second man to compete in fifty ABC Tournaments in 1960 at Toledo. Because he was in ill health, Baumgarten's participation that year was limited to one ball.
- A peak at the 1914 issues of *Bowlers Journal* reveals that bowlers were already calling three successive strikes a turkey. And back then, two-in-a-row was sometimes referred to as a chicken.
- Politicians have often sponsored bowling teams, but only one team has been bankrolled by a former First Lady. The sponsor was Mamie Eisenhower, widow of our thirty-fourth president. In 1977 Mrs. Eisenhower invested in $60 worth of bowling shirts for a team of navy personnel in California. In honor of their new sponsor, the Compartment Acceptance Team adopted the name "Mamie's CATS."

- One of golf's most familiar maxims is borrowed from bowling. Golfers often claim that, "You drive for show, but you putt for dough." Back in the old wooden ball days of the 1890s, knowledgeable bowlers said, "You strike for show, but you spare for dough."
- In 1932 the Long Distance Bowling Championship was staged by the town of Bexley, Ohio. To celebrate the opening of a new street, a crowd of more than 30,000 people gathered to watch 2,782 contestants roll bowling balls down the pavement. The winner of the contest was teenager Paul Bender. His shot traveled over one-third of a mile, until officials stopped it from rolling onto an open highway. Bender's prize was $25.
- When Don Carter was the king of bowling, *Championship Bowling* was the leading televised bowling show. Between 1954 and 1960, Carter appeared on the syndicated film series six times. He lost all six matches.
- The first recorded damage suit against a bowling establishment occurred in 1902. John J. Reycraft was bowling at the Bedford Rest in Brooklyn. While he was retrieving his ball from the return, another ball rolled up and smashed his fingers. Reycraft sued the proprietors and won a $90 judgment in Municipal Court. *The Bowler's Journal* (New York) thought this decision was outrageous, and started a fund to defray the costs of future suits. And shortly afterward, signs began to appear in local alleys, advising patrons to pick up their bowling balls with their hands on the sides of the return.
- Bowlers react to the pressure of a possible 300 game in many ways. In 1951 John Ross of Monterey Park, California, opened a game with the first eleven strikes. He decided to roll his twelfth ball between his legs. He hit the pocket perfectly—and left the 10-pin.

The First ABC Tournament

(February 2001)
On the evening of January 5, 1901, the regular Chicago Limited of the Pennsylvania Railroad steamed out of Manhattan Transfer Station. For this trip, three extra coaches had been added to the train. New York's

bowlers were on their way to the first American Bowling Congress Tournament.

That 1901 ABC drew forty-one teams from nine states, and was scheduled to run four days. Entry fees were $5 per-man per-event, with a total purse of $1,592. Top prizes for each event—Team $200, Doubles $80, Singles $80. Not officially recognized, the nine-game All Events had no prize.

"Tenpin Knights Arriving" read the headline in the *Chicago Inter-Ocean*. The local papers recognized that a major sporting event had come to town, and gave the tournament considerable coverage, complete with cartoons and photographs. Many printed a complete schedule of each day's competition. The *Post* even ran an article on how a bowling alley was built.

Just as today, some people worried that bowling scores were becoming too high. "It will be remembered when Mr. So-and-So was called a great spare bowler and was a factor in tournaments," the *Post* complained. "Now the competition has become so keen that captains look for strike bowlers, and the men who can make 'turkeys' are mostly in demand. This causes crack bowlers to think of professionalism, and that thing will sooner or later disturb the game of bowling."

At 12:30 on the afternoon of January 8, at the Masonic Temple, President Henry Timm called the ABC Convention to order. After some minor business, the meeting was adjourned for the day and the delegates trooped the two blocks to the tournament site, the Welsbach Building. Six regulation lanes had been installed, courtesy of the Brunswick-Balke-Collender Company. At 3 o'clock, officials stepped onto the lanes for the "opening ball" ceremony. Nobody rolled a strike, but the tournament was off and running.

Three squads of teams bowled the first day. When play ended that evening, the Interstates of Erie, Pennsylvania, were on top of the leader board with 2678. And after just one day, it was obvious that the ABC Tournament was a success. According to the *Chicago Tribune*, the event was special in every way. The only thing wrong was that there wasn't enough room to accommodate all the fans eager to witness the show. "There's definitely an interest in bowling," the *Tribune* said. "The noise made by the crowd would put a bleacher delegation at a baseball game to shame."

The second day saw the rest of the teams roll their games. On the final squad, Standard of Chicago counted 2720 and became the first ABC champion team. Meanwhile, at the convention, business went on.

President Timm announced his retirement, and Godfred Langhenry of the host city was elected to succeed him. The delegates approved plans to hold a second tournament in 1902 at Buffalo. A proposed ban on three-hole bowling balls was defeated.

When they weren't bowling or conventioneering, many bowlers wandered over to Mussey's Alleys to watch the first National Women's Bowling Tournament. Others engaged in round-the-clock matches at various venues. For his part, local favorite Cap Anson was having a tough time. After bowling badly at the ABC, the retired baseball star lost a billiards match to a 13-year-old upstart named Willie Hoppe.

The third day brought the Doubles event. Doubtless celebrating his election, President Langhenry rolled the highest game of the tournament, 258. However, the championship went to a New York duo, C.K. Starr and Johnny Voorhies, the famed "Little Wizard." Their winning score was 1203. A protest that Voorhies had used an illegal ball was tossed out.

That left the Singles. Besides the prize money, the winner would be awarded a gold medal proclaiming him National Bowling Champion. Everyone agreed that three games was too short a test for such a prestigious title. But logistics dictated the limit, and all 115 entrants took their turns in a single day.

As the squads wore on through evening, Chicagoans R.D. Jones and P.H. Thorson were tied for the lead with 606. Then another hometown hero, Frank Brill, began bunching strikes. He posted 648 to squash the roll-off talk. On the final squad, New York's great John Koster made a run at Brill, but came up short. (As a footnote, Brill also had the best nine-game total with 1736. Years later, he was given retroactive recognition as the 1901 All Events champ.)

The first ABC Tournament was history. The bowlers could hardly wait for the next one. Sound familiar?

Joe Norris, R.I.P.

(April 2001)
I didn't know Joe Norris as long or as well as most of the people who are remembering him in print. But the man was so engaging that, once you met him, you felt you'd been friends with him forever. I sure did.

It was 1963, and I was sixteen when I first read a profile Mort Luby, Jr., had written about Joe. All the famous Norris stories were there—I particularly liked the one about the dead fish under the massage table—and I was impressed. Here was a guy zanier than any of my friends. Joe was retiring from Brunswick, and had told Mort, "Now I'm gonna sit on my butt and just watch the world go by." We all know how that worked out.

Years later, when I started writing historical pieces about bowling, he was the logical person to contact. I remember the first time I called him. Nervous about disturbing a living legend, I stammered a little when he came on the line, saying I hoped Mr. Norris could spare me a few minutes.

"I read your stuff all the time; I was wondering when you'd get around to calling me," he said. And by the way, he added, there was no Mr. Norris at that number. "Call me Joe—or just Norris." And then he burst into a high-pitched little giggle that let me know all was right with the world.

After that, I would phone him every few months. Fortunately, those Chicago-to-San Diego long distance calls were a tax-deductible business expense, because Joe never knew the meaning of a short conversation. His memory was always vivid and sharp. Sometimes I suspected that a few of his memories were a bit too vivid to be absolute truth. But that was part of Norris Experience.

Once he really scared me. We were talking about his first 300 game, and he excused himself to get a scrapbook. A few seconds later, I heard a loud crash on the line. Then nothing.

A full minute went by. Then two minutes. By now my mind was racing—I had killed Joe Norris! Nobody in any bowling alley would ever speak to me again! I was about to hunt up my rosary when Joe finally came back on the phone. "Sorry for the delay, Jake," he said casually. "I knocked over the TV set."

I finally got to meet him in the flesh in the summer of 1999. That was when I spent a memorable day at Mort's home, working with Joe and a few more living legends on our list of the one hundred Bowlers of the Century.

Joe was in top form. He had an opinion and anecdote on just about everyone. What impressed me, though, was when he asked Tom Kouros for some advice on getting a different bowling ball. Joe might be over ninety, but he was still a competitor.

The next day, our work finished, Mort had a dinner party. My wife,

Terri, had been listening to Norris tales for years, and wasn't sure what to expect. We had just entered the house, and were still greeting Mort and Pat, when suddenly Terri felt someone grab her arm and start kissing it from her hand up toward her shoulder. That was her introduction to Joe Norris.

Joe was in even better form with the ladies present. Now his stories were R-rated. One of them was about a famous star of the '40s, whose wife caught him in bed with another woman and promptly divorced him. Joe's summation was priceless: "That man's wife was really narrow-minded."

On the way home, I wondered what Terri would be thinking about this old goat Norris. And her response was priceless: "That's what I want you to be like when you're ninety-one."

The last time I talked to Joe was just after last year's ABC Tournament. I had written about the leg brace he had to wear, and said that if you asked him, he might show it to you. "You clown!" he roared at me. "I must have had fifty guys at Albuquerque asking me to roll up my pants!" And then he giggled—someone had put something over on the great practical joker.

And now he's gone. And I wish I had called him more often. And I wish that, just once more, I could hear that giggle.

Style and Substance

(November 2001)
They used to say that no bowler could be as great as Joe Kristof looked. He was the finest stylist of bowling's golden age, with the graceful perfection of a Michelangelo statue come to life. Pick up an instruction book in the 1950s or '60s, and chances are you would find line-drawings based on Kristof's classic form. Watch him in action, and you immediately understood the meaning of the cliché poetry in motion.

Joe Kristof is now eighty-one years old. He hasn't bowled seriously in nearly twenty years. But visit his pro shop in Columbus, and you will find that he still carries himself with elegance. The memories are there, too.

He came out of the Hungarian East Side of Toledo, Ohio. As a fourteen-year-old schoolboy, he wandered into Larry Gazzolo's lanes one day in 1935, intent on trying another sport. Joe put his first four shots in the gutter, then switched balls and finished with 121. And did anyone ever learn bowling quicker? His next three games were 200, 212, and 256.

Young Master Kristof went to work for Gazzolo and began perfecting his game. The exquisite form that would become his trademark was developed through observation, trial-and-error, and long, unglamorous practice. Always looking for an advantage, he quickly found a way to make the best use of that time.

"Gazzolo allowed us a half-hour of practice time," Joe says. "I had the pinboy set up the 5-pin only. Then, the last five minutes, I would shoot at the full set. That way I could get more shots." The payoff was a 200-plus average and a 300 game at the age of seventeen. At the time he was celebrated as the youngest bowler ever to roll a sanctioned perfect game.

He began impressing the big boys in 1943. World War II was on, Joe was in the Army Air Corps, and came to Chicago on leave to bowl the Petersen Classic. With the country's best bowlers gathered together, there were plenty of after-hours matches going on. He soon found himself rolling against ex-Petersen champ Vince Mikiel.

"I beat Mikiel five or six games," Joe recalls. "Mort Luby [Sr.] was there. He liked to bet on matches, and asked me if I'd mind bowling the next day. So he set up three matches. The first was with Junie McMahon, the second was with Paul Krumske, and the third was with Connie Schwoegler. Well, I took all of them. I don't know how much money Mort finally won."

After that, Luby stayed in touch with Joe. When the war ended and Luby was helping put together the Lustre Crème Shampoo team, he advised sponsor Harry Daumit to sign Kristof. So in 1946 Joe moved to Chicago.

Lustre Crème was captained by Buddy Bomar and featured an all-star lineup. Joe stayed with Bomar for the next eight years, through various sponsors and changes in personnel. The Bomar teams became a power in the Chicago Classic League, and were ranked among the country's best. For two years they held the BPAA Team Match Game title. In the 1949 matches Joe rolled a 300 game, one of the few perfect games ever in that event.

He won a number of individual tournaments, including the Midwest

Singles, the Du-Bowl, the Petersen 2-in-1, and the Blong Classic. At the All-Star Tournament, his greatest success came off the lanes. In 1949 the BPAA inaugurated a Women's Division in their showcase event. One of the bowlers was a young lady from Columbus named June Zimpfer. Joe met June, and romance developed. They were married in 1951.

But it was television that made Joe Kristof a household name. The medium was brand new, and televised bowling was just becoming popular. On the evening of February 12, 1955, Joe rolled a perfect game during a telecast from Faetz-Niesen Recreation in Chicago. It was the first 300 game ever rolled on a live-television singles match. Joe won a new Pontiac and earned national headlines.

The event was particularly memorable because it happened to be Joe and June's wedding anniversary. "Whispering Joe Wilson was the announcer and he got really excited," Kristof says with a chuckle. "He was crying and shouting, 'What a night! What a night!' And then he told the audience that this was our third wedding anniversary, and that we had a four-year-old son. I had to tell him he had it backwards."

After the 300, Joe seemed to be everywhere. Whenever a new bowling program hit television, the word went out to get Kristof. His classic form appeared in glorious color on the cover of the widely circulated *Bowler's Handbook*. He was featured on the All-Sports Conditioner Spray bottle, with the likes of Bob Feller and Sam Snead. And he rolled exhibitions with June. The Kristofs became nearly as famous a "bowling couple" as Don and LaVerne Carter.

In the spring of 1955, Pabst Beer approached Joe about sponsoring a team in the Classic League. He had left Bomar and was bowling with Rudy Habetler's team. As part of the deal, Pabst wanted the magic Kristof name in the captain's slot. Habetler, one of the nicest men in bowling, agreed to make Joe co-captain.

The Pabst story has an unusual sidelight. "The brewery wanted me to do a lot of exhibitions, so we needed seven men for the team," Joe says. "So for the last spot, I signed Dick Weber. He was a mailman from Indianapolis, and wasn't well-known. Then I got a call from Pat Patterson that they wanted Weber for the Budweisers. Well, Dick wasn't going to bowl very much for us, so I mailed his contract back to him. And the rest is history."

The Pabst bowling team earned a lot of goodwill for its sponsor and won a collection of middle-range tournaments, but never captured one of the major titles. Joe's record was similar during these years.

"No bowler could be as great as he looked": stylish Joe Kristof.

Though he added to his impressive list of sweepers and jackpots, the major titles eluded him. The closest he came was second place in the 1955 Masters, when Buzz Fazio nipped him by two pins.

Then, in 1961, the ABC Tournament started a Classic Division for pro bowlers. Joe had become a charter member of the PBA, so he automatically rolled in the new division. He paired with Don Ellis to post 1331 in the Classic Doubles and claim his long-awaited eagle.

That was a year of decision for Joe. He was well-established in Chicago, but there were other opportunities—the PBA Tour was starting to take off, and the National Bowling League looked promising. Meanwhile, AMF was after him to open a pro shop in Columbus, June's hometown. Joe finally chose the last option, and never regretted it.

After making the move, he continued bowling in tournaments and doing exhibitions for AMF. But in 1963 he was involved in a serious auto accident. His right hand never fully healed, and Joe's competitive days were over.

He now poured his considerable energy into his business. The Joe Kristof Pro Shop was a trend-setter, one of the first to offer ball-resurfacing and to feature its own stub lane. Precision drilling and personal service were stressed, reflecting Joe's belief that "a bowling grip should be as personal as a fingerprint." The shop drew customers from such far-flung places as Jamaica, Japan, and Saudi Arabia. When *Bowlers Journal* visited Joe's operation, they labeled it the "Palace Among Pro Shops."

So went Joe's life. He took care of business, raised a family, and bowled in leagues. In 1968 he was elected to the ABC Hall of Fame. Before he left the lanes he rolled in 40 ABC Tournaments. His lifetime average in the big show was a shade under 193, one of the better marks for 40-year men from his era.

About a dozen years ago, the "palace" building developed a leaky roof, and the business was moved to its current Indianola Avenue location, not far from the Ohio State campus. Today the shop is run by Joe's son Karl—the "four-year-old from the third anniversary." Last February the Kristofs celebrated their Golden Anniversary, along with their three children, three grandchildren, and some friends. Officially, Joe is retired. But he still comes in to the shop almost every day.

Always known for speaking his mind, Joe is critical of modern scoring conditions. "The averages today are ridiculous," he declares. "The pins fly all around. It's not bowling anymore—it's tiddly winks!" Looking back over sixty years in the game, he still thinks the best bowler he ever saw was Ned Day.

All things considered, it has been a good run. "I always liked the people and I always liked the competition," Joe says. "I always liked the game. Where would I have been without it? Bowling has been my life. And it always will be."

Brunswick or AMF?

(January 2002)

In Chicago, where I come from, baseball loyalties are sharply divided. You are either a Cubs fan or a White Sox fan—never both. It's mostly a geographic thing, North Side versus South Side. When I was growing up in the 1960s, there was a similar schism among the city's bowlers. The question then was, are you Brunswick or AMF?

Affiliation had nothing to do with geography. Your bowling loyalty depended on the house in which you'd learned the game, and the type of equipment they had. It was like your religion or political party, something you were born into. In my own case, I started bowling at Habetler Bowl. So, naturally, I was a Brunswick man.

Everything was ordered. Like all my friends, I bought my Black Beauty at Buddy Bomar's store. Don Carter won all the tournaments, and guys like Lillard and Nagy and Day ruled on *Championship Bowling*. And if you were of the female persuasion, there was Marion Ladewig to follow. That was our world.

Our one apostate was Steve the Greek. For Steve, being cool was the most important thing in life. His favorite bowler was Johnny King, the coolest dude this side of the *77 Sunset Strip* television show. So when Cool Johnny joined AMF, Steve dumped all his Brunswick gear, replacing it with anything that had the Magic Triangle logo. But then, Steve always did things backwards—he was left-handed. And who ever heard of a lefty bowler?

When you grew up in a Brunswick house, there were certain things you knew. It was an established fact that Brunswick alleys hooked more, producing higher scores. Furthermore, AMF approaches were always tacky—except when they were too slippery, and you fell down. AMF may have invented the automatic pinsetter, but their machines looked dumb, with the pins hanging out in the open in those cheesy slots. And they were too noisy. As for the T-square ball returns, they were a disaster if you took a five-step approach. There was also the matter of color. AMF was all yellow and red and brown, like stale scrambled eggs. The true color of bowling was Brunswick Blue.

If we needed any further proof of Brunswick superiority, there was *Championship Bowling*. For years it was a showcase for high scores and Brunswick stars. Then, around 1962, the program abruptly switched to AMF. Fred Wolf was still doing the commentary, but now guys were winning matches with 590s. What did that tell you?

Still, there was Dick Weber. By this time he had become the World's Greatest Bowler, and he was AMF. How to explain that? You couldn't—except to say that Weber might have won even more tournaments if he'd had the right equipment.

Eventually, we started to question our parochial attitudes. During my last two years of high school, I bowled on the Habetler teen traveling team in an eight-house league. A majority of the places were AMF, and they weren't bad. I suppose my experience was similar to the knee-jerk bigot who gets involved with other racial groups, and discovers they are human after all. When I rolled my first 700 series, it was in an AMF house. That gave me something to think about.

College opened even wider perspectives, and induced a large dose of skepticism in traditional beliefs. My classmates were protesting the Vietnam War, challenging all aspects of American society. The times, they were a-changin.' In that spirit, I finally went out and bought an AMF three-dotter.

Yet old superstition dies hard. At the ABC Tournament, I would always bowl badly in the odd-number years, when AMF was in charge. The pattern was obvious, and a few times I seriously considered sitting out. Then I broke the string by doing even worse in a Brunswick year, and I had run out of excuses.

Today I can happily report that I have learned an important lesson in tolerance. Unthinking prejudice is a terrible thing, and I have a completely open mind on the merits of bowling equipment. So now I announce it to the world, loud and clear—I will bowl on any lanes and use any ball that gives me higher scores with less effort.

Billy G.

(May 2002)
I found it in Hawaii last summer, when my thoughts were a million miles away from bowling. It was a Saturday morning flea market in a little town on Maui. There, among the sacks of macadamia nuts and piles of Polynesian bric-a-brac, was an ancient LP record album—*How To Be a Better Bowler* by Billy Golembiewski.

Billy G! His picture had been on the cover of the first *Bowlers Journal* I ever saw, over forty years ago. A vision flashed through my mind, of that scrawny little man charging down the approach, screeching to a halt and lofting the ball onto the lane, right arm upraised like the Statue of Liberty. I paid the 78 cents and bought the record. And I remembered.

Even when he was one of the biggest stars in bowling, Billy always had a hollow-eyed, hungry look. Maybe it came from being in kid in a family of eleven children during the Depression. He grew up in Grand Rapids, worked as a pinboy, started bowling. In 1950, when he was twenty-one, he made his first headline with an 826 series, highest in the nation that year.

Offers came from the big Chicago teams. But Billy preferred to remain in his little pond, happy to be "the singing counterman" and local wiz. Eventually the Stroh's Beer team enticed him to Detroit. He bowled one season, became the 1958 King of Detroit Bowlers, and wound up broke. He was ready to move back to Grand Rapids when the Pfeiffers signed him.

With the Pfeiffers, Billy rolled anchor and became known for his gutsy, clutch performance. The 1959–60 season saw him scale the heights. At the World's Invitational he gave Don Carter a scare before settling for second place. A few months later he beat Steve Nagy to win the Masters. The last big event of the season was the Champion of Champions in Madison Square Garden, and Billy took that one, too. Carter was the defending champ, and when Billy knocked him off head-to-head, people were impressed.

But not quite impressed enough. The voting for Bowler of the Year found Carter on top, as usual. Billy actually polled more first-place votes, but in the total count he trailed the great man by three points. It remains the closest-ever B-o-Y election.

Billy did some mighty things over the next few years. He won a second Masters and a Classic Doubles eagle with Joe Joseph in 1962. He also copped another Madison Square Garden shoot-out and a total of four PBA events. He was named an All American six times.

Could he have done even better? Some folks thought so. Mr. Bowling of the '60s turned out to be Dick Weber, who was Billy's age, Billy's size, and had a similar record until his own breakthrough in 1961. The critics noted that Billy liked to play the ponies, liked to take a drink, and was so carefree that he once slept through his squad time at the All-Star. Dominant players do not oversleep at major tournaments.

Still, it's hardly an insult to say you weren't as good a bowler as Dick Weber. Or, for that matter, as good as Don Carter. Billy faced down the game's finest, and he never blinked. And he enjoyed it. All things considered, it would have been nice for him to have been Bowler of the Year that one time.

As the '60s wound down, so did Billy's bowling. He dropped off the Tour and into obscurity. When he was elected to the Hall of Fame in 1979, he was juggling three part-time instructor jobs in Detroit and still having money problems. The next time Billy made the national bowling news was in 1998 ... with his obituary.

The record in on the turntable now, and across the decades I once more hear the voice of Billy Golembiewski. "Winning is exciting, but it isn't everything," he says. "So I'm going to show you how to get some fun out of bowling—not necessarily to be the world's best bowler, but maybe one of the happiest."

It's not what Vince Lombardi would have said, but it's pure Billy G. Let it be his epitaph.

Jerry Lewis Goes Bowling

(September 2002)
For nearly forty years, Labor Day weekend has meant the *Muscular Dystrophy Telethon* hosted by Jerry Lewis. The event has become a tradition for millions of viewers. Few of them know there is a bowling connection.

Sam Weinstein, the Tenpin Tattler of Chicago radio and television, used to operate a downtown bowling supply store. In January 1957 Lewis showed up to buy a ball. He was in town playing a local night club. Sam and Jerry hit it off, and in the course of their conversation, Sam spontaneously wrote a check to the Muscular Dystrophy Association. He knew about the comic's devotion to that cause.

That touched Lewis. "Jerry became another guy," Sam recalled. "He stopped clowning around and became very serious, and wanted to know what he could do for me."

Of course, Sam had only wanted to contribute to a worthy charity. But now the happy thought came to him—why not have Lewis on his television bowling show and solicit MDA donations? Lewis liked the idea, and agreed to appear on the next Sunday broadcast.

The program was *Bowl the Professor*. Paul Krumske was the professor, and the half-hour format called for him to give bowling tips and roll a one-game handicap match against a local amateur. When Sam told station executives that Jerry Lewis was going to be his surprise guest, they were skeptical. They figured no big Hollywood star would make time to appear on a local bowling show.

Sunday arrived, and so did Lewis. Wearing a shirt emblazoned with "Jerry 300 Lewis," he nonchalantly puffed a cigarette as Sam introduced him as "the man who in three days has become the most feared, most respected champion bowling has ever known." Lewis refused the offer of a handicap, and declared he would bowl scratch. "I don't want to embarrass Paul," he said.

As a bowler, Jerry Lewis was a great comedian. His preferred shot was a straight ball fired from the right corner. After an open in the first frame, he blasted a strike.

As Krumske took the lanes, Lewis began offering him advice in a steady banter. Krumske was known as one of the great pressure bowlers of all time, but Lewis's routine had him laughing so hard he could barely roll the ball. At the end of the second frame, Lewis was actually out in front.

The match went on. Lewis ran through his whole *shtick*, yelling at the pins, sprawling on the approach, sticking his head in the ball return, patting Krumske on the butt while he bowled. During the live commercial, he wandered over to harass the announcer. The audience was in hysterics.

The second-frame strike proved to be the high-point of Lewis's game. He managed to "convert" the 4–6 split with some aid from the pit, and posted one legitimate spare, for a score of 93. Krumske never did regain his composure and wound up with 172.

At the end of bowling, Weinstein presented Lewis with a plaque and another check. But the real payoff came later. A film of the match had been made, and for a $25 donation, local clubs and lodges could rent it for an evening's entertainment. Universal Bowling, Sam's company, organized distribution and also matched the contributions. Over $10,000 was raised the first year, quite a sum in 1957.

The success of the project convinced Lewis to schedule a rematch with Krumske. To maximize the live gate, this second exhibition was filmed at a commercial center, Strike 'n' Spare Lanes. The new video

Jerry Lewis mugs with Paul Krumske before their 1957 television match.

was circulated nationwide, and quickly brought in over a quarter of a million dollars.

Sam Weinstein had become the godfather of celebrity bowling. But more than that, he had demonstrated how Jerry Lewis could use television to raise money for his favorite charity. It was a lesson that Lewis would build on.

Church Alleys

(December 2002)

St. John's Evangelical Lutheran Church is a dignified old building in a quiet residential area on the Northwest Side of Chicago. For the daily commuters along Montrose Avenue, it is a familiar landmark on the way to the "L" or expressway. Most of these people would be surprised to learn that the Gothic edifice is the home of four regulation bowling lanes.

During the first half of the twentieth century, many urban parishes built recreation centers. The idea was to get men out of the saloons and off the street corners, and into a wholesome environment. Bowling was often part of the mix, and "church alleys" were once quite common.

In those days the sport still had an unsavory image. Nearly all cities had laws banning minors from bowling alleys, so if a teenager wanted to bowl, he could sign up at a church league. Many of the stars of the Golden Age got their start that way. The most notable was Junie McMahon, whose father managed the St. Francis de Sales Rec center in Lodi, New Jersey.

Nobody knows how many churches had bowling lanes; probably there were hundreds. The number seems to have peaked around 1950. Then they began closing.

Bowling was cleaning up its act. Now if you wanted to bowl in a "family" atmosphere, you could go to a commercial establishment—you didn't have to stick to the parish lanes. Automatic pinsetters were becoming popular, and churches didn't want to spend money for the new machines. Finally, more women were now working outside the home. Daycare centers replaced the bowling lanes in many parishes.

As late as 1960, Chicago had over two dozen church alleys. The number was down to two by the end of the century. When Peace Lutheran closed its lanes last year, that left St. John's alone in the city.

The main church sanctuary dates from 1929. The bowling lanes were installed in the basement at the time of construction. They were immediately popular, and soon St. John's was busy with open play and had a full complement of leagues. Because there were only four lanes, the leagues had to bowl in shifts.

"They had something going on every night," says Bob Snell, who grew up in the parish in the 1960s. "The place was always packed. You didn't have any really good bowlers. But everybody in the parish was out there. And they all had a good time."

The pattern was unchanging through the decades. A major innovation came in the early 1970s, when St. John's installed automatic pinsetters. The machines came from a Texas center that had gone bankrupt. Within five years, they were entirely paid for.

The St. John's alleys have known their own hard times. Some of the leagues broke up, and lineage declined. By 1990 the future of the facility was in doubt. There was talk of ripping out the lanes and using the room for a library.

In recent years, things have bounced back. The church school continues to use the lanes for Physical Education classes, and league play goes on. The room is regularly rented for private bowling parties. Volunteers from the parish manage the business. A mechanic keeps the pinsetters in shape.

Why has St. John's kept its bowling lanes when so many other churches have abandoned theirs? Henry Knueppel, a retired teacher from the school, has a simple answer. "This is a very large, active parish with a good, active group of people who like to bowl," he says. "They just weren't going to let the lanes close down."

So it seems that St. John's Lutheran will continue to host the most distinctive tenpin facility in Chicago. Still, there are those busybodies who ask whether it is appropriate to have a bowling alley in a church. In answer, we can remind them that Martin Luther himself liked to bowl. And who are we to argue with history's first Celebrity Bowler?

The Stuff of *Dreamer*

(January 2003)
In the spring of 1979, I was not yet a powerful and influential member of the bowling media. I had not yet heard the industry buzz. So I was pleasantly surprised when my March issue of *Bowlers Journal* arrived. It was there on the cover. Hollywood was making a feature film about bowling.

Dreamer, they called it. Starring was Tim Matheson, a promising young actor fresh from his triumph as one of John Belushi's wild fraternity brothers in *Animal House*. Veteran character actor Jack Warden played the grizzled mentor, and Susan Blakely provided the romantic interest. The director was someone named Noel Nosseck.

Of course, there had been movies with bowling vignettes. But nobody had built a film around the game. Baseball, football, golf, tennis, soccer, swimming, you name it—they all had their cinema. As far as Hollywood was concerned, bowling was the Rodney Dangerfield of the sporting world. It never got any respect.

But now the moment had come. And thoughts went back to 1961, and *The Hustler*. That film had sparked a revival in the billiards business. Would *Dreamer* provide the same magic for bowling?

The industry got on the bandwagon. Every bowling alley and pro shop seemed to have a poster for the film. There were *Dreamer* T-shirts and *Dreamer* tournaments. Some proprietors gave away tickets to the movie. In a savvy marketing move, Twentieth Century–Fox scheduled the premiere for the week of the Firestone Tournament of Champions, when spectator interest would peak. But before we go on, we should pause and describe the movie's plot in some detail.

Harold Nuttingham (Matheson) is an ex-pinboy who dreams of making the PBA Tour—hence the nickname "Dreamer." He works as a counterman and mechanic at the Bowl Haven in Alton, Illinois. When we meet Dreamer, he has just won his first PBA Regional tournament.

Harry White (Warden) runs the local pro shop. A former Tour bowler, he is Dreamer's backer, teacher, and father-figure. The two men plan on buying their own bowling center with the money Dreamer earns on Tour.

Complicating matters is Karen Lee (Blakely). She is Dreamer's girlfriend. Although she also works at the Bowl Haven, and tries to be supportive, she doesn't understand her man's obsession with the Tour.

The supporting cast includes a mixed bag of characters. Taylor is the money-hungry proprietor we all run into sooner or later. Spider is a small-time pool shark who disses Dreamer and lusts after Karen Lee. As comic relief, there are two Mexican pin-chasers whose roles might have been scripted by the Frito Bandito. Finally there is Lady, a traveling pool hustler. She is portrayed by Azizi Johari, one of *Playboy*'s first African American playmates. Appearing in a painted-on T-shirt and slacks, she provides—for male viewers—perhaps the most cinematic three minutes of the entire movie.

Anyway, the PBA rejects Dreamer's membership application. With Karen Lee in tow, he storms PBA headquarters in St. Louis (!) and get his card. Harry, meanwhile, has taken out an option on the bowling center that he and Dreamer want to buy. This distresses Karen Lee. She walks out on Dreamer.

Dreamer goes to Chicago, wins his first Tour event, and qualifies for the Firestone—er, Grand Championship. Harry has a heart attack and dies. Karen Lee and Dreamer reconcile, and together go to the Grand Championship.

Naturally, Dreamer makes the television finals. Since it's 1979, Chris Schenkel and Bo Burton are on hand to do the commentary. But for some reason, Dick Weber is bowling under the name Johnny Watkin. In the final frame, Dreamer converts the 5–10, then follows with a strike to beat Weber—er, Watkin—by one pin. The movie closes with Dreamer and Karen Lee, now married, as proprietors of the Harry White Memorial Bowl.

Dreamer, the movie, opened to mixed reviews. It bombed at the box office. Tim Matheson's career was set back a decade. Susan Blakely was never heard of again.

In the wake of the debacle, Mort Luby, Jr., wrote that *Dreamer* was a bad, dishonest film. Certainly, the technical mistakes were laughable—to cite one example, our hero carries only one bowling ball. The characters weren't always believable, either. Personally, I always wondered why Dreamer didn't dump that whining Karen Lee and take up with Lady instead.

I've written my own nasty comments about *Dreamer* over the years. But in preparing this article, I dug up the old cassette and popped it into the VCR for the first time in nearly two decades. And the truth of the matter is, the film is not nearly as terrible as I remembered.

For one thing, Tim Matheson actually looks professional on the lanes. When a character in a movie or television show is reputed to be a "great bowler," you know what to expect—the person will have a style so godawful, he'd be lucky to keep the ball on the lane, even with bumpers. Matheson, though, did his homework. He reminds me of Don Johnson, with a bit of Bo Burton thrown in.

Granted, the plot is simplistic. But the little-guy-hits-it-big angle has been around since Aesop. It's a staple of sports movies. If the storyline of *Dreamer* seems familiar, that's because it's basically a bowling version of *Rocky*.

Parts of *Dreamer* are quite good. The opening credits offer a montage of vintage bowling photos, backed musically by a delightful set of variations in period idiom. The score is by Bill Conti. He later earned an Oscar for adapting Tchaikovsky and Holst in *The Right Stuff*.

To sum up, I would give *Dreamer* two stars. It is an average movie. Leaving aside for a moment my love of bowling, my desire to see a bowling movie succeed, *Dreamer* is still better than a lot of the stuff at Blockbuster.

Yet the movie remains a symbol of failure within the bowling business. I think this is a result of Great Expectations Unfulfilled. Bowling leaders were hoping for *The Hustler*. That movie had Paul Newman, George C. Scott, and Jackie Gleason. It was directed by Robert Rossen. Compare that talent to the people who made *Dreamer*.

Twenty-five years after *The Hustler*, Paul Newman starred in a sequel called *The Color of Money*. For his reprise of Fast Eddie Felsen, Newman won an Academy Award.

The silver anniversary of *Dreamer* is coming up in 2004. If history is any predictor, a sequel is due. Perhaps some adventuresome producer will make it. Perhaps bowling will finally have a cinema classic.

I wonder what Azizi Johari is doing?

Beware the Count!

(May 2003)

Forty years afterward, Billy Sixty still remembered it like yesterday. It was a warm spring day in the summer of 1915, and the regulars were having lunch at the Langtry-McBride Bowling Café in Milwaukee. Then the stranger walked in.

The man was in his thirties, tall and sandy-haired. He was dressed in a tuxedo coat with striped pants, and a bowtie on a winged-collar dress shirt. He wore white spats and a derby, and wielded an ornate walking stick in his right hand.

He made his way to the bowling room, where four men were getting in a few quick pot games before heading back to work. The stranger was a friendly guy, and soon had joined them. He spoke with a thick German accent. An obvious beginner, he bowled palm-ball and took only one step.

The stranger lost a few dollars that day. But he kept returning for more action. The stakes went up, and gradually his game improved. By the end of the week he was ahead several hundred dollars. Then he vanished.

In the words of reporter Sixty, "That was the impressive introduction to Milwaukee of John (Count) Gengler."

Bowling has always had hustlers. In 1915, local knowledge meant everything. Standardization was still new in the game, so gambling action stayed within one house—or at most, was crosstown. How could anyone travel around the country and take on the best bowlers on their own lanes?

Gengler did. Not that he wanted the publicity. Billy Sixty was a teenage stringer for the *Milwaukee Journal* when the mystery man came to Langtry-McBride. The only personal information that Sixty could pry out of him was that he came from Luxembourg and had learned bowling as a youngster in Bavaria. He wouldn't even tell Sixty his right name.

Today, we know that Gengler left Europe at the outbreak of World War I, in the summer of 1914. Arriving in America, he began his hustling routine and moved through most of the major bowling cities, from New York to California and back to the Midwest. Besides tenpins, he would take bets on duckpins, billiards, poker, pistol-shooting, or a dozen other pastimes. The Count was a one-man traveling casino.

Bowling news traveled slowly in 1915. Rumors of the dapper gambler began to drift from city to city. After Gengler passed through Omaha, local reporter C.J. Cain put the pieces together. Cain, also a *BJ* correspondent, alerted publisher Dave Luby that the Count might be heading for Chicago.

On November 20, 1915, Luby ran the following announcement—"WATCH OUT FOR THE COUNT! The 'Count,' from Luxembourg, has arrived and is cleaning up Chicago bowlers, the same as he has done with all other pin followers from coast to here. He is making a tour of this country, and in every big bowling city, stops off to take a share of the bowlers' easy dough. He will bet you anything from one ball to fifty games, and will place any amount you wish. Watch out for the 'Count!'"

The Count had been pulling his usual hustle on the local talent. Now that was ended. And yet, even after Luby's warning, he still found plenty of prospects eager to take him on. The one-step approach and palm-ball delivery were enough to tempt men who should have known better.

Still, Gengler managed to retain some of his mystique. At a time when few people owned cars, he often arrived at a bowling alley in a limousine. Sometimes he was accompanied by a man and woman who stayed out in the limo while he rolled his matches. And he still would not give his name. Stories in *BJ* refer to him simply as "Count."

Most of Gengler's matches went unreported. The one that got the most publicity was his battle with Ed "Pop" Blouin, father of superstar Jimmy Blouin. They bowled on neutral lanes, and the old man clobbered Gengler over ten games. Then Blouin came back and beat him again in a three-game set.

Of course, it's possible Gengler dumped those matches to set up some other suckers. Or maybe Blouin really was too much for him. We'll never know. What we *do* know is that immediately afterward, the Count was taking on all comers in the house—and winning handily.

He continued popping up at various bowling alleys and billiard halls. In one arranged match, he met brash Bob Rolfe of the famous Chambers-Detroit auto team. The Count threw a 280 at him, and Rolfe slunk away with his tail between his legs. By early December, the *Chicago Herald* was telling readers that "Count D'Alleys" had gathered in over $8,000—in 2003 money, about $100,000.

And then he was gone from Chicago. There had been talk about setting up a match against Matty Faetz, the reigning ABC All Events champ. The Count's often-stated motto was, "A match well-made is a match half-won." He wasn't sure he could beat Faetz, so he left.

The Count was moving east. He was sighted at South Bend, at Toledo, at Cleveland. But the big news came on December 25, when *Bowlers Journal* exploded its Christmas bombshell—the "traveling Count" had finally been identified! Someone had recognized the mystery man, registering in an Ohio hotel as John Gengler. When confronted, the Count admitted that was his true name.

With his cover blown, Gengler decided to go straight. He was settling in Toledo. The ABC Tournament was coming to town in a few months. He planned to enter.

He had not reckoned with ABC secretary Abe Langtry, who already knew the Count from Milwaukee. He had been following the stories of Gengler's odyssey. Langtry had no intention of letting such a notorious character bowl in his tournament!

Gengler was officially barred from the ABC. A Cleveland newspaper took up his cause, claiming that bowling leaders were afraid of Gengler, that he might win all the championships. Langtry stood firm. Gengler was not a member of a sanctioned league. Therefore, he could not compete in the ABC Tournament.

That was not the end of Count Gengler—not hardly. Within a short time he had embarked on an exhibition tour with match-game king Jimmy Smith. Gengler won the Atlantic Coast Doubles championship.

He slaughtered Frank Caruana in a home-and-home match. He bowled a 300 game in the dark. And he even made it into the 1920 ABC Tournament, though with little result. From there, the Count passed into legend.

If he was angry at *Bowlers Journal* for unmasking him, he got over it. When he later ran a bowling alley in a Chicago suburb, Dave Luby became one of his friends. In 1934 he sat for a series of interviews with Mort Luby, Sr. He was also honored as a member of *BJ*'s 1910–1925 Special All American team.

At the same time Gengler was roaming the country and beating bowlers on their home lanes, so was Jimmy Smith. But Smith did it openly, in exhibitions and arranged matches—and he was proclaimed the match-game champion of the world. In a sense, Gengler was Smith's dark shadow.

Inevitably, the two men joined forces. And inevitably, they broke asunder. Smith could not redeem Gengler. The climax came in 1926, when Smith annihilated Gengler in a 40-game match, and exorcised his demon.

Wow! People always seem to get carried away when the subject is Count Gengler. Leaving aside all the hyperbole, he remains an important figure in the history of bowling. He also set in motion the circumstances that made *BJ* the game's first national voice. Today, more certainly than ever, we know that the Count's arrival was one of bowling's Defining Moments.

The Buds Shoot 3858

(June 2003)
In January 1957, as was done every year, the Matt Hermann & Sons Undertaker Company of St. Louis issued a calendar. The Hermann calendar never carried a picture. Instead, it featured the scoresheet of the record 3797 series rolled by the company's bowling team on January 27, 1937.

For the twentieth anniversary in 1957, sponsor Cone Hermann organized a team reunion at a local hotel. The oldtimers feasted and relived their glory. They were confident their score was untouchable. "Let 'em shoot," one of them scoffed. "They can't break our record!"

Their sponsor had somewhat less bravado. "If the record is broken," said Cone Hermann, "it will be by the St. Louis Budweisers."

By 1957 the Budweisers were being talked of as the greatest team in history. Their story had started three years earlier, when Whitey Harris and Ray Bluth convinced the Anheuser-Busch Brewery to put together a world-class bowling team. All-Star champ Don Carter was lured home from Detroit to join a lineup that included Bluth, Billy Welu, Don McClaren, and Pat Patterson. Harris was captain and sixth man.

The team had repaid the brewery's investment in the best way possible—with publicity. They captured the BPAA Team Match Game title and most every team tournament of consequence. For three straight seasons they recorded the highest series in the nation. When the Buds went out on exhibition tours, they played to packed houses. They even made a movie.

Along the way there had been some changes in the roster. McClaren was dropped after the first season and replaced by a little-known Indianapolis postman named Dick Weber. Welu left the next year. His place was taken by a returning St. Louis favorite, Tom Hennessey.

The lineup was now Carter, Bluth, Patterson, Hennessey, Weber. When the Hermanns staged their reunion, many in the bowling world figured the Buds would one day shatter the record. The only question was, how high would they go?

The answer came of March 12, 1958. Besides their exhibitions and tournaments, the Buds competed in the St. Louis Masters League. The league's home was Floriss Lanes, an ancient three-story establishment hidden on a side street on the North Side of the city. Floriss had sixteen lanes, divided between the second and third floors. The Masters bowled on the second floor. On this frosty Wednesday evening, the league-leading Buds were facing the second-place Pulaski Savings team. The match was scheduled for everyone's favorite pair, Seven and Eight.

"Ray Haefner ran the place and he was a throwback to the old days," Ray Bluth remembered. "Sometimes he'd do the lanes, sometimes he wouldn't. But the carry was really good—he just had a high-scoring house. On Eight you could swing the ball and had a large area to play. On Seven you had to be more direct. We knew we could hit them, and we always looked forward to bowling on Seven and Eight."

Unlike the previous three seasons, the Buds had not yet posted the nation's highest series. The leading score so far was the 3696 rolled by the Rochez Brothers team of Pittsburgh. The Rochez captain had recently run into a few of the Buds at an exhibition, and had kidded them about the situation.

Setting their sights on the Rochez score, the Buds charged out of the box. The first three men—Carter, Bluth, Patterson—each started with the first five strikes. By the end of that frame, the team already had 39 marks. In the sixth, Hennessey blew a 10-pin for the first open. But the Buds quickly regrouped and finished with 1265. The Rochez series was within easy reach. And the Buds were only two pins off the Hermanns' pace.

The second game began. Patterson caught a rail in the first and struggled. But his teammates stayed hot. Bluth and Hennessey each strung the first eight. Then Bluth left a 10-pin and missed it. Meanwhile, Hennessey went all the way for 300. When the dust settled, the Buds had 1300. Forget Rochez—now they were running ahead of the Hermanns. They needed 1233 for the record.

Whitey Harris was not present this night. Not needed for the match, he was busy at Airport Bowl, the house he owned in partnership with a few of his teammates. But with the team closing in on the Hermanns, the other Buds put a phone call through to their captain, and he listened to a play-by-play from the Floriss counterman.

Oddly enough, both Bluth and Weber had triplicates going, Bluth with 267 and Weber with 258. As the final game began, Hennessey gave Bluth the needle. "Come on, get going," he said. "I've got *my* 300."

Now the strikes were coming harder. Through the first few frames, only Bluth was stringing. Would the Buds again come up short?

And then—suddenly—the avalanche. They all struck in the fifth frame ... in the sixth ... in the seventh ... in the eighth ... and the first three in the ninth, until Hennessey was tapped. Add in Weber's anchor strike in the fourth, and the Buds had reeled off 24 in a row.

Now the Buds needed only a few marks. They got them, and more. They closed with 1293 for a total of 3858, and a new ABC record. Their opponent, Pulaski Savings, set an unwanted record of their own. With 3494, the Pulaskis had the highest series by a team which lost all three games. The previous "wrong night" record of 3457 had been set by the Hermanns' opponents of 1937—a team called Budweiser Beer.

On the 1958 Buds, Patterson was low man with 736. Carter had 754 and Hennessey 759. Weber lost his triplicate with a 259, which gave him 775. Bluth also lost his triplicate—with a 300 game, for an 834 series. "I never could beat you," Hennessey told him.

Each of the new record-holders talked to Captain Harris on the

The Buds Shoot 3858

The Budweiser Beer team with their record 3858 scoresheet. Front row: Dick Weber, Pat Patterson, Tom Hennessey; rear row: Ray Bluth, Don Carter, captain and sixth man Whitey Harris.

phone. Then Hennessey yelled, "Budweiser for everyone!" and the rest of the league—plus the hundred or so spectators—joined in the celebration. The brewery happily picked up the tab.

The Hermann Undertaker calendar would never be the same. Unlike today's custom, none of the old Hermann bowlers sent congratulations to the Buds. Cone Hermann himself had died shortly after the reunion dinner, and never saw the cherished record broken.

The 3858 marked the high point of the Great Team Era. Little more than a year later, the Professional Bowlers Association was launched, signaling the beginning of the end for big-time team play. Budweiser dropped its sponsorship in 1961. The bowlers stayed together a few more years as the Don Carter Bowling Gloves, then went their separate ways.

The Buds' record lasted nearly thirty-six years, until a Pennsylvania team topped it by 10 pins. Considering the explosion in scoring, it's a wonder it held up so long. Then again, maybe there's no cause to wonder. For when was there ever a team like the Budweisers?

Gibby's Big Jackpot

(September 2003)

Jackpot Bowling debuted on NBC-TV in January 1959. The show was designed to fill air time whenever the Friday night boxing broadcast ended in an early knockout. That air time varied from week to week, so a flexible format was needed. The solution was simple—bowlers would shoot for strikes only. Each contestant rolled nine balls, and the man with the most X's won.

The jackpot was a special prize given to the bowler who rolled six straight strikes. Starting at $5,000, it added $1,000 a week until somebody got the six-bagger. To the surprise of network execs, *Jackpot Bowling* became a huge hit.

As the second season drew to a close, the fill-in show was getting a bigger audience than the boxing bout. That convinced NBC to pull out all the stops. For the 1960–61 season, *Jackpot Bowling* was given a half-hour time slot on Monday evening. Now there would be two matches every show. In the second match, when the king-of-the-hill defended, the jackpot would start at $25,000 and go up in $5,000 increments.

That was serious money—multiply the figure by seven, and you get the 2003 equivalent.

The program would also have a new host, legendary comic Milton Berle. NBC had Berle under contract, and was looking for a vehicle to revive his career. If Groucho Marx could run a quiz show, why not bowling with Uncle Miltie?

Jackpot Bowling Starring Milton Berle—that was now the official name of the show—got off to a fine start. Berle did his routines and schmoozed with his celebrity guests, while sportscaster Chick Hearn handled the actual bowling matches. The fourth week in, Frank Clause hit the jackpot for $40,000.

The season went on, and the jackpot began to build again. For ten weeks, no one could manage that sixth strike. By January 2, 1961, the prize was up to $75,000.

This particular Monday was the New Year's holiday, and that caused a problem. *Jackpot Bowling* was normally taped in the afternoon a few hours before air time. But announcer Hearn was also calling the Rose Bowl college football game, and got hung up in traffic on the way to the bowling lanes. He arrived late, so the show had to go out live.

The first match featured Don Ellis and Bob Kwolek, with Ellis winning in ten frames. Then celebrity guest Jack Dempsey rolled a ball for his favorite charity—he got seven pins. With that, it was time for Ellis to challenge the reigning king-of-the-hill, Therm Gibson.

Closing in on his forty-fourth birthday, Gibson was on the downslope of a distinguished career. In his prime he'd been one of the mainstays of the Pfeiffer Beer team. Now he was operating a pro shop in Detroit and making a few tournaments. He was a big, bald, bear of a man who liked to run out his shots, clapping his hands loudly as the ball hit the pocket.

The match started. And it was immediately clear that Gibson was off his game. He pushed his first shot too high, and just did carry the 7-pin for a strike. In the second, he hit full on the nose but got another lucky break, caving in the 6–7 split. Meanwhile, Ellis had rolled two perfect strikes.

Third frame. For the first time, Gibson put the ball where he wanted it. And for the first time, he clapped his hands. Strike! Ellis, rolling like a machine, cleared the deck again. Each man was halfway. And now the crowd was buzzing.

Gibson in the fourth. Now the adrenalin was flowing. He bowled, he clapped, he struck. Over to the Ellis machine. But this time, something went wrong. The ball skidded past the headpin to the right, and he got seven pins. Loud groans from the audience.

Back to Gibson. Another perfect shot, the clap of the hands—and Gibby had number five! By now, Ellis was eliminated from the jackpot. But if Gibson missed, he could still win the match. Ellis rolled in the fifth, and once again sent the ball too far to the right. Another miss.

Suddenly, it was deathly quiet. Chick Hearn told the home audience, "Ladies and gentlemen, it's time for all of us to sit back and say a little prayer." Gibson stepped on the approach, and a faint smile crossed his face. On television screens across America, "$75,000" flashed below his image. He seemed to be taking a little more time. Then he was gliding to the line, and the ball was away.

Gibby didn't like it—there was no hand clap. The ball hit light, and the pins scattered. The 2-pin slashed left, hitting the 4-pin, which fell sideways into the kingpin. The 7-pin stood—but then that hardworking 2-pin clipped the crown of the 7, and it slowly toppled. As the sweeper came down, there were three pins lying on the deck. But Gibson had his strike.

Chick Hearn was the first to reach him, jumping into his arms like Yogi Berra at the end of Don Larsen's no-hitter. Then came Berle, who did the same thing. The audience hollered and hooted. When the cheers started to die, Berle yelled, "That's not enough applause!" and everyone gave the new hero another salute.

The match was over. Of course, if the bowlers continued on for the full nine frames, there was still the mathematical possibility that Ellis might win, 7–6. But that would have been an anticlimax. By hitting the jackpot, Gibson automatically won the match and the weekly prize of $1,000. That gave him a total purse of $76,000.

In a little under four minutes, Therm Gibson had earned more money than Mickey Mantle got for playing an entire season in the Yankee outfield. It was more than Johnny Unitas made on the gridiron, or Arnold Palmer on the golf course, or Wilt Chamberlain for a year in the NBA. In fact, the only American athlete to cash a bigger paycheck from his sport that year would be Floyd Patterson, the heavyweight boxing champ.

And yet, Gibson's fete was ignored by most of the media. It was a case of bad timing—remember, this was the same day the college football bowl games were being played. Though the wire services carried news of the "$76,000 strike," it was buried by the sheer bulk of football reporting. The only place where the jackpot story rated headlines was Detroit, Gibby's hometown.

Therm Gibson, right, winner of the *Jackpot Bowling* television jackpot, is congratulated by the show's host, comedian Milton Berle. In four minutes Gibson earned more money than Mickey Mantle got for playing an entire season in the Yankee outfield.

By summer, *Jackpot Bowling* was gone forever. Therm Gibson died a few years later. In the decades that have passed, that television show and Gibson's exploit have become bowling legend. The digits 1–2–61 stand for a red-letter day, the one moment in time when tenpins was a big-money sport.

But part of this Defining Moment must also be the aftermath, and the silence of the media. In 1961—even at the peak of the Golden Age of Bowling—our sport did not get the respect it deserved. The pattern was set. And we are still trying to do something about it today.

Bowling's Defining Moment

(November 2003)

George Bailey was on his way to the 2004 American Bowling Congress Tournament. He was excited that the tournament was being revived—this last gap of seven years was the longest yet. The only problem was that George was not very good at Glow Bowl, and that's what the manufacturer had chosen for the format.

George preferred Straight Bowling. He was currently carrying a 288 average, which ranked him fifth in the Potter Bank League. Years before, George had cashed with an 876 Singles in the National Bowling Association Tournament. But the NBA had given up Straight Bowling when its backer decided to emphasize Carom Bowling.

Six of the national governing bodies were holding tournaments this year. None would be Straight Bowling. Still, George was excited. The ABC Tournament at Terre Haute would be the biggest in memory, with over 100 teams competing! He certainly did have a wonderful life …

\# \# \#

Confused? We've merely been engaging in the pluperfects of history—the "What Ifs." The foregoing is what bowling today might have looked like if a few things had gone differently.

As we've seen over the past several months leading up to this Anniversary Edition, there have been many defining moments that produced the game we enjoy. Yet there is one entity which—from its very beginning—has defined just what bowling is. That would be the American Bowling Congress.

So how do we identify the number one defining moment in bowling history? It makes sense to look at ABC's early years, a time of many crises. ABC chose a particular path that has made all the difference in what the game has become.

Like many a nation-state or ancient religion, ABC has developed an elaborate Creation Saga. The story goes that bowling was a chaotic, unregulated pastime in the late nineteenth century. No one could agree on rules, scoring, or equipment specifications. Then, in September 1895, bowlers from various New York clubs gathered at Beethoven Hall to bring some order to the situation. The result was the American Bowling Congress.

In later years, the last survivor of the founding fathers, Louis Stein, delighted in reliving that historic meeting. Stein was quite a storyteller. He related a colorful tale of argument and compromise, of grand debates lubricated by ponies of beer into the small hours of the morning. You could almost smell the sauerkraut and cigar smoke.

As Huck Finn might have said about Louis Stein, "He told the truth, mainly." But as Paul Harvey said, "Now for the rest of the story."

The place to look is Rick Kogan's book, *Brunswick: The Story of an American Company from 1845 to 1985*. According to Kogan, the man most responsible for founding the ABC was Moses Bensinger, president of the company then known as Brunswick-Balke-Collender. During the early 1890s, Bensinger tried to convince proprietors and club leaders that if bowling were to prosper, it needed to be organized. It was Bensinger who put together the meeting at Beethoven Hall. And as Kogan writes, "After hours of debate and eloquent speeches by Bensinger, the American Bowling Congress was born."

Bensinger's work was just beginning. A few years later, he was the driving force behind the first ABC Tournament. Brunswick also provided the equipment, and helped publicize the event by way of newspaper advertisements. The company even paid for printing the tournament schedules and prize books.

Kogan's book is a company-sponsored corporate history. Did he give Bensinger too much credit? The final answer to that question requires more research. But of course, Bensinger would want to organize and promote bowling. Promote the game, and Brunswick would sell more equipment. Standardize the rules, and Brunswick could produce that equipment cheaper.

This was the dawn of America's sporting age. Al Spalding was already building an empire by providing equipment for baseball, football, golf, and other games. Bensinger's Brunswick was doing the same thing. The company had made its name in billiards; now it was moving into bowling.

Most bowling leaders were glad to have any help Brunswick could offer during those first few years. They didn't seem worried about manufacturers having too much influence on the game. Once ABC was launched, the most visible problem facing organized bowling was sectionalism.

ABC's original members were the bowling clubs of New York City. Copies of their model rules had been sent to every city known to have bowling. With a few exceptions, that meant the East Coast and the

Midwest. In 1895 most of the country's population was still concentrated there.

Chicago was the great metropolis of the West—that is, the far side of the Alleghenies. The bowlers of that city received the ABC rules with enthusiasm, and immediately pledged their loyalty to the new organization. But the Chicagoans had their own ideas about the game. In 1899 they started the Illinois Bowling Association as their own "local branch" of the ABC.

The Easterners were alarmed. Were the Chicagoans going to break away and form a rival group? Partly to placate them, the 1901 ABC Convention was awarded to Chicago. The ABC also reversed policy and voted to stage a tournament along with the convention.

The East-West split involved more than geographic rivalry. The Easterners were "old club," where membership was restricted and cozy. The clubs generally followed a loose schedule. Only a few matches were bowled at a session, and some teams might go weeks without playing. To use a political analogy, the Easterners wanted ABC to remain a "small government."

The Westerners were more progressive. They believed in tournaments, in promotion, in growth. You didn't have to be accepted into a special club if you wanted to bowl—the leagues of the West were open, and they usually bowled every week. The more people who bowled, the better the Westerners liked it. They wanted ABC to be bigger and more active.

Inevitably, the balance of power within the ABC shifted to the West. The Easterners had started the Congress, but had become a minority. They didn't like it. When Chicagoan Frank Pasdeloup was elected ABC president at the 1902 Convention, the Easterners walked out in protest, forcing Pasdeloup to resign after a "term" of three hours.

Now the annual convention became a battleground. Each year the two factions squared off, and the West outvoted the East. The Westerners threw an occasional bone to the minority. But the long string of defeats left the Easterners bitter. They finally ran out of patience in 1906, the year the 1907 Convention was announced. The East had been promised that the 1907 show would go to Philadelphia. Instead, St. Louis was voted in.

Feeling double-crossed, bowlers from the Eastern cities met in Newark a few weeks later, and organized the National Bowling Association. In November, the NBA gave notice that it was withdrawing from the ABC.

After little more than a decade, organized bowling was being torn apart. And now another long-smoldering question was coming to a boil. What role would manufacturers play in the game?

Of course, the ABC was still little more than a letterhead. In 1907 there were only a few thousand sanctioned bowlers in the whole country. Yet the potential growth was there. And just who would direct that growth?

Everyday leadership in the ABC was vested in Samuel Karpf. As a columnist for *The Bowler's Journal* (New York), Karpf had helped promote the 1895 Beethoven Hall meeting. In recognition of his services, he had been elected Secretary of the new organization. He'd continued to hold that office when he moved to Dayton in 1898. Karpf had relocated to take a job with Crawford, McGregor, and Canby Company, a builder of bowling lanes. As we've seen, in the first few years of the ABC, nobody was concerned about conflicts of interest. But that was changing.

The Eastern bloc had fired the first shot. Seeing the manufacturers as a threat to grass-roots control of bowling, the Easterners had demanded that manufacturer's reps—and even bowling proprietors—be banned from sitting on the ABC governing board. The Easterners had introduced such legislation at the 1904 Convention. As usual, it had been voted down.

Over the next few years, more and more bowlers had begun to feel that maybe the manufacturers did have too much clout. Then Karpf's company was given the contract to install lanes at the 1907 tournament. That deal seemed to confirm the suspicions. The outraged Cincinnati bowlers announced they would oppose Karpf in the next election.

The leader of the Cincinnati group was August "Garry" Herrmann. A colorful rogue of good fellowship, Herrmann was one of the chieftains of the city's political machine. He was also a national celebrity—president of the Cincinnati Reds and *de facto* commissioner of baseball. And Herrmann had a reputation for getting what he wanted. Hadn't the posh Waldorf-Astoria Hotel added fried pigs' feet to its breakfast menu?

Rather than fight, Karpf gave up. He claimed that his other interests did not leave time for the ABC job. "There is no need of ... the slightest uneasiness on the part of the bowlers of Cincinnati or elsewhere as to my again trying to secure the office of Secretary," he said. "I am simply not a candidate, and will not allow my name to be placed before the meeting in St. Louis."

Karpf was not the only official stung by the manufacturer controversy. W.V. Thompson was an ABC vice president, respected and well-liked. He was also known as Brunswick's man on the executive committee. Seeing the way the wind was blowing, Thompson stepped down.

And with all that was going on, the presidency of the ABC had become an issue. Robert H. Bryson was the incumbent, and he wanted another term. Everybody loved Bob Bryson. But was he the man to fill the ABC's top office? "We should have a big man, a man of national stature as president," said one convention delegate. Perhaps somebody like Garry Herrmann.

"Red Hot Political Fight On at ABC" read the headline in the *St. Louis Post-Dispatch* as the bowlers gathered in St. Louis for the 1907 Tournament and Convention. Though the calendar said it was the first week of spring, the city sweltered in 90 degree heat. Behind the scenes, the maneuvering quickened. What about the Eastern schism? What about the manufacturers? And who would lead the ABC?

At 2 o'clock on the afternoon of March 20, the Convention was called to order at the Southern Hotel. The expected fireworks never did develop. Business was transacted quickly and amicably—it was just too hot for long speeches.

Cincinnati was awarded the 1908 Tournament. Then came the election for president, and Herrmann swamped Bryson, 103 to 55. At Bryson's request, the vote was made unanimous.

Meanwhile, three candidates were on the ballot for secretary. G.H. Rautenberg and Dennis Sweeney were both from St. Louis, while Abraham Lincoln Langtry came from Milwaukee. Many delegates remembered Langtry for the superb job he'd done running the 1905 Tournament—in those days, local committees were in charge of the event. When the vote was taken, the totals read: Langtry 78, Rautenberg 40, Sweeney 17.

The withdrawal letter sent by the NBA was read to the Convention. Now that the long-feared schism had finally happened, it was accepted with practicality. The delegates gave President Herrmann authority to appoint a three-man committee which would meet with NBA officials. Playing rules had to be coordinated, conflicts in tournament dates resolved, and so on.

A few more minor issues were dealt with. After that the delegates adjourned, and went off to bowl in the tournament. The 1907 ABC Convention was over. The decisions made there had far-reaching consequences.

Consider the way the sectional crisis was handled. The break with the East was amicable. Over the next decade, the ABC and the NBA avoided stepping on each other's toes. The two groups kept in contact through liaison committees, and sent observers to each other's conventions.

Garry Herrmann did much to keep tempers cool. The new ABC President had a politician's instinct for conciliation. He might have roused the 1907 delegates to an all-out war against the East, but he didn't. It happened that one of the NBA leaders was Charles H. Ebbets, president of the Brooklyn Dodgers and one of Herrmann's baseball cronies. Whatever their friendship meant, the fact is that the NBA eventually rejoined the ABC.

The anti-manufacturer movement is also significant. Even though no official action was taken, the forward-thinkers knew it was time for the ABC to become independent. Today, historic companies like Brunswick and AMF remain an important part of the bowling world. But they do not dominate it.

The ABC has not wielded the power of some of the other sports governing bodies. For example, it does not have the clout of the United States Golf Association, which has been unafraid to take on golf equipment manufacturers in court. Yet the ABC has still tried to live up to its self-professed mandate. It has not become a toothless tiger like the Billiard Congress of America, or a joke like the various boxing commissions.

And think for a moment about the game of tenpins itself. In the billiards room, the traditional championship game of 14.1 continuous pool—the game of Greenleaf and Caras and Mosconi—is fast disappearing. Now it's all eight-ball or nine-ball. If the ABC had remained under the thumb of the manufacturers, what would bowling look like today? Would our introductory tale of George Bailey really be an outrageous fable?

Now look at the Convention's choice of secretary. A.L. Langtry ran the ABC as a virtual one-man show for a quarter-century. As much as any person, he shaped organized bowling, and bowling has been the better for it. But suppose Dennis Sweeney had been elected instead of Langtry—the same Dennis Sweeney who later helped start the Women's International Bowling Congress. Might bowling have had a single membership organization eighty years ago?

Going back to the sectional issue, what if the Eastern secession had been handled differently? Cave in to their demands—have peace at any price—and bowling might have remained just another diversion for social clubs, with little growth. Or go the other way and have a full-scale war, ABC vs. NBA. Maybe bowling would now have two or three or even more governing bodies, each with its own rules.

Some of these scenarios contradict one another. We can only speculate on what might have happened. All we know for sure is what did happen.

Our sport has evolved in a particular way. A large number of strands lead back to one crucial point, where momentous decisions were made. The process was set in motion. That's why the defining moment of modern bowling is the 1907 ABC Convention.

Time for a Bowling Postage Stamp?

(January 2004)
I went to the post office the other day and bought some stamps. The latest issue honors Red Grange, Bronko Nagurski, and some other football demigods. I was reminded once again that bowling has never had a proper postage stamp.

In the forty-odd years I've been mailing my own letters, I've pasted a bunch of sports heroes onto my envelopes. I can recall stamps featuring Babe Ruth, Babe Zaharias, Bobby Jones, Joe Louis, Jim Thorpe, Roberto Clemente—well, you get the idea. Athletes have become as popular a subject of postal art as dead presidents and movie stars.

Once upon a time, we did have a sort-of bowling stamp. In 1971 the Federation Internationale des Quilleurs World Championships came to Milwaukee, the first time that event had been held on U.S. soil. The Postal Service responded by issuing a postage-prepaid envelope, with a red square in the appropriate place. The square had white letters which simply read "Bowling." I still have one of those things buried in a drawer somewhere.

About ten years ago there was a stamp for Harold Lloyd, the silent-screen comic. Lloyd was an avid bowler. He was also co-owner of a famous bowling palace near Hollywood, and was a frequent spectator at the All-Star Tournament. He even rolled a 300 game when a perfect score was about as rare as air conditioning in an automobile.

I think it's safe to say that the Postal Service was not honoring Lloyd for his accomplishments on or near the lanes. So it's time bowling had a *real* stamp.

As with the other sports, the bowling stamp should honor a person. Three obvious candidates are Marion Ladewig, Dick Weber, and Don Carter. The trouble here is that you have to be dead to get your picture on a U.S. stamp, and we don't want to hurry anyone. Only those who have entered the Great Beyond need apply.

We could start with Earl Anthony. His record speaks for itself— he may have been the greatest bowler ever. But more important, he symbolized the sport to the general public. You didn't have to be a bowler to know who Earl Anthony was. Even the hip television show *Mystery Science Theater 3000* reference him in some of their bits.

Half of the bowling population is female, so we might want to consider the first woman star of the sport, Floretta McCutcheon. She could compete on the same level with the best men. And Mrs. Mac also made things respectable. Before she came along, a bowling alley was no place for a lady. She was like the schoolmarm in the old Western movies who brings civilization to Deadwood or Dodge City.

Among the men pioneers, we could honor either Jimmy Smith or Hank Marino. Smith was the first person to earn a living as a bowler. He brought bowling to the far corners of the country, helping make it more than a regional pastime. Marino was all about talent. In 1941 he led the voting in the first Hall of Fame election. Ten years later, he was named Bowler of the Half Century.

Then there were our first Hollywood bowling stars, Ned Day and Andy Varipapa. Like Mrs. Mac, Day helped polish bowling's image, showing that a bowler could be a gentleman. Varipapa had a few rough edges, but was the finest trick-shot performer who ever lived. Both men gave bowling great visibility through their film shorts. And they could knock down a few pins in competition, too.

But my choice for the one bowler to put on a postage stamp is Joe Norris. At the beginning of his career, he was hailed as the youngest person to roll a 300 game. Nearly seventy years later, in his twilight years, he became the oldest bowler to turn the trick. In between he organized the first great brewery team, won tournaments all over the world, was an All American eight straight years, and rolled in seventy-one ABC tournaments.

The Norris proposal has an additional advantage. Remember when the Postal Service had the public vote on two portraits of Elvis Presley, to decide which one should go on his stamp? We'll offer the bowlers of America *three* Norris pictures—Young Joe, Middle-aged Joe, and Old Joe—and let them vote on that.

I Remember Billy Welu

(April 2004)
I met Billy Welu twice. In my memory, he will always be linked with sudden, unexpected death.

The first time was a Sunday morning in November 1963. President Kennedy was lying in state at the Capitol, killed by a sniper named Lee Harvey Oswald. But in Chicago the bowling gods had come to town for the World's Invitational. I was a teenager and had gone down to McCormick Place to see them. I had just entered the building when the Great Welu appeared in my path, all 6-foot-5 of him.

"Did you hear?" he asked me in a vacant voice. "They just shot Oswald." Like old friends we chatted about the president's assassin for a few moments. Then Welu wandered off.

He finished down the list in that tournament, something that didn't happen often in those days. Welu was one of the best, at the top of his game. ABC Doubles champ ... winner of the All-Star Tournament ... charter member of the Budweisers ... captain of the Falstaffs ... PBA champion ... many-time All American ...

His was a Hall of Fame resume—and he was barely thirty. But it was the way Welu bowled that was most impressive. A big man was supposed to charge the line and overpower the pins with brute force. Welu seemed to glide down the approach like a man on skis, the ball flowing noiselessly onto the lane. How could he get so much power out of so little effort? It made the rest of us want to give up bowling and go play croquet.

By 1963 Welu was already launched on his second career as color analyst for the *Pro Bowlers Tour* telecasts. The teaming of the "aw-shucks" Texan with the polished Chris Schenkel was inspired. A few years later, Roone Arledge would give us *Monday Night Football* with the unlikely trio of Gifford, Cosell, and Dandy Don. I'll always believe that Arledge got that idea from his Saturday afternoon bowling show.

Welu could play the part of the cornpone philosopher perfectly.

It didn't matter that Billy was a college graduate who'd worked on a Master's degree. He was Jed Clampett in a bowling shirt. We came to treasure all the little Welu-isms, like "Hit 'em thin and watch 'em spin," or if that wasn't appropriate, "Hit 'em high and watch 'em fly." And the ultimate compliment—"Good speed!"

Still, among all the clichés, the Welu wit was ready. It might peak out at any moment, particularly when the conversation strayed from bowling:

SCHENKEL: "Billy, if I had your money, I'd retire."
WELU: "And if I had *your* money, I'd throw mine away."

As it happened, Welu the Broadcaster was not quite through as a player. When the 1964 television season wrapped up, he went off and won the Masters. That felt good, so the next year he did the same thing.

His credentials re-established, he could relax. He settled into the color role, describing the talents and triumphs of lesser bowlers. The only place we could now enjoy the wonderful Welu style was on reruns of *Championship Bowling.*

The years passed. From time to time Welu came to Chicago for a sportsmen's show. I went to a few of these, and would see him there, but I never approached him. The crowd was always too thick.

Then, one day in 1974, I was walking through O'Hare Airport when I saw him coming toward me. I had aged from a crew-cut teen to a long-haired-and-bearded grad student. But when I started to tell Welu that we had met once before, he immediately said: "When Ruby killed Oswald, right?" We reminisced for about thirty seconds, then each of us walked off into our separate lives. A month later, one bright spring morning, I opened the *Sun-Times* sports section and read the headline: "Billy Welu Dead at 41."

The First National Tournament

(May–June 2004)
Before there was an ABC Tournament, there was a wild and wonderful extravaganza known as the International Bowling Tournament. The bowling world had never seen anything like it. That's still the case, more than a century later.

The story begins in the fall of 1899 with Louis F. Schutte, publisher of *The Bowler's Journal* (New York). The nineteenth century was drawing to a close, and everyone seemed to be planning some sort of celebration. Schutte believed a "monster tournament" would be a good way for bowlers to celebrate.

Bowling tournaments were still rare events. The ABC refused to hold one. But out in Chicago, the new Illinois Bowling Association had just completed a successful tournament, and was planning to make it an annual affair. That was enough to convince Schutte.

Bowling in New York City was run by the United Bowling Clubs, a loose alliance of forty leagues. Schutte outlined his plan to club leaders, and they agreed to back it. An International Bowling Tournament (IBT) committee was formed, with Schutte as president. To get the ball rolling, *The Bowler's Journal* contributed the first $100 to the tournament fund. The Illinois tournament had been small, with only Team and Singles events. The IBT would be much grander. Besides tenpins, competition was planned for duckpins, candlepins, headpin, and other popular games. There would even be a Ladies Division.

In 1900 a typical bowling venue had only three or four lanes. No ordinary establishment could hope to accommodate the IBT, so the promoters decided to erect temporary facilities on the grounds of Schuetzen Park, a popular target-shooting resort across the Hudson in Union Hill, New Jersey. They scheduled the tournament for the week of July 16–22, 1900.

Skeptics hooted that such an elaborate show would never succeed. That made the IBT committee more determined. New York City and environs were divided into a dozen districts, each with a "captain" in charge of drumming up entries. ABC Secretary Samuel Karpf, with his wide contacts, was given the job on enticing the out-of-towners. Beginning in March, each weekly issue of *The Bowler's Journal* ran a lengthy front page article on the joys of the upcoming IBT.

At first the entries trickled in. Alarmed, the promoters extended the deadline. The also began to publicize some of the other available attractions, like the pistol marksmanship competition. There would be gymnastic exhibitions and circus acts, afternoon band concerts and dancing under the stars. Each day's festivities would close with a fireworks show.

Then came the big announcement. Admiral George Dewey, hero of the recent war with Spain, had agreed to be the Grand Marshall of the opening parade, and roll the ceremonial first ball. A special lignum

"Hit 'em thin and watch 'em spin!" Billy Welu lifts off during the All-Star Tournament.

vitae wooden bowling ball, with the admiral's portrait inlaid, was being prepared for his use.

And now the pace of entries gathered speed. When the June 1 deadline arrived, 255 teams had signed up, including forty-nine in the ladies event. Although the majority of entries were from Greater New York, there would be bowlers on hand from Baltimore, Pittsburgh, Cincinnati, Chicago, St. Louis, and even Houston, Texas. And the IBT would be truly international, with two Canadian teams coming from Toronto.

Out at Schuetzen Park, the tournament buildings were completed. The main bowling hall contained sixteen lanes donated by Brunswick. The separate Ladies Building had six more. A traditional German "centerboard" alley had been constructed outdoors, along with an Italian bocce court. *The Bowler's Journal* tent was in place. The illustrated programs had been printed.

With everything ready, Louis Schutte offered a benediction. "And now one last word for those Doubting Thomases," he wrote. "The tournament is already an assured success. Therefore, ye bowlers, gird up your loins and prepare for the fray. Give your hearty support to the first great bowling tournament ever held in this country, in order that you might be able to say, 'I have done my duty. I have contributed my mite.'"

As it happened, Grand Marshall Dewey sent his regrets at the last minute. But the IBT committee pressed forward, and nobody seemed to miss him.

The festivities opened with a banquet for the out-of-town bowlers at Beethoven Hall in New York on Saturday evening, July 14. The next morning, a little worse for wear, the officials and their guests made their way across the Hudson to Schuetzen Park. After a few speeches, sixteen bowlers stepped onto the sixteen lanes and rolled the tournament into action. Then everyone went back to New York for a nap.

The big parade came on Monday. At 9 a.m. they stepped off from Beethoven Hall, moving through lower Manhattan to the Hoboken ferries. Buglers led the way, followed by mounted police and bicyclists. The bowling clubs marched in their uniforms, carrying banners. Interspersed among the bowlers were four bands pumping out favorite German melodies and John Philip Sousa's latest hits. Last came the pinboys, carrying the tournament pins on silk pillows.

Once they crossed the river, the marchers reassembled and rode chartered trolley cars to the park. Most of them would not be bowling until later in the week, so they wandered around the grounds, and took in the attractions. The shooting galleries were particularly popular.

The IBT was divided into Team and Singles competition. The Team event was run on a set schedule, like a modern tournament. Each five-man team rolled a single game and posted a score. Most teams opted for "strike and spare" tenpins, and only a few tried duckpins, cocked hat, or the more exotic games.

The First National Tournament 137

In contrast, the various Singles games operated like a carnival midway. A bowler bought a 25-cent ticket for each game he wanted to bowl. He then selected the prize he was interested in—silver cups, souvenir medals, merchandise, or cash—and moved to the pair of lanes offering that prize. He could bowl for as many games as he paid for, whenever the lanes were open, and count only his best score.

Over at the Ladies Building, only tenpins was offered. The big draw was the five-woman Team competition, like the men's event a single game. A separate pair of lanes was devoted to the Ladies Individual Championship, total pins over three games. Finally, there was something called What Falls Counts. This event, it was frankly stated, was for women who could not figure out how to keep a bowling score.

By far the greatest interest was in the Inter-City Championship. The purpose here was to settle, once and for all, the vexing question of which city produced the best bowlers. Entries were limited to one all-star team per city, total pins for three games. Nine teams eventually signed up.

The IBT organizers hoped that spectator admissions here would help the tournament's bottom line. As the week moved on, temperatures soared into the 90s, and paid attendance ran only about a third of expected. But the committee had also announced that lanes would be available for "private play" when not in tournament use. Pot games and challenge matches sprang up, and the lineage from them erased some of the red ink.

And then it was over. The bronze medals and silver cups and little sacks of gold coins were passed out, and the bowlers went home. For the record, the Chicago team won the Inter-City Championship with a three-game series of 2615. Future Hall of Famer Frank Brill was their big gun, blasting an opening 246, the highest game rolled during the entire eight-day tournament.

The IBT had lost money, but that wasn't the point. Bowling had been promoted. More important, it had been proven that a national tournament could be made to work.

Among the post-mortems, the most prophetic came from Samuel Karpf. "One [mistake] was that it was not strictly a bowler's festival," he wrote. "I would like to see a strictly American game affair, with contests arranged for teams of five, teams of two, and individual contests."

Six months later, the first American Bowling Congress Tournament rolled into action.

Strange Inventions

(October 2004)
Part of the enduring appeal of bowling is its simplicity. You roll a ball at a bunch of sticks. The more stick you knock down, the better you are. Of course, just how you go about knocking down those sticks is the key to success. To accomplish this goal, bowlers have come up with some ingenious devices.

The first bowling aide was finger holes. They were invented in the 1890s as a way to make the ball easier to handle. Soon after that, bowlers discovered that finger holes allowed them to impart all sorts of useful spin on their shots.

By the 1940s many "scientific" grip styles had become popular. These were based on various specifications of pitch and offset. Some featured curved drillings or indentations within the holes. The grips had names like Curval, Collier, Easter, and Bates. Always the goal was to produce the strongest shot with the least effort.

Ned Day went to far as to get a patent for his particular grip—look at one of the old master's instruction books, and you'll see that the patent notice was engraved right on the ball. Since the Ned Day Grip was a simple arrangement that any ball-driller could duplicate, I've often wondered how Day enforced his rights. Did he visit a bowling alley in disguise, measure the balls on the rack, and confiscate any that had bootleg drilling?

About 1970 the retractable-handle ball made news. These had been used by disabled people for years, but now one manufacturer decided to market them to the general public. Our local proprietor bought a few of these for house balls, and soon my friends and I were rolling handle-ball pot games. The big drawback was that a handle-ball took spin the opposite of a normal bowling ball. Turn it to the left, and the darned thing would back up.

If a slippery grip were your problem, there were various stick-ums you could apply to your fingers to achieve a solid delivery. Joe Kristof sold a popular spray, the All-Sports Hand Conditioner. But we preferred the grip cream called Claro. We abandoned Claro when Gary the Haig got his fingers stuck in the ball and went down the lane with it.

Sometimes an invention you thought would be a sure-fire success never caught on. I remember seeing ads for bowling blinders—goggles with side-shades that shut out distractions on adjoining lanes—but I never saw anyone actually using them. For a while, back in the days of black hard-rubber bowling balls, AMF had a model with a red line that went around the ball on a full-roller track. A friend of mine owned two of them, which probably accounted for half the total sale.

Star endorsements were important. Early in his career, Dick Weber used a black leather sheath that snapped over the thumb. I watched him wearing it in the television finals of the All-Star Tournament one year, while he was losing to Don Carter. Later, when Weber became the dominant player in the game, he no longer depended on that big black thumb.

Among his many accomplishments, Don Carter popularized the bowling glove. But does anyone recall that he was also responsible for Don Carter 300 Bowling Slacks? At one time, it seemed like every bowling magazine featured a full-page ad for this remarkable product, a wash-and-wear design with nyloton supreme pocketing and "swing action" that made it suitable for bowling, office, or otherwise. They did look classy.

Still, my favorite bowling aide has to be the Joe Wilman Timer. After searching for over forty years, I finally found one at a flea market last summer. It looks something like a wrist watch. Inside the watch case is a little metal ball. You strap the timer on your bowling wrist, and while you bowl, the ball slides around and makes loud clicks. By adjusting the timer and monitoring the clicks, you develop proper timing.

The Joe Wilman Timer retailed at $4.95. That's the equivalent of over $40 today. Who says high-priced, high-tech bowling equipment is a recent development?

Dick Weber, R.I.P.

(April 2005)
They told me that Dick Weber has died. But I don't have to believe it if I don't want to.

Too soon, too soon. He was only seventy-five. He should have gone on for another fifteen or twenty years, celebrated like Joe Norris as a Grand Old Man, until all of us could get used to the idea that there would one day be a world without Dick Weber.

He had been such a monumental part of our sport for so long that we tend to forget Weber first came to big-time bowling as an outsider, little known beyond the Indianapolis borders. In 1955 he moved to St. Louis and the Budweisers. He had already been scouted and rejected by Buddy Bomar, who said that Weber "didn't have a big enough ass for the ball he throws." Not signing Weber, Bomar later admitted, was the stupidest thing he'd ever done.

On the Buds, Weber was immediately installed in the anchor spot. Topflight bowlers liked to track the lanes by watching each other's shot, and the rest of the team couldn't learn much from following Weber's wide looping curve, so why not put him on the bottom? Anyway, the Buds were so far above the rest of the competition, it didn't matter that they had a rookie rolling in the position of honor.

But funny things happen. A few weeks into the season, Weber teamed with Ray Bluth to set a new ABC record in a doubles league. By the end of that first year, it seemed the most natural thing in the world to have the little man with the big bender anchoring bowling's super-team.

The irony is that Weber soon had to overhaul his game and develop a straighter shot. Lane conditions were changing, and he made the adjustment best of anyone. A whole generation of bowlers who came of age then—my generation—remembers the patented Dick Weber Strike. This was not the vicious ripper, slashing the 5-pin into the 7, the characteristic of a Junie McMahon. Now we had the "wall shot," with the headpin going to the left sideboard, then rebounding to take of the 2–4–5, with the 5-pin falling to the right, or even forward. It looked messy, but it worked.

Big-time team bowling was on the way out, and Weber made that transition, too. He didn't win the first PBA tournament, but he did take the next two, and that was symbolic of what was to come. The statistics are there: the four All-Star championships, the many PBA titles, the Bowler of the Year awards, and all the rest. By 1970 he had ascended into legend.

For its seventy-fifth anniversary that year, ABC polled writers to name the greatest bowler in history. The only unanimous selections were Don Carter—and Dick Weber. From that time on, any list of all-time greats has Weber among the top three or four. Often he is ranked the best ever.

I once referred to Don Carter as bowling's Joe DiMaggio. Sticking to the baseball analogy, the player Weber calls to mind is Stan Musial.

Both arrived at St. Louis from the hinterlands, made it big there, and came to symbolize the city in their given sport. Both were known for their friendliness and cheerful manner. Baseball's Perfect Knight and Bowling's Greatest Ambassador.

And yet ... look into the eyes of the two men at their respective peaks in the old black-and-white photos. You can glimpse the fire that makes a champion. You don't accomplish as much as these two competitors did without kicking some butt.

Over the years I had occasion to contact Weber perhaps a half-dozen times. He always returned my phone calls promptly, and answered my questions in detail, as if he had all the time in the world, and talking to me was the most important thing in his life. He was everything that I had hoped Dick Weber would be.

The one time I met him in person was in 1999, at Mort Luby's home. As everyone had told me, Weber had a mischievous, irreverent sense of humor. After about an hour, I remarked to him with a laugh, "You're not totally like your public image, are you?" And he chuckled and said, "You don't know the half of it."

Dick Weber dead? I don't have to believe it if I don't want to.

Candy Mac

(July 2005)
Try picking the greatest bowler in history, and you're likely to get an argument over whether his name is Don or Dick, Earl or Walter Ray. But the identity of the world's greatest bowling fan is not open to debate. It is Frank McKeever, better known as "Candy Mac."

The dapper little man with the Western hat and gravel voice was a familiar sight at nearly every big bowling gathering for six decades, until his death in 1963. Someone once said that if you wanted to have a successful tournament, you needed two things—an ABC sanction and a visit from Candy Mac. During 1956 alone he traveled over 80,000 miles, visited 624 bowling establishments, and watched forty-three tournaments in forty-two states, Canada, and Mexico.

His introduction to bowling was one fantastic story. The way he told it, ten-year-old Mac left his native California to go traveling with an uncle in 1895. While they were in New York City, Unk attended an important meeting—the founding of the American Bowling Congress! "They wouldn't let me in because I was too young," Mac later recalled. "But I made up my mind right then to follow bowling."

Back home in San Francisco, Mac started setting pins for a living, and knocking them down for fun. Then he took a job as a brakeman on the Southern Pacific railroad. With free travel on the SP and courtesy passes on other carriers, he began visiting bowling events. In 1902 he attended his first ABC Tournament in Buffalo.

He became known as Candy Mac around this time. Finishing lunch at a diner one day, Mac reached into his pocket and realized he had no money to tip the waitress. All he had was a bag of gumdrops, so gave them to her. The waitress chuckled, and Mac chuckled back.

Soon afterward, he started passing out candy to people he'd meet as his personal calling card. Then Mac found a purse containing $244 in gold coins, quite a fortune in those days. In a strange coincidence his payroll number happened to be 244, and he was working out of caboose #244. For Mac, it was an omen.

"I wanted to share my good fortune with my fellow bowlers," he later said. "So one night, when a woman rolled a 244 game, I bought her a box of chocolates. Then I started giving out packages of cigarettes to men who bowled 244." If the man didn't smoke, he got a pencil flashlight instead. But the score had to be exactly 244. Mac said that he was giving the gifts, so he made the rules.

Now, whenever work and finances permitted, Mac would show up at bowling events, awarding small prizes and other mementos for different accomplishments. In return he collected scoresheets, pictures, newspaper clippings, calendars, matchbooks—and the names and addresses of bowlers. An accident forced him to give up active bowling. That only made him more eager to expand his travels.

Mac kept a record of his hobby. If questioned, he could whip out a notebook and report that he had attended forty-seven of the first fifty ABC Tournaments, or had given away 11,128 cases of Coca-Cola, or had been present at the grand opening of 430 bowling centers. He was especially proud of designing the World's Largest Bowling Birthday Cake, a tasty morsel that measured 30 inches square at the base, stood 39 inches high, and weighed 222 pounds.

There was a price to be paid for his wanderings. Married and widowed twice, by 1960 Mac was living alone in a single room in a scruffy San Francisco hotel. Relations with his nine children were strained.

"They told me I shouldn't go running around the country at my

Frank McKeever, the beloved "Candy Mac," arrives at another tournament.

age," he explained to a writer. "I told them I saw no harm in doing what I wanted, as long as I didn't drink or smoke or swear or get into trouble." Mac rarely saw his kids, and wasn't even sure if they were all alive.

But by then, he already had another family. During his travels, Mac estimated that he had met more than 12 million people. They were his real family. As for the life he had led, he wouldn't have traded it for anything. And who's to say that a life bringing a bit of joy to others was not well spent?

The Baseball-Bowling Connection

(October 2005)
Baseball and bowling, our twin national pastimes, have enjoyed a long and loving relationship. Garry Herrmann, Charles H. Ebbets, Al Spalding, and Charles Comiskey are among the baseball pioneers who also helped shape America's tenpin sport. And there have always been baseball players who enjoyed bowling. Lots of them.

It was natural that ballplayers got involved in bowling. In the days before aerobics and professional training regimens, bowling was a good way to keep in shape during the off-season. Some players took things a step further and opened their own bowling alleys. Major league ball didn't pay very well a century ago, and even the stars needed a second income.

Nobody knows who was the first big-time ballplayer to become a regular bowler. Among the players who became proprietors, the earliest to be widely publicized were John McGraw and Wilbert Robinson of the Baltimore Orioles. In 1897 they launched the Diamond Café in their home city. The two partners eventually went their separate ways, and neither returned to the bowling business.

During this same era, Cap Anson was operating a series of emporiums in Chicago. Anson was a pretty fair bowler, and shared in the 1904 ABC Team title, to make himself the answer to a classic trivia stumper ("Who is the only member of the Baseball Hall of Fame to win a national bowling championship?"). Cy Falkenberg and Kip Selbach were other major leaguers of the day who could hold their own on the lanes. Selbach will never make it to Cooperstown, but he did win two ABC eagles, 1903 Doubles and 1908 Team.

One of the best bowlers among the early ballplayers was Frank Kafora. After two short hitches as a catcher for the Pittsburgh Pirates, Kafora turned his attention to tenpins. In 1915, at the Chicago City Championship, he shook the bowling world by becoming the first person ever to win three events in a single tournament. Seven years later, he was part of the select field of twenty-four invited to compete in the first World Classic. Kafora was only thirty-nine when he died, cutting a distinguished bowling career way too short.

Kafora's contemporary, Everett Scott, was an all-star shortstop with the Boston Red Sox and New York Yankees, setting the consecutive game record that Lou Gehrig and Cal Ripken eventually broke. Scott bought a Fort Wayne bowling alley after hanging up his spikes. In 1940 he became the first major leaguer to roll a sanctioned 300 game. However, his greatest claim to bowling fame came in 1931, when he whipped Hank Marino in a 20-game match.

Perfect games were once very rare. A few years after Scott turned to trick, old-time pitcher Kid Nichols rolled a 299 while bagging the Kansas City Singles championship. He was sixty-four at the time. The first sanctioned 300 by an active major leaguer was posted by A's second baseman Cass Michaels in 1952.

In June 1935 *Bowlers Journal* ran its first cover displaying a ballplayer, White Sox third baseman (and Philadelphia proprietor) Jimmy Dykes. As bowling expanded over the next decades, more and more players went into the business, and every city on the major league circuit seemed to have at least one bowling center with a ballplayer-proprietor. Though it would be impossible to put together a comprehensive list, a few places come readily to mind.

Besides the Dykes establishment, Philadelphia had Del Ennis Lanes. In Boston there was Sammy White's. Metro St. Louis had Stan Musial and Joe Garagiola's Red Bird Lanes, and—across the river in Illinois—the famed Playdium, owned by outfielder Terry Moore. Brooklyn featured Freddie Fitzsimmons Recreation, immortalized in the film *Desperate Characters*. Also in Brooklyn was Gil Hodges Lanes. The beloved Dodger first baseman is long gone, but the bowling center bearing his name lives on.

For some reason, most of the Chicago proprietors were catchers. Kafora, Jimmy Archer, and Bob O'Farrell were the earliest. Later the city had two suburban showplaces, each run by a Hall of Fame backstop, which nicely mirrored the local baseball rivalry. Ex-Cub Gabby Hartnett owned Gabby Hartnett Recreation in Lincolnwood (north), while ex–Sox Ray Schalk operated Evergreen Towers Bowl in Evergreen Park (south). Schalk's center was home to the well-regarded Ray Schalk Holiday Team Classic.

The boom times of the 1950s were the heyday of the ballplayer-proprietor. White Sox teammates Nellie Fox and Sherman Lollar had hometown lanes in Pennsylvania and Missouri, respectively. Yankees Yogi Berra and Phil Rizzuto were partners in a $1.2 million New Jersey showplace. Bobby Shantz and Joe Astroth, the star battery of the Philadelphia A's, operated Pit-Catcher Lanes. Other major leaguers who owned lanes were Nelson Potter, Irv Noren, Hank Sauer, and Ralph Branca.

With the dawning of the 1970s, as free-agency brought megabucks into baseball, the number of players who doubled as bowling proprietors dropped sharply. Other ventures now offered greater cash return with less effort. Mickey Mantle, the biggest star of an earlier era, once owned a piece of a Dallas tenpin palace. Somehow, I don't think that I'll be seeing Barry Bonds or A-Rod at the BPAA Convention any time soon.

Still, ballplayers have always liked to bowl. During the 1930s, *Bowlers Journal* regularly ran articles about how Babe Ruth was taking to the lanes to reduce his "spare tire." White Sox pitcher Billy Pierce saluted the tenpin game in a 1956 *Parade* magazine article titled "I Love Baseball—But Bowling Is More Fun." A few years later, retired star Lou Boudreau became so good with the three-hole ball that he rolled as sixth-man on a team in the Chicago Classic League. When the Baseball Hall of Fame phoned Boudreau to tell him he'd been elected, his wife had to take the call—Lou was out bowling.

In 1962, to determine the top bowler among major leaguers, AMF teamed with *The Sporting News* in staging the BaseBowl Championship. The Tampa tournament was scheduled to coincide with spring training, and drew a large field. Cardinal outfielder Don Landrum won the first trophy with a two-game scratch set of 422. A popular event while it lasted, some of the later editions of the BaseBowl Championship were telecast.

Bill Stafford was a pitcher on the great Yankee teams of the early 1960s. He also carried a 208 league average, a lot of wood in that pre-chemical era. Stafford earned a PBA card when he retired from baseball. However, he never got around to bowling in a Tour event. "Those pins were a lot harder to carry," he said. During the 1987–88 season, a bowling team called the Minnesota Twins earned national publicity for its St. Paul league when two of its bowlers, Kent Hrbek and Tim Laudner, missed two weeks of bowling while helping the baseball Minnesota Twins win the World Series. Business commitment or not, each man was fined $2 for being AWOL.

Mitch "Wild Thing" Williams, a top relief pitcher a few years back, was so serious about the tenpin sport that he carried several bowling balls along for practice when his team was on the road. Like Stafford, Williams talked about joining the Tour, but with no result. Tom Candiotti, another avid pitcher-kegler, did follow through with his post-baseball bowling plans, and has rolled in at least one PBA event. In recent times, the most famous ballplayer-bowler has been John Burkett. Over the years he has competed in a number of PBA events. His most notable foray has been the 2004 Masters, where he finished 185th out of a field of 590.

To conclude, we should note that the baseball-bowling connection goes both ways. Many prominent bowlers spent time in organized baseball. Frank Brill, Joe Wilman, Don Carter, and Earl Anthony are four members of the bowling Hall of Fame who played professional baseball. All were pitchers. Only Brill made it to the major leagues, achieving an unremarkable 2–10 record with Detroit in 1884.

And then there is Ed Lubanski. Hall of Famer, Bowler of the Year, and four-time All American, he was also a minor league pitcher. In 1947 he posted a 22–8 record in the Class D Wisconsin State League. He moved up to Class C the following year, and already had sixteen wins by July. When the front office refused to promote him, Lubanski walked out.

Ed Lubanski was only eighteen years old when he quit baseball. Would he have become the greatest combination of "basebowler?" There's no way of knowing. But if I had to choose the one man who achieved the highest level of performance across both sports, I'd pick Everett Scott.

The Buzzer

May 2006)
My father was not a bowler. Still, he would sometimes sit with me and watch *Championship Bowling* or one of the other television tenpin shows. And every time, he'd ask the same question, "Who's that little Italian guy who jumps around all the time?"

The answer is easy, Dad. It's Buzz Fazio.

During the 1950s, everybody knew The Buzzer, and loved to watch him. He'd trot to the line, push the ball toward the pins, then go into his gyrations—running around the approach, punching the air, dropping to his knees in prayer. When a strike resulted, his grin lit up the room. And afterward, there was always a ready quip for the announcers, Freddy Wolf or Whispering Joe Wilson.

But the jokes and the clowning were only part of Buzz Fazio. He seethed with competitive fire. One magazine called him "The Ty Cobb of Bowling."

Like Joe Norris, Fazio was born in 1908. Unlike Norris, Fazio was no boy wonder; he slowly developed his game while working in the rubber plants of Akron. In 1945 Norris crossed paths with Fazio at the

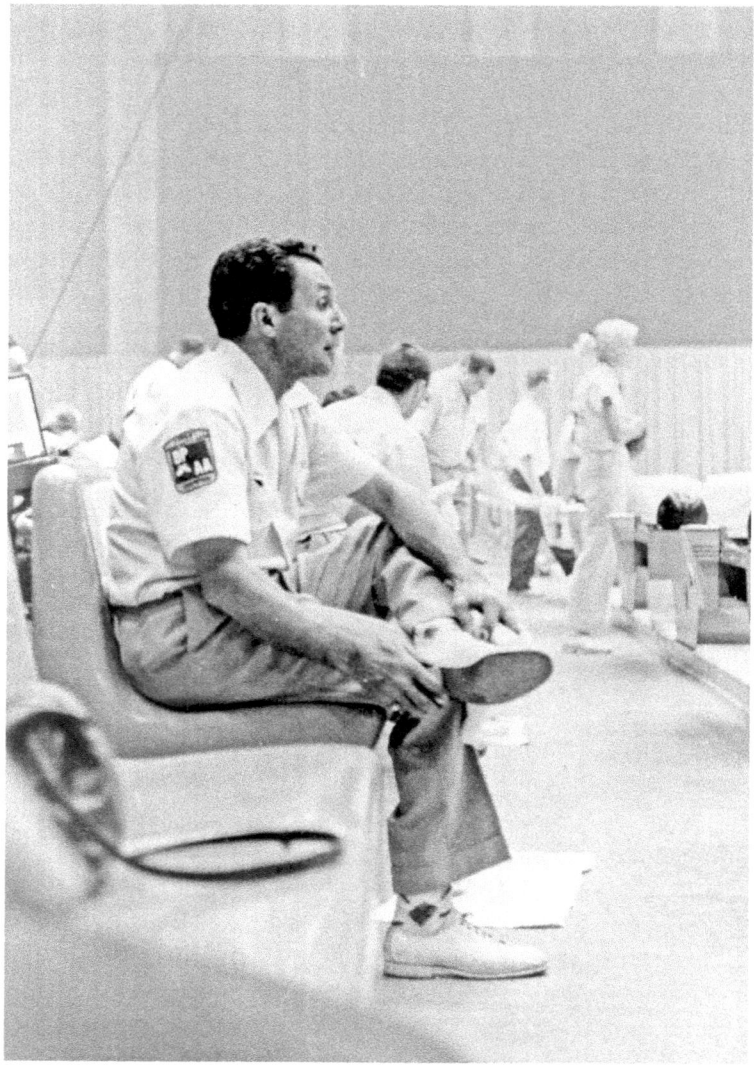

Buzz Fazio, argyle socks and all, getting ready to move into action at the World's Invitational Tournament.

All-Star Tournament, was impressed, and brought him to Detroit to bowl with the Stroh's Beer team. Two years later, when Norris left, Fazio became captain of the team.

During his nine seasons at the Stroh's helm, Fazio became a national star. He won the Match Game Doubles with Tony Lindemann twice, and was in the thick of the battle at the All-Star every year. In 1950 he became the first man to roll a 300 in the finals. Fazio's crowning achievement was the 1955 Masters. He was named an All American five times.

His television charisma has already been mentioned. For objectivity, we will mention two statistics. In 1955 Fazio won seven straight television matches in Chicago. That same year, in Detroit, he became the first bowler to roll an 800 series on a live broadcast.

With Fazio as captain, the Stroh's continued their winning tradition. But again unlike Norris, Fazio was not very popular with his peers. His aggressiveness and sarcasm stung his opponents—Ty Cobb of Bowling, remember? "You can bowl against someone and still like him," Joe Kristof said. "Nobody liked Buzz."

While acknowledging his toughness, Fazio's teammates recognized that it brought results. "Buzz was a good guy," Tony Lindemann said. "But he was a taskmaster. He always wanted you to do your best."

Ed Lubanski echoed the sentiment. "Buzz was tough, no question about it," Lubanski said. "If you didn't want to bowl, you didn't stay with him. I liked him because he was a competitor. He never gave up. He was putting out 100 percent all the time."

Harry Smith summed up his captain's fierce spirit memorably: "I think he'd swim across Lake Erie for a quarter."

In the summer of 1957 Fazio surprised the bowling world by resigning as Stroh's captain. He moved to St. Louis, taking over the reorganized Falstaff team. The Falstaffs won the ABC team title the next spring. But after two seasons, Fazio quit and returned to Detroit.

He spent the next several years touring for Brunswick, with a season out to captain the Omaha team in the National Bowling League experiment. Elected to the Bowling Hall of Fame in 1963, he had the pleasure of being inducted with his longtime friend and sometimes doubles partner, Steve Nagy. Fazio also bowled a full schedule on the PBA Tour and won two titles. In 1968 he nearly grabbed a second Masters championship. He was sixty years old at the time.

He lived another quarter-century, and some of it was rough. A serious auto accident put him in the hospital for two months. Later there were a couple of brain tumors. He kept bowling, now with a 12-pound ball. "What's the use of stopping?" he told *Bowlers Journal.* "You do that when they bury you."

Buzz Fazio died in 1993. But if they have bowling in heaven, I know The Buzzer is still at it. And my dad will be watching him.

Unusual Injuries

(August 2006)
Kingpin, the movie, drew mixed reviews from the bowling world. Still, most everyone got a chuckle out of the scene where Woody Harrelson's kegling career is abruptly terminated. Woody has just beaten some guys out of some pot money, so the sore losers decide to get even—by shoving his bowling hand into the ball return.

This was obviously a takeoff on *The Hustler*, in which Paul Newman has his thumbs broken by a group of hustlees. Then again, maybe the writers of *Kingpin* knew something about bowling history. Many famous stars have endured bizarre injuries.

One of the oldest tales dates from the 1920s, and may be mere legend. The bowler in question is a big fellow—it could have been Nick Bruck, or Frank Kafora, but the usual suspect is Otto Stein. Anyway, Stein gets tapped. He happens to be bowling on the end lane, so to vent his frustration, he kicks backward at the adjoining plywood wall. With that the wall collapses, and knocks our hero cold.

The story of Billy Knox is better-documented. In 1929 the future Hall of Famer was using a knife to sharpen a pencil. He cut his bowling thumb and it became infected. The result was six surgeries and the loss of a half-inch of that thumb. Knox was out of action for three years. The good news is that he did come back, as fine as ever.

If you noted that Knox was using a knife instead of a pencil sharpener, remember we are talking about a low-tech era. Hank Marino, for one, often employed a razor blade to trim the callus on his bowling thumb. One day Marino cut too deeply. Teammate Billy Sixty found him soaking his hand in hot water, gritting his teeth while blood spurted over the sink. Marino wound up in the emergency room.

It's worth mentioning that Marino was a onetime barber and presumably knew how to handle sharp implements. But as Buzz Fazio found out, even barbers make mistakes. Fazio had entered a barbershop for a quick shave-and-a-haircut. He was sitting with his hands folded under the sheet. The barber took a swipe at the sheet to knock some lather off the razor, and sliced the Buzzer's thumb open to the bone.

Then there was the case of Carmen Salvino and the Invisible Door. Salvino was in a Michigan bowling center for a PBA event. He was ambling along, minding his own business, when a friend called to him. Carmen turned, saw his friend, and walked over to greet him ... through a plate glass door. His face, hand, and arm were badly cut, and the squad was delayed while he was patched up. Oh, by the way, Salvino won the tournament.

Trips to the ABC could be dangerous, particularly at hotels. In 1970 Jim Spalding fell in the shower and tore up his hand. Some years later, at Niagara Falls, a bowling ball rolled off a bed and broke Ed Lubanski's toe.

Weird wounds are not limited to male stars. In 1992 Donna Adamek caught her hair in a drill press while working on a ball. She lost a three-inch section of scalp and had severe whiplash. It took Adamek a long time to come back from that one.

Perhaps the most famous injury to a celebrated bowler was suffered by Joe Falcaro in 1933. On the day before he was to defend his match game title, Falcaro was hit in the groin by a flying metal projectile, which had been propelled by high speed from a device known as a gun. Falcaro had become involved with a gangster's lady, and the gangster didn't like it.

My own story of mishap took place about twenty years ago. I had stopped at my mother's house on the way to bowling to look at whatever was making strange noises under the hood of her car, and proceeded to stick the middle finger of my bowling hand into the whirling blade of the engine fan. Fortunately, all I lost was a chunk of callus, and I did roll 670 that night, a lot of wood in those days. But I don't recommend the method. Better you should stick to razor blades.

The Quiet Man

(November 2006)
At eighty-seven, Tony Lindemann has seen a lot of bowling history. He has made a lot, too. Born in 1919 as Roland Marvin Lindemann, he grew

up in Beaver Dam, Wisconsin, adopting the named Tony "because it sounded more macho." He started bowling in the local four-lane house as a teen.

Then World War II came. Lindemann was rejected from military service on medical grounds, but late in 1941 he moved to Detroit to do war work as a draftsman. He had no friends or relatives in the big city. With nothing much to do in his free time, he bowled.

He'd arrived in Detroit sporting a 175 average. That gradually rose to 200 and beyond. After the war ended, Lindemann moved up to the better leagues. In 1949 he was offered a spot on the nationally famous Stroh's Beer team—and turned it down. "I didn't think I was good enough," he says. "I wanted to make sure I wasn't just a flash in the pan." So Lindemann bowled another year, and had another good season. This time, when Stroh's renewed its offer, Lindemann accepted.

The new Stroh was a quiet, affable man of medium build. He had a simple style, and liked to roll a small hook from the outside. He was the first to admit he lacked the color of some of his flamboyant teammates. Tony sort of snuck up on you.

Take the 1951 ABC Tournament. As the Stroh's time on the lanes wound down, everyone was watching to see whether anchorman Lee Jouglard would set a new record in Singles. Jouglard closed with 278, and beat the old record by a single pin. Only when the shouting was over did anyone—even Tony—notice that Lindemann had rolled to the top of the All Events. His three series were 656, 663, and 686. None of the scores were spectacular, even by 1951 standards. But the 2005 total was good enough for the eagle.

The 1950s was a good time to be a Stroh. Along with Lindemann and Jouglard, the lineup included Ed Lubanski, Pete Carter, and Captain Buzz Fazio. The Stroh's set a Team All Events record at the ABC, and were the BPAA Match Game champs for four years. They rolled exhibitions and appeared on television. In 1955 they were the stars of a widely circulated, profusely illustrated instruction book, *Bowl to Win*.

Lindemann did his part. He led all Detroit bowlers in composite average during the 1950–51 season. He earned a first-team spot as an All American. He joined with Fazio to capture the BPAA Doubles. With one interruption, they held that title a total of three years.

During the summer there were barnstorming trips to the West Coast. "Lee would put together a team and we'd drive out west for a couple of months," Lindemann recalls. "We'd give exhibitions and bowl all the tournaments, like the Fourth of July Singles in San Francisco.

Tony Lindemann takes over as captain of the Stroh's Beer team in 1957— and yes, they did misspell his name.

We met a lot of interesting people and really got to see the country. It was great."

In 1957 Fazio resigned as Stroh's captain. Lindemann succeeded him. He held the post four years, until he was recruited as captain of the San Antonio entry in the National Bowling League. But the financing fell through, the team folded, and Lindemann wound up in Dallas. After a few years, he returned to Detroit.

When he was elected to the Hall of Fame in 1979, Lindemann had just about given up bowling. But the old fire remained, and he started to come back. And at the 1994 ABC, he was again in the headlines. After some low scores in the Team event and the first two games of the Doubles, Lindemann suddenly began to strike ... and strike ... and strike ... and ... twelve-in-a-row! Two months shy of his seventy-fifth birthday, he became the oldest man to roll a perfect game in the ABC Tournament. "And then, in the Singles, it was back to the 160s," he laughs.

Tony Lindemann still bowls twice a week in suburban Detroit. And he still carries a 200 average.

Pioneer Don Scott

(February 2007)
February is Black History Month. That makes it an appropriate time to remember one of bowling's pioneer African American pros, Don Scott.

A native of Cleveland, Scott learned his bowling as a teenage pin-boy in Akron. He began making a name for himself in local leagues and money matches during the 1950s. He also won a number of events sponsored by The National Bowling Association, the black-oriented group created during ABC's segregated days.

When the PBA was launched, Scott was one of the first blacks to join. His proudest moment on Tour came in 1961. The premier PBA event was the National Championship, and that year it was being held in Cleveland. Charging out of the box in front of a hometown crowd, Scott topped the qualifying field of 192 entries. He finished ninth in the tournament.

The 1960s was a time of transition for America. Many large businesses which had ignored African Americans suddenly awoke to the fact that there was huge untapped market out there. With his tournament success and outgoing personality, Scott was a natural to spread the gospel of bowling. AMF signed him to its advisory staff to roll exhibitions and stage clinics, and the Cleveland-based Carling Brewery hired him for similar work.

In 1964 Scott became the first African American to appear on the *Championship Bowling* television show. The series was at the peak of its popularity, and carried at least as much prestige as the still-new PBA Tour. "We bowled in Akron, and Harvey Firestone from the tire company was one of the sponsors," Scott remembered. "He told [the producers] that he had a lot of black customers who were buying his tires, and they got the message. It came down to J. Wilbert Sims and me. I had been competing around Ohio, and most of the white bowlers knew me. AMF was sponsoring the show, I was with AMF, so I got the nod."

Admittedly nervous, Scott still did respectably. He bowled against two future Hall of Famers, George Howard and Carmen Salvino, beating Howard and losing to Salvino. His 1216 six-game total put him in the middle of the show's 24-man standings.

Though he belonged to the PBA for nearly twenty years, Scott never bowled a full Tour schedule. He had a bowling center and other businesses to run in Cleveland, and didn't have much free time. So he stuck to those events "a tankful of gas away" in places like Detroit, Buffalo, and Waukegan.

Besides, the competition was getting tougher. "When I first went out there, if you carried a 203 or 204 average like I did, you cashed," Scott said. "Then it started to go up to 205, 206, 211, 212, just to cash. I was still the same, but instead of cashing, now I was on page eight of the standings."

Scott encountered very little racism in his PBA days. The other bowlers were generally welcoming and supportive. Scott remembers one episode with a chuckle. He was sitting at the lunch counter at a tournament venue in Miami, and the waitress repeatedly ignored him. Scott happened to mention it to Bill Allen, one of the Tour's leading stars and a native Southerner.

"Allen got really excited," Scott says. "He told me, 'You don't have to put up with this! We're going to tell Eddie [Elias]! We don't have to stay here!' I finally had to tell him, 'But Bill, it was a black waitress.'"

Scott eventually moved on from bowling into other ventures. For more than thirty years he operated the country's largest black-owned nightclub. He and his wife, Val, raised three children "who never caused me the grief I caused my parents," and who carved out successful professional careers of their own.

In 2000 Don Scott received the Congressional Black Caucus's Unsung Hero Award to honor his bowling achievements. He still lives in Cleveland, and plans to get copies of his old television matches, "so my grandkids can show off to their friends."

The Hitchhikers

(June 2007)
The year was 1954. It was spring, and as the poet might have said, it was the time when a young man's fancy turned toward ... the American Bowling Congress Tournament.

The young men we're concerned with were eighteen-year-old Dick Lutz and nineteen-year-old Dave Junker, both from Stillwater, Minnesota. The ABC was in Seattle that year, with their Bill's Junior All-Stars team scheduled to bowl on May 1. But complications developed, and the team suddenly found itself without transportation. Three of the bowlers managed to arrange a ride with a man who was driving friends to the West Coast. That left Dick and Dave. With $17 between them, they couldn't afford a plane, train, or bus. So they decided to hitchhike.

Ahead of them were 1,800 miles of sparsely settled, pre-interstate America. Entrusting their bowling equipment to their teammates, on April 24 Dick and Dave set out with their suitcases and their thumbs. It was Saturday morning.

They started out fine, covering the 200 miles to Fargo, North Dakota, in a single jump. After a nice meal, Dave phoned home to report their progress, and to tell their buddies to bring the entry form he'd forgotten. Then things began to go wrong.

In Fargo they caught a ride with a man who turned out to be drunk. More than once, the driver nearly ran the car into a ditch, then overcorrected by swerving across the two-lane highway into oncoming traffic. When he finally stopped to take a nap, the boys quickly left.

They spent the next two days making slow progress across North Dakota. Valley City ... Jamestown ... Crystal Springs ... Menoken ... Mandan. On they went, following the sun, a few miles at a time. At Richarton they were stranded outdoors through a cold, windy night. They eventually wound up in Dickinson after forty-eight sleepless hours, still 1,200 miles short of their goal.

And now their luck turned. They met two truckers who were hauling a load to Vancouver, and who were happy to take them to Everett,

Washington. Dick and Dave found it hard to sleep while bumping along in the rig, but now figured they'd make Seattle on time. As a thank you, they treated the truckers to lunch before they were dropped off.

The boys found shelter in the Everett YMCA and promptly collapsed on a couple of benches in the lobby. Dave was just drifting off to blessed sleep when he was awakened by a rough hand on his shoulder. Now what?

But it was only one of the truckers. The man had earlier borrowed two quarters in change from Dave, and forgotten to repay him. He'd backtracked ten miles just to return the fifty cents.

On Wednesday evening, the travelers finally rolled into Seattle. Dick had a friend in town and they crashed at his house, sleeping for twelve straight hours. The rest of the team arrived on Friday. By that time, Dick and Dave's bankroll was down to twenty-three cents.

The next part of the story should say that Bill's Junior All-Stars posted a high total in the tournament and earned a large prize check. Actually they rolled a 2383, which was pretty weak, even by 1954 standards. The minor events weren't much better.

There was room in the car going back to Minnesota, so our two intrepid hitchhikers were able to return home in comfort. There's no record that either of them made an impact in later ABC Tournaments.

But for over a half-century, the saga of the two teenagers from Stillwater and their odyssey across the top of America has endured. It reverberates with all true bowlers, who each year answer that gentle obsession to compete in our great national tournament, come hell, high water, or hitting the highway. Dick Lutz and Dave Junker, we salute you—wherever you are.

The Greatest Action Match

(August 2007)
"I liked your issue on action bowling," the Oldest Bowler said. "It reminded me of a match in Peoria, Illinois. It might have been the greatest action match of all. It sure was the strangest."

I hugged my wallet closer to me, sat back, and listened.

"It was 1934, and the ABC Tournament was in Peoria," the Oldest Bowler began. "In those days, the tournament ran only about a month.

It was the middle of the Depression, and nobody had anything better to do. So the bowlers would hang around town and bowl pot games. They'd find a local house and gather every night. It was like a hustlers' convention. In Peoria, the place for action was Peoria Auto Parts."

They bowled in an auto parts store?

"You've been living in the suburbs too long," the Oldest Bowler said. "They had the auto parts store on the ground floor, and put the thirty bowling lanes on the second floor. Anyway, every night, after the last ABC squad, there'd be pot games all over the place. And maybe a hundred guys would wander in to watch and bet on the bowlers.

"This particular night, Andy Varipapa, Joe Falcaro, Jimmy Smith, and Joe Bodis were shooting. But the real action came down to two guys. There was Mort Lindsey, the old moose from Connecticut, and a young guy from Texas, Nelson Burton."

Funny, I didn't think Bo looked that old.

"Nelson Burton *Senior!*" the Oldest Bowler snapped. "Bo's father! Now, this was a great match-up because both these guys bet their own money—they didn't depend on backers. Lindsey was a millionaire, Burton, well, he just had guts. It was like that poker movie, *The Cincinnati Kid,* where the kid Steve McQueen goes up against the old master, Edward G. Robinson.

"They get started. Three games for $300—a lot of cash during the Depression. Most of the smart money was on Lindsey, who already had three ABC titles. And he could still bowl— later that year, he won the richest prize in bowling, the Petersen Classic. But Burton could bowl, too, and he stomped Lindsey."

Wait a minute. In the movie, Edward G. beat McQueen ...

Nelson Burton, Sr., around the time he faced off against Mort Lindsey in Peoria.

"So now, they decide to bowl duckpins," the Oldest Bowler went on. "They had a Brunswick office in the building, so they get out some duckpins. Well, Burton wanted to bowl against the rubber band duckpins, with that rubber bumper around the middle of the pin. Lindsey wanted to bowl regular duckpins. Anyway, they finally work it out. Three games for $300 against the rubber bands, then three for $300 against the regular ducks. And Burton wins both of those matches!"

I said that it was a great story. But the Oldest Bowler wasn't finished.

"By now, it's 4 a.m. Lindsey's getting dressed to leave, and he happens to say, 'Too bad we didn't play candlepins. That's my real game.'

"Well, Burton had never bowled candlepins, and Lindsey knew it. But Burton figured he was already up $900, so he says okay. Back to Brunswick, and they get a couple sets of candlepins. So they bowl again. And Burton wins *again.* After that, Lindsey says he's had enough. From that time on, he'd tell anybody who'd listen that Nelson Burton was one of the country's finest bowlers."

I had to agree. But the Oldest Bowler had one final thought on action bowling.

"Jimmy Blouin was the greatest money bowler of his day. He'd bowl a three-game set for $10,000 back when you could get a nice bungalow for half that price. Blouin said bowling for $10,000 wasn't the greatest pressure he felt. The greatest pressure was bowling for ten dollars, when he only had *one* dollar."

It's an old maxim. But worth thinking about.

The Fred Wolf Story

(November 2007)

A century ago, the most popular American author was Horatio Alger. His novels generally told of a poor young man who—through talent, hard work, and a little bit of luck—became rich and famous.

It's not known whether Fred Wolf ever read a Horatio Alger story. If he did, he would have recognized his own life.

Born in 1910, Wolf grew up in modest circumstances in Detroit. As an honors graduate of the city's top high school, he might have gone to college. As a sandlot baseball star, he might have accepted a minor league contract. But times were tough. He needed a job, so he apprenticed as a toolmaker.

In the evening, he earned extra cash by setting pins. And he started to bowl. Wolf's style wasn't pretty—a mad rush to the line, a screeching stop, and a little hop as he delivered the ball. But within two years he had rolled a 300 game. In 1938 he signed with the Stroh's Beer team.

Stroh's was bowling's glamour team. Wolf did his part, and more. He helped the team recapture the match game title, led the Times Classic League in average, and won a collection of sweepers. In 1943 *Bowlers Journal* named him an All American. "A lot of people have forgotten just how good a bowler Freddy was," his captain, Joe Norris, said years later. "If he hadn't gotten hurt, he probably would have won the All-Star."

During a match in 1944, Wolf stuck on the approach and wrenched his back. He wound up in bed for four months with a ruptured disk. Although he eventually returned to the lanes with a gentler style, his competitive days were over.

But then another door opened. A few months after his injury, Stroh's defended its title, and a local radio station aired the match. Ex-Stroh Wolf did the broadcast commentary. Audience reaction was enthusiastic. Who'd imagine someone could make a bowling match exciting? Wolf soon had his own weekly program.

Detroit's favorite radio deejay of the 1950s, and the man behind the mike on the *Championship Bowling* television series, Fred Wolf.

Radio station WXYZ hired him for its morning drive-time slot in 1950. Wolf conceived the stunt of doing the show from a glass-fronted hut on Detroit's busy Jefferson Avenue. Later he moved "Wolf's Wacky Wigloo" around town on a trailer. By the mid–1950s he was the city's favorite deejay. Meanwhile, he broadcast a variety of sports on both radio and television. Any history of Motor City media contains his name, writ large and often.

In 1956 he became host of the nationally syndicated *Championship Bowling* television show, the program for which he is best remembered. There he set a standard that has seldom been equaled, and never surpassed. Off the air, Wolf was not exactly the humble sort—he was good, and he knew it. But his broadcasts were knowledgeable, witty, and relaxed, with none of the self-importance often associated with an ex-jock. Most viewers probably never realized that Wolf himself had once been a champion bowler.

Wolf's WXYZ radio career ended in 1965. The usual reason cited is that he didn't like to play Beatles music. The *Championship Bowling* run ended about the same time. By then he was well-fixed, with partnership in a large suburban bowling center. In 1975 Wolf surprised himself and the bowling world by rolling another 300 game. His first had come in 1931, and the 44-year gap was an ABC record.

Then a stroke felled him. Restless, dynamic Fred Wolf spent his last years a shell of his former self. "He couldn't speak, he was paralyzed on one side," Anita Cantaline recalled. "He'd come into the bowling alley with a cane. You'd have to do the talking for him. It was so sad, you'd want to cry."

Fred Wolf died in 2000. He often signed off his bowling broadcasts with the words, "You don't have to play a sport good to be a good sport." Perhaps that quotation was not original to him, but it's a nice thought to remember him by.

Big Steve

(January 2008)

Steve Nagy loved to tell people about his first bowling ball. The year was 1939, and he had just plunked down five hard-earned dollars to buy a beautiful, red plastic ball. One cold night he arrived at the lanes with only a few minutes to go before league time, so he set the ball down on a radiator to warm up. Came the first frame, Steve grabbed the ball, sprinted to the line, and rolled a strike.

"Of course it was a strike!" he'd laugh. "As soon as it hit the headpin, the ball split in two, and took out the pins on either side!"

That tale pretty much sums up the image of Steve Nagy we have today—down-to-earth, a bit disorganized, funny, yet effective. "Nagy didn't look like much, he had a sloppy style," Buddy Bomar once observed. "But he had great instinct, and was one of the best."

Nagy was a broad-shouldered, black-mustached, fun-loving Hungarian who looked a lot like television's broad-shouldered, black-mustached, fun-loving Hungarian, Ernie Kovacs. He came from Cleveland, and was a cabinet-maker by trade. Again like Kovacs, he always put on a good show. Nagy ran out strikes, jumped ball returns, yelled at the pins. More than once, he pulled off his belt and whipped his ball if it was performing badly. Off the lanes, he was never too tired or too busy to sign an autograph or chat with a fan. The public loved him. So did the other bowlers. And as Bomar said, Nagy could knock down some pins, too.

He had rolled a few games as a kid, but Nagy didn't take bowling seriously until he went to the ABC Tournament with a Booster team. That was in 1939, the year of the split ball. During the next decade, he gradually built himself into a national star. In 1952 he was named Bowler of the Year. That honor was based mostly on his performance at the ABC. He teamed with Johnny Klares to win the Doubles with a record score that would stand for forty years. Along the way Nagy also picked up the All Events eagle, nearly setting another record.

His 1954–55 season made Nagy a household name in the greater sports world. In October he traveled to Chicago for the *Championship Bowling* television show and proceeded to roll a 300 game. It was the first perfect game captured on film. Half-a-century and half-a-million 300s later, it's still exciting to watch.

A few months later, he was back in Chicago for the All-Star Tournament. Starting slowly, Nagy managed to tie Graz Castellano for the last spot in the finals, won a 2 a.m. roll-off, then got his game together. Over the next few days, he moved up steadily in the standings until he met Ed Lubanski in the ultimate showdown. Lubanski caught a split at a crucial juncture, and Nagy swept the match to be crowned All-Star champion.

Once more, Nagy was elected Bowler of the Year. He also became the first bowler featured on the cover of *Sports Illustrated*. He's still the only bowler with that distinction.

Nagy bowled an occasional season with some great teams—Stroh's and Pfeiffer in Detroit, Falstaff in St. Louis, the Toros of the National Bowling League in Los Angeles. But always he came back to Cleveland. Not that it mattered much. His tournament, exhibition, and television work kept Nagy on the road. One year he slept in his own bed all of thirty nights. He was one of the organizers of the PBA and served a term as president.

During a 1965 Tour event in Boston Nagy suffered a stroke. A year later he was dead at fifty-three. In his memory the PBA instituted a Steve Nagy Award to recognize the "good guys" of pro bowling. It might be considered the Durocher Rebuttal Award. As much as anyone, Steve Nagy showed that nice guys could finish first.

Johnny Small's Magic Ball

(February 2008)
Most knowledgeable bowlers know the origin of the high-tech bowling ball. In 1973 PBA pro Don McCune discovered that soaking a plastic ball in the chemical solution MEK improved the lane-gripping qualities of the ball's surface. Thus began the era of Chemical Bowling.

Yet McCune was not the first person to demonstrate the scoring potential locked in the shell of a bowling ball. For that part of the story, we have to go back further in time.

In 1939 the Raybestos-Manhattan Company began making bowling balls. The firm was an old, established manufacturer of rubber products, and the booming bowling market provided a logical opportunity for expansion. As one bit of advertising copy promised, the new Manhattan ball would be the finest ever made. It would "offer greater resistance to wear, and maintain its original spherical shape longer than any pellet ever offered to the tenpin world."

In Chicago, radio broadcaster Sam Weinstein had just gone into the bowling supply business. He became the first distributor of the Manhattan ball. The factory sent Weinstein a batch of 100, and he sold most of them. Then problems started to develop.

The new balls had an excess of static electricity. And as we learned in junior high science class, rubber that has an excess of static electricity gets sticky. "Those balls gripped the lanes like no other ball ever did," Weinstein remembered years later. "But they really got dirty and the bowlers couldn't keep their hands clean."

That didn't bother Johnny Small. A member of Joe Wilman's Budweiser team, Small was one of that large group of bowlers who ranked just below the elite—"a good team bowler," the expression went. He was a rugged competitor who rolled so many pot games that friends called him The Marathon Man. Two things about Small stood out. His backswing was ridiculously short. And though just in his early thirties, he was almost completely bald.

Small had purchased one of the new balls from Weinstein. He was in the electrical business himself, so presumably he understood why his Manhattan got so greasy so quickly. What mattered to Small was that he was suddenly cleaning up in all his money matches. At a time when the best bowlers averaged a shade over 200, he was regularly rolling 240s and 250s.

Meanwhile, Manhattan had been working to correct the rubber problem. The company issued a recall of its "electric" balls, replacing each one with a new model. At first, Small didn't want to turn his in. Weinstein finally convinced him, and Small got a different ball. Just as he'd feared, his game reverted to its previous level.

Now Small went back to Weinstein to retrieve the original ball. A search of the shop revealed that it had been shipped back to Manhattan. The factory was contacted, and an exhaustive search of those premises was undertaken. After weeks of uncertainty, the news finally came back—the magic ball had already been melted down.

The next part of the tale should say that Small spent the next thirty years, and thousands of dollars, trying to replicate that lost ball. Maybe he did. But if he did, he never admitted it.

Manhattan continued to manufacture bowling balls for decades. Sam Weinstein's supply business became a success. Johnny Small's bowling resume eventually included three ABC eagles, a share of the BPAA Doubles title, and an eighth-place finish in the All-Star Tournament.

Of course, we may presume that Small would have done even better if he had managed to keep that special ball. Had that been the case, today we might all be using rubber bowling balls ... and washing our hands between frames.

Two Secure Records

(August 2008)
During the 1930s and '40s, William "Jake" Lenzen was one of the better bowlers around Chicago. Yet today, we remember him for two unusual incidents, which produced two records that may never be broken.

Lenzen was born in 1893 and started making a name for himself in Chicago leagues around 1925. His breakthrough came in 1930, when he won both the Peterson Classic and the Chicago Singles championship. *Bowlers Journal* put him on its cover twice that year.

His hot streak continued into 1931 as he captured the International Bowling Association All Events championship. Then, in 1932, Lenzen became a charter member of the Chicago Classic League. He led the league in average that first season with a mark of 222, a figure that would remain a Classic record for thirty years. He eventually paced the league in average three times, and won numerous city and state titles, before retiring to rural Wisconsin. He died in 1960.

Quite a resume. Now, let's get to those unusual incidents.

In 1940 Lenzen was anchorman for the Monarch Beer team. Besides Lenzen, the Monarch lineup included such talent as Bill Flesch, Dick Winsberg, and the Faetz brothers, Leo and Matt Jr. The team had won the Classic League championship the previous season. When the Monarchs stepped on the lanes at the ABC Tournament in Detroit, they were considered one of the favorites.

Then—disaster! Two frames into the first game, Lenzen sprained his middle finger and wrist. He tried to keep going. At the end of the fourth frame, his score read "41." Obviously, he couldn't continue.

The Monarchs now put Harry Angel, a bowler of only moderate ability, into Lenzen's spot. Angel managed to come through with a double and finished the game Lenzen had begun for a score of 170. The team counted 996. Rolling for himself in the second game, Angel had 187. Meanwhile, the four regular Monarchs caught fire and combined for a gaudy 902. With Angel's score that gave them 1089, the best single game of the tournament. Though the team cooled off to 962 the third game, Angel did his part with 192.

The 3047 series moved the Monarchs into the Team event lead. The score was still on top when the tournament ended a few weeks later. In accordance with the rules then in place, Jake Lenzen had won an ABC eagle—by bowling four frames.

By 1945 Lenzen had become anchorman of the Thompson Restaurant team. On October 30 that year, the Classic League rolled at Pla-Mor Lanes. Lenzen opened his session with games of 222 and 194. In the third game he found the range. He strung twelve perfect strikes for 300.

Pla-Mor Lanes erupted. Perfect games were rare in 1945—there would be only 111 of them posted in the entire country for the entire year. It was also Lenzen's fifth sanctioned 300, more than any other bowler in Chicago history up to that time. After the excitement concluded, Lenzen picked up his ball and started for the locker room.

Except that wasn't the end of it. In all the commotion about the perfect game, the team match had been temporarily forgotten. The scoresheet showed a tie game, and in those days ties were settled by a one-frame roll-off.

Lenzen was summoned back to the lanes. When his turn came, he naturally got a strike. And though those rules said that roll-off scores should not be added to the original totals, Lenzen's friends always claimed that he had rolled the world's only sanctioned "310" game.

So there you have it. Will anyone ever win an ABC championship with a score lower than 41? Will anyone ever roll thirteen legal and legitimate strikes in a single game? In the record book of bowling trivia, Jake Lenzen's place is secure.

Movie Star Bowler

(November 2008)
During the 1920s, Harold Lloyd was one of Hollywood's biggest stars. As a comic actor, he was spoken of in the same breath as Charlie Chaplin or Buster Keaton. Today, many film historians consider him the funniest man on the silent screen. But more to our point, Harold Lloyd was also a serious bowler.

Born in Nebraska in 1893, Lloyd moved to California as a teen and got started in the movies in 1918. After a few false starts, he settled on the screen persona of a fresh-faced young man in glasses who always seemed to get himself into some outrageously dangerous situations. Ever see the picture of the guy in a straw hat dangling from the hands of a clock a hundred feet above a city street? That's Harold Lloyd.

How he got started bowling is unknown. By 1924, when he was at the height of his fame, Lloyd was regularly on the lanes three nights a week. He said that bowling gave him "the health, strength, and agility which comes in handy in the strenuous motion picture business." If he hired a chauffeur, the man had to be a bowler, so Harold would have a companion for open play.

He served as a league president and sponsored his own team. The Harold Lloyds won the Southern California Team Tournament two years running. Harold himself contributed more than celebrity value or a sponsor's check, averaging in the 190s when the best players were barely over 200. In 1940 he rolled a perfect game in a Los Angeles tournament.

And all the time he was dealing with a major physical handicap. Early in his film career, an accident with a prop bomb blew off the thumb and index finger of Lloyd's right hand. From that point on he wore a prosthetic glove on screen. So when he bowled he was using—literally—a three-finger grip.

By 1940 Lloyd had stopped making movies. He had met Ned Day several years earlier, when Day first came to Hollywood. Day introduced Lloyd to his teammate, Hank Marino, who was a successful proprietor in Milwaukee. The three men soon decided to build their own bowling center.

They called it Llo-Da-Mar Bowl, taking the first letters from each of their surnames. Located only a few miles from Hollywood in Santa Monica, the Streamline Moderne showplace attracted many of the glamorous people of the film industry. Harold Lloyd competed in a few of the leagues, and chuckled when he told friends he couldn't bowl well in his own house. But in 1946, one of the Llo-Da-Mar teams went to the ABC Tournament and came back with the Team championship.

Lloyd rolled in the ABC four times, with little success. Still, he did earn a footnote in the history of the event. Until 1942 the big tournament had never been held west of Kansas City. At the ABC Convention that year, Harold's speech helped convince the delegates to award the 1944 show to Los Angeles. World War II delayed things a bit, but in 1947, the first West Coast ABC was held. And Harold Lloyd was featured on the cover of *Bowlers Journal* to promote it.

He couldn't get enough of the game. Whenever the top bowlers gathered for an important match or tournament, chances were good that Lloyd would be in the audience. The All-Star Tournament was his favorite. "We'd look around first thing in the morning and there would be Harold Lloyd," recalled Buddy Bomar. "Then we'd look around at night, and there would be Harold Lloyd, still there, and just as keenly observant as though he'd just come in the place."

As the years passed, Lloyd gradually withdrew from the public eye. In 1961 the Bowling Writers Association of America gave him its

Hollywood comic legend (and serious bowler) Harold Lloyd promotes the 1947 ABC Tournament at Los Angeles, the first to be held on the West Coast.

Rip Van Winkle Award. Because of a sanction technicality, his 300 game had not been recognized by ABC.

Harold Lloyd died in 1971. Some years later, Llo-Da-Mar closed its doors. But the building still stands, now housing a number of small businesses and designated an architectural landmark.

A Christmas Story

(December 2008)

To many people this time of year brings back cherished memories of the magic Christmases of childhood. But I always remember the Chicago Classic League, and its annual visit to Habetler Bowl.

The time was the early 1960s. The PBA Tour was on the rise, and the Classic League had passed its peak. Yet the league still loomed large on Chicago's bowling scene. It had a history. Twice a week, our four daily newspapers carried the scores of the Classic's two divisions.

And there were the bowlers! The league boasted many of the legends we had grown up watching on TV—Joe Norris, Paul Krumske, Harry Lippe, Eddie Kawolics, and more. Those demigods would be performing on the same lanes as our Saturday morning junior league.

The Classic came to our house the last Tuesday before Christmas. That date was important, for with school on vacation, it was easier to talk parents into letting us stay out to watch a 9:15 league. Our proprietor, Rudy Habetler, was a former president of the Classic. I like to think he secured that special date so his junior bowlers could attend the session.

The hype began around Thanksgiving. Large posters were hung on the Habetler Bowl walls proclaiming that the Classic League was coming. The message was echoed on the outside signboard for the enlightenment and edification of the motorists along Northwest Highway. Then, about the middle of December, the Classic League Yearbooks appeared. These were digest-size booklets crammed with pictures, statistics, and schedules, and we eagerly scooped them up.

The big night finally arrived. Portable grandstands had been set up behind the last eight lanes, and spectators began filling them as early as eight o'clock—which produced some nervousness among the 150-average bowlers in the early league who suddenly had an audience. Then, a little before nine, the Classic Leaguers began drifting in.

Everything about them said *class*. They were freshly barbered, spoke in low voices, and smoked seven-inch-long cigars. They carried leather bowling bags and wore silky shirts with the finest embroidery. When they took to the lanes to warm up, even the bottom-rungers managed to get a devastating curve out of a hard-rubber ball with no apparent effort.

Each year there seemed to be some new phenom who had been

tearing the league apart. His name might be Jim Stefanich or Don McCune or Les Zikes, Jr.—with the final suffix, since Les Sr., still bowled in the Classic. One year the promising rookie was our own Don Eberl, a graduate of Habetler's Friday night scratch league.

Of the actual bowling I recall very little. There was too much to take in. My most vivid memory is of Eddie Kawolics coming out of the box with the first seven strikes. Another time there was an old-timers' match. Rudy bowled along with some other vets. What made this special was I got to watch the great Adolph Carlson in action. It was the only time I would ever see him bowl.

And then it was over. My friends and I came out of our trance. We drifted sleepily into the night toward our homes, declaring that we would show up a half-hour early for league next Saturday, so we could try out the tricks we gleaned from observing Andy Rogoznica or Lou Cioffi.

Going home from one of these sessions, I had the aura of the Classic League reinforced for me. It was long past midnight, and as I walked down Foster Avenue, a police car pulled up next to me. Vacation or not, Chicago youth had a strict 10:30 curfew.

When I told the officer where I had been, his face brightened, and he asked me how the Biasetti Steak House team had done. He then told me to get into the squad car—and gave me a ride home. He spent the trip talking about Vince Grzelak, Biasetti's young phenom.

Merry Christmas and Happy Holidays.

Who Was Ned Day?

(January–February 2009)
"Who was Ned Day?" The question was asked by a thirty-year-old friend, and it surprised me. My buddy knew enough bowling history to talk about Andy Varipapa and Joe Norris and some of the other stars of the pre–PBA era. It never occurred to me that a person who knew those names would draw a blank on Ned Day.

This is who Ned Day was ...

He was born Edward Gately Day in Los Angeles in 1911. The family moved to the Milwaukee suburb of West Allis when Ned was a toddler. There he grew into a smart, cheerful, friendly teen, of average height and wiry physique, who played three varsity sports and was the fastest sprinter in his high school conference.

His parents had warned Ned about the sordid atmosphere of the town's bowling alleys. Curious, he wandered into one place when he was fifteen, and was hooked. Day spent the next few years developing his game. He finally came under the care of Gus Steele, who applied the finishing touches.

The Ned Day style would become the most admired in bowling. Ned stood at the left side of the approach and advanced to the line on four measured steps. He released the ball with a full follow-through across his body. The ball rolled out toward the gutter, grabbed the shellac lane surface, then arched back into the pocket with pent-up fury. He crossed more boards than any bowler of the time. All this was accomplished with fluid grace. He never strained; he seemed so natural. Watching Ned Day practice bowling was like watching a fish practice swimming.

Day began to make his national reputation when the Heil Products team signed him in 1934. The Heils won the team match game title, the International Tournament in Germany, and numerous other events. Day was usually top scorer, or at worst second-best. He became a particular favorite of sponsor Julius Heil.

In 1938 Heil captain Hank Marino relinquished his individual match game crown. Day entered the eliminations and won the title. He was officially certified as the best bowler in the world, and he knew how to cash in on it. He bought a bowling center in West Allis. He signed with Brunswick and toured the nation. He wrote instruction books—there would eventually be four—and a syndicated newspaper column. He even secured a U.S. patent for the particular grip that was drilled on his bowling ball.

And he went to Hollywood. Day starred in a series of instructional shorts and made friends among the film crowd. His polished manner and good looks belied the idea that a professional bowler was some sort of Neanderthal. One smitten actress gushed that Ned Day seemed like "Cary Grant with curly hair."

Of course, all the good life depended on Day's continued success on the lanes. With Mort Luby, Sr., as his manager, Ned came up with another publicity coup. He posted $5,000 for anyone who would meet him in a home-and-home match. Joe Wilman, Marty Cassio, Adolph Carlson, Tony Sparando, and various lesser lights eventually took up the challenge, although for lesser sums. All of them went down in defeat.

172   Who Was Ned Day?

In 1941 the BPAA launched the All-Star Tournament to provide Day with an opponent for the match game title. Johnny Crimmins won, then faced off against Day. Ned successfully defended again, though this time it was close.

By now World War II was raging. Day enlisted in the navy. Not

"Cary Grant with curly hair": Ned Day, 1938.

knowing when he might return, he surrendered his match game title to the BPAA. From that point on, the winner of the All-Star would become match game champ.

In less than a year, Day received an honorable discharge from the navy for medical reasons. He entered the 1943 All-Star and easily won back his title. Once more, Ned Day was on top of the bowling world.

The next year, as match game champion, Day accepted a challenge from Paul Krumske. Krumske won, becoming the first man to defeat Day in a home-and-home match. One incident is noteworthy. In the blocks at Day's lanes, the hometown crowd began hooting and trash-talking Krumske whenever he bowled. Day, always a sportsman, stopped the action and made his supporters shut up.

Even without his title, Day remained the biggest name in bowling. He was chosen Bowler of the Year two years running, and *Sport* magazine ran a five-page feature story on his life, complete with full-page color photo. His fame reached the general public, too. In one of his sketches, radio comic Jack Benny talked about a bowling friend who "thought he was the new Ned Day."

The exhibition tours for Brunswick continued to occupy his time. He was no longer a full-time league bowler, but rolled in the major tournaments with Buddy Bomar's teams. Day and Bomar became fast friends and won the BPAA Doubles title. The pair also helped President Truman open the new White House bowling lanes.

Times were good. The money was rolling in. Besides his bowling lanes in West Allis, Day held a one-third share of a mega-center in California and owned three Milwaukee pro shops. He collected a royalty on all Brunswick supplies sold in Wisconsin. There were more films, more books, more ladies to be courted.

Of course, the other bowlers respected him. And better still, they liked him. Day was always generous with his time—and when needed, with his money. He did not complain, did not demean others, and was always ready to share the credit for any accomplishment.

In 1948 Day finally achieved his ambition of capturing an ABC eagle, when he won the All Events. But he no longer contended in the All-Star. In the smaller tournaments, he blew hot and cold. His career was entering a long decline.

The game was changing. Lacquer had replaced shellac as lane dressing. The new conditions proved difficult for Day's big, slow, rainbow curve. He adjusted the best he could. Going to the line he was smooth as ever. At the moment of truth it all fell apart. Now his release reminded one observer of a man yanking the cord on an outboard motor.

His last victory was *Championship Bowling* in 1959, a match game tournament filmed as a television series. The next year he appeared in the ABC for the last time. His lifetime average in the big tournament was a shade over 200, and he didn't want to jeopardize that record by continuing.

Day's prize for the television tournament had been the biggest of his career—over $14,000. Announcer Fred Wolf later remarked, "I'll guarantee, the next day, that money was either in the stock market or on a horse." Ned had always been a reckless gambler. Now, like advancing age, his vice began to catch up with him.

The Brunswick contract ended and one by one, the businesses were sold. In 1965 he was down to a single pro shop. That year Day was named an unindicted co-conspirator when a gambling operation in his basement was raided.

He retreated from the bowling world—fat and balding, he wanted his fans to remember him as he had been. By the fall of 1971, he was divorced and eking out a meager living operating a used bookstore.

On the morning of November 26, his ex-wife phoned him and didn't receive an answer. The police were called and found his body. He had suffered a stroke. Ned Day had died alone on Thanksgiving Day.

So, who was Ned Day?

In the 1999 *BJI* ranking of twentieth century bowlers, he placed fifth. And there is one more thing. When I conducted oral history interviews with a dozen veteran pros, he was the one person nobody could criticize. And in describing him, these stars all used the same word. Ned Day was a "gentleman."

Ed Lubanski's Double 300

(June 2009)

In 1959 bowling balls were made of hard rubber, and most bowling pins were solid maple. The American Bowling Congress counted about 3,000,000 members. Out of all the millions of league games rolled that season, the number of perfect games recorded was 426. Keep those facts in mind while you continue reading …

Ed Lubanski's Double-300

In June of 1959, Ed Lubanski was completing one of the greatest seasons in bowling history. The previous November he had won the 100-game World's Invitational Tournament, scoring a decisive triumph over Don Carter and an all-star field. Then, in February, he had taken his Pfeiffer Beer team to the ABC Tournament and put on a spectacular show. The result was three eagles for Lubanski—Team, Singles, and All Events. In the process he had posted a record All Events total, and come within one strike of the Singles record.

Lubanski was a member of AMF's advisory staff. On June 22 he was in Miami along with Billy Welu, Carmen Salvino, Anita Cantaline, and various other AMF stars. The bowlers were finishing up a four-day series of clinics at ten area centers. This evening there would be a Scotch Doubles match featuring Lubanski and Welu, telecast live from Bowling Palace.

In Scotch Doubles, two bowlers share in bowling a single game. One person rolls the first ball, and the partner picks up the spare. The next frame they switch order, and continue on alternating this way until the game is over. But if one of the bowlers gets a strike, that same bowler rolls first again the following frame.

Lubanski and Welu were bowling a three-game match, each pro teaming with a different local amateur in each game. Welu and his first partner opened with 224. Meanwhile, the Lubanski duo ran into splits and errors and posted 149.

They started the second game, and suddenly, Lubanski found the range. He rolled a strike. Then another. And another. Now it was easy. "I was a baseball player, and sometimes I'd see that ball, and it'd be coming up there big like a beach ball when you wanted to hit it," he says today. "Well, it was the same with bowling. Sometimes, it was just like you knew that nothing could stop you."

This time he *was* unstoppable. Lubanski rolled twelve strikes for 300. With the final strike, Bowling Palace erupted. There had been only a handful of perfect games bowled on TV. The last one had been rolled two years before in Detroit—by Ed Lubanski.

They stopped the action and congratulated Lubanski. Then everyone exhaled. It was back to normal, everyday bowling. Or was it? The third game got under way, and Lubanski was still rolling strikes. "After the first [300], they told me to just keep going," he remembers. "Well, my confidence went up. So I just concentrated on where I was going to stand and where I was going to throw the ball. I thought if something was going to happen, it was going to happen."

The strikes continued. Once again, Lubanski's amateur partner rode the bench as the X's stretched across the scoreboard. The string reached eleven. On the twelfth shot, as the ball curved into the pocket, Lubanski dropped to his knees. The hit was perfect. All the pins fell. And Lubanski had his second consecutive 300.

Today, at seventy-nine, Ed Lubanski does some instructing in suburban Detroit. Looking back on his double-300, he still chuckles at one memory. "I called my wife to tell her the news, and the first thing she said was, 'How much money did you make?'"

But let the final word go to Lee Jouglard, the announcer for the match. As the show signed off, Jouglard told viewers "You've seen something on television that you may never see again." And so far, Jouglard has been right. In the half-century since Ed Lubanski's historic feat, no one else has bowled consecutive 300s on TV.

Andy Varipapa Stories

(August 2009)

Twenty-five years ago this month, Andy Varipapa died. He was ninety-three years old. Whether he was the greatest bowler of his era is open to debate. But nobody can deny he was the greatest showman. Andy created memories—and not just among the fans. Some years ago I had the pleasure of conducting oral history interviews with a dozen veteran stars. Sooner or later, there would always be an Andy Varipapa story.

Shirley Garms described her first exhibition with Andy. As part of the act, Shirley was supposed to stand out on the lane with her feet apart, and Andy would roll the ball between her legs. Once she was set, Andy told her to move her feet closer together. Shirley followed orders, but Andy wasn't satisfied.

Andy had Shirley adjust her stance a few more times. As the space between her feet narrowed, she began to wonder what would happen if Andy's aim were off. "Finally, he said 'All right!'" Garms remembered. "He threw the ball and I closed my eyes. That ball just barely went between my legs."

At the height of his fame, Andy was one of the best-known athletes in America. That became apparent to Joe Norris when the two men made a European exhibition tour. Andy did a lot of shopping and returned home with thousands of dollars in merchandise—and didn't bother to keep any receipts. For anyone else, that might have been a problem.

"We landed and we're waiting for the customs inspection," Norris said. "This agent walks by, recognizes Andy, and takes him off to meet his supervisors. Well, Andy's gone about twenty-five minutes. When he comes back, they pass us right through and don't check anything."

Ray Bluth recalled a Varipapa incident from a television match at Faetz-Niesen Recreation in Chicago. The two men were loosening up before going on. "We're in the process of practicing, and Andy took his bowling ball and sanded it," Bluth said. "That's against ABC rules, so they took his ball away from him."

Andy lost the match, but it didn't faze him. Afterward he told Bluth, "They wanted you to win the show."

Before one of the BPAA Doubles events, Andy found himself without a partner. He phoned his friend Buddy Bomar, and Bomar fixed him up with a very young Bill Lillard. "It was in Buffalo during practice on Friday night," Lillard said. "Andy walked in and calls out 'Hey kid, help me carry my bowling balls in.' He had eight balls and we brought them all in, and I think he used all eight of them in the tournament."

"Number One and Number Two": Andy Varipapa (left) introduces Carmen Salvino (center), the newest inductee of the Chicago Sports Hall of Fame.

Varipapa and Lillard finished second. For Andy, that was a disappointment. "Andy didn't bowl as well as I did," Lillard recalled. "So when we're finished, he said to me, 'Kid, here's $50—buy [your wife] a new hat.'"

Carmen Salvino observed that "Andy had a way of talking arrogant, yet you loved him for it—he never sounded boastful." He often kidded Salvino that Carmen was "Number Two" after the Great Varipapa.

When Salvino was inducted into the Chicago Sports Hall of Fame, Andy was brought in to introduce him. "They hand me the trophy and Andy grabs it out of my hand," Salvino chuckled. "I try to pull it back, and he grabs it again. It looked like Abbott and Costello up there. I say 'Andy, it's my day!' But he says, 'Number Two, settle down!' So what can you do?"

The only time I met Andy Varipapa was in 1970, at the last All-Star Tournament. He'd been having some wrist and arm problems, and had started bowling left-handed—and was doing pretty well, even at age seventy-nine. When I complimented him on his switch, he looked annoyed. "What am I supposed to do?" he snorted. "Sit home and grow tomatoes?"

Then he laughed. And I had to laugh, too.

Earl Breaks Through

(January 2010)

Earlier this year, Earl Anthony was voted the greatest player in PBA history. He won forty-one Tour titles and two Masters championships. His name led the career win list for thirty years, and he still ranks second behind Walter Ray Williams.

It had to start somewhere. So let's go back to the beginning.

As 1970 began Anthony was thirty-one years old. His major bowling accomplishment was a share of the 1968 ABC Team All Events championship. He had tried the Tour once before, and earned exactly $0. But after working in a grocery plant and practicing 180 games a week, he was ready to try again.

The Winter Tour made thirteen stops in 1970, with the finals on network TV each week. The first event was at Wichita, and Anthony led the 40-game qualifying. When the broadcast began, millions of viewers rubbed their eyes in astonishment. A lefty from out of nowhere, with horn-rimmed glasses and a buzz-cut that had gone out of style three presidents ago, had been suddenly dropped into the mod '70s and was on his way to winning his first PBA event. It was storybook stuff—except that reality didn't follow the fairytale script. Skee Foremsky climbed through the stepladder television format and beat Anthony for the title, 217–209.

Anthony was out of the money the next two tournaments. Maybe he had been nothing more than a one-week wonder. Then, at San Jose, he qualified second—behind Foremsky. Time for the rookie's revenge? Not quite. On the television show, Dave Davis polished off Anthony before he could get to Foremsky, 244–237.

Now it was February. Anthony cashed at Denver without making the broadcast. He bowled the next four events and didn't win a penny. March came, and the pendulum swung back. At New York Anthony was back in the finals, and finally won a game on TV—beating Dick Weber, no less. Then Mike McGrath edged him 200–198, and Earl had to settle for third place.

Miami next, and a no-cash week. On to New Orleans—and for the second time Anthony emerged as the tournament leader going into the Saturday broadcast. Once again, the stepladder format killed him. Don Johnson took the title, 216–214. For the fourth time Anthony had lost a televised match, each of them by fewer than 10 pins.

The Tournament of Champions concluded the PBA's broadcast schedule. Since he had still not claimed his first title, Anthony was not eligible. Like most of America, he had to watch Don Johnson's 299 finish on the tube.

The 1970 Winter Tour was history. Johnson was the leading money-winner, mostly on the strength of his T-of-C victory. Anthony stood eleventh in the prize rankings. But reading into the statistics further, it was revealed that the new boy non-winner had topped the average list, with 213.3 for 367 games in twelve events.

The pro caravan moved on to Chicago for the All-Star Tournament. Though it carried a ton on prestige, the All-Star was not an official PBA event. For a variety of reasons Anthony did not bowl.

The Summer Tour kicked off on June 4 at Seattle. That was just a couple of gallons of gas from Anthony's home in Tacoma. And since the Summer Tour was not on TV, there was no stepladder format. You bowled your 40 games, counted up the pins, added in the bonus-points from the match game portion, and the high man got the biggest check.

A picture that would become familiar—Earl Anthony with trophy and prize check.

This time, Anthony took no chances. At the end of the opening 24 games he had 5825 pins for a new PBA record. The next 16 games were match-play, and when that was over he had another record, 9564 in actual pinfall for 40 games. Adding in the bonus pins for games won, and he had a third record—10,064 total pins.

Earl Anthony finally had his first PBA title. It took him another year to win his second. And after that ...

The Petersen Classic Turns 100

(February 2010)
You may have seen a bowler's towel with the words "I Survived the Petersen Classic." That sentiment is appropriate. With its 100th edition of the tournament set to run this spring, the Petersen itself is a survivor.

Louis B. Petersen was one of Chicago's pioneer bowling promoters. He was founder of the first local proprietors' association, and the driving force behind what was then the largest-ever bowling event, the 1918 National Patriotic Tournament. In 1919 Petersen moved to Los Angeles to enter the oil business. But two years later he was back in the Windy City with another grand idea.

Petersen planned the richest bowling tournament in history, with a first-place payoff of $1,000. That was a gigantic prize for a sporting event in 1921. That same year, the winner of golf's U.S. Open had collected only $500.

To put together his big pot, Louie had to charge a hefty entry fee of $20—a week's pay for many men. Scoffers said he'd never recruit enough bowlers to finance his prize list, and Louie did have to hustle to get the sixty-four entries he needed. When he finally reached his goal, he deposited the money with *Bowlers Journal* publisher Dave Luby.

The first Petersen Classic rolled out at Archer-35th Recreation in Chicago on October 2, 1921. Two squads of thirty-two bowlers each rolled eight games. There were just three prizes—$1,000 for first place, $500 for second, and $100 for high single game.

The tournament turned out to be a thriller. Going into the final game of the second squad, at least five men had a shot at the top prize. Then Harry Steers broke out of the pack with a closing 245 for a winning total of 1629. Matty Williams placed second at 1594, and Larry Dunn took the high-game award with 257.

Louie's Classic was a success. Bowler demand was so great that the next year he staged two tournaments, one in the spring and a second in the fall. As the entries poured in, the prize list expanded to more places. By 1926 the spring Classic was attracting more than 500 bowlers.

The tournament went on the road for the first time that year, when the fall edition was held in St. Louis. The main Petersen Classic remained in Chicago, but some years a second tournament was bowled in places like Milwaukee, Detroit, Cleveland, or Buffalo. That's why the 2010 Classic counts as #100.

The road Classic was only one of the experiments Louie tried during the tournament's first decade. One year there were three divisions, based on entering average. Another time the bowlers rolled five games, instead of the customary eight. The top prize also fluctuated, going as high as $3,000, and dipping to $500 per division in the three-division year.

Most of the early champions were well-established stars. Besides Harry Steers, the big check was taken home by such future Hall of Famers as Jimmy Smith, Hank Marino, Sykes Thoma, Charley Daw, and Mort Lindsey. The master of the Classic was Dom DeVito, with three victories in six years. In 1927 DeVito won with a record 1924 series—that's a 240-plus average with a hard rubber ball against solid maple pins.

Then the Depression hit. By 1934 the entry list was down to eighty-two. Louie suspended the tournament for four years, then resumed in 1938. Once more, the Classic offered the richest prize in bowling. Once more, the finest bowlers of the era earned the right to have their portraits hung in the gallery of champions—Ned Day, Adolph Carlson, Tony Sparando, Russ Gersonde, Nelson Burton, Sr.

Then, as the 1940s ended, the Classic began to change. Maybe Louie got the idea in 1947 when Buddy Bomar won both the spring and fall events. The better bowlers had always dominated the Petersen, rolling their usual high scores. But what if conditions were toughened up? If the winning score were low, then anyone might be tempted to take a crack at the tournament.

The 1951 event was the turning point. Out of nearly 2,000 bowlers, not one could break 1600 over eight games. The winner was John Quinzi, a good bowler from Rochester, but hardly a household name. He had averaged 199.

The pattern was set. A few famous stars continued to compete—Ned Day always showed up, and always took home a some cash—but others were scared away by the thought of rolling 120s in front of a packed house. Dick Weber gave up after bowling fifteen years and never cracking 1450. It was about this time that the management began selling those "I Survived" towels.

Now came all the folklore. The tournament pins were stored in the open on the roof, to make them water-logged. The first pair of lanes went uphill at a 6 percent grade. At the other end of the house, the last pair was six feet longer than standard. The approaches were cured with shellac, causing bowlers to stick. Louie had a special button at the counter, so he could order an equipment breakdown when someone was bowling well. And so on.

If anything, the legends grew more outrageous after Petersen died in 1958. He was succeeded by his son-in-law, Mark Collor, who seemed to glory in the bowlers' complaints. But Collor knew how to read the bottom line. As the Petersen Classic got tougher, and the grumbling grew louder, the bowlers kept returning.

In Collor's first year at the helm, entries passed 10,000 for the first time. That number kept rising steadily. By 1981, more than 36,000 bowlers were climbing the rickety stairs at Archer-35th to take their shot at the pot of gold. The event stretched over ten months, from October to July.

More bowlers meant more money. Now a contestant could collect $1,000 by finishing in 100th place. New features were added, like the optional doubles. First prize passed $10,000, then $20,000, then $30,000. The peak was reached in 1987, when one man earned $55,000.

The names changed each year, yet the story was usually the same—some unknown bowler would grind out eight games, and triple his year's income in a few hours. The 1968 champ, Mike Berlin, did go on to a Hall of Fame career. But during the Collor era, the winner of the Petersen was almost always a one-year wonder.

Buddy DeLuca of Pittsburgh was a special case. He earned first prize in the 1976 event with a towering 1731, the highest Petersen score since Buddy Bomar in 1947. Eleven years later, DeLuca topped the standings again. That made him the first Petersen repeater since Bomar. (The lesson may be this—if you want to do really well at the Petersen, call yourself "Buddy.")

The tournament had become a bowling tradition. Then, in 1993, Collor announced that the Petersen was being discontinued. The reasons were simple. The 90-year-old building on 35th Street was falling apart, and he was ready to retire. For the bowlers of the world, all that would be left would be the nightmares.

The Petersen Classic had been buried in 1934, only to rise again after four years. This time, the resurrection came more quickly. A group of investors purchased the tournament and its assorted physical properties. They moved the site thirty miles northwest to Hoffman Lanes in suburban Hoffman Estates. In the summer of 1994, the latest version of the venerable Classic made its debut.

As much as possible, the new owners tried to recreate the feel of old Archer-35th. The giant posters of past champions and all the other hokey décor were retained. Lane conditions were still tough, and scores still low. When AMF took over the event in 1998, it continued the time-honored Petersen formula.

Like most of the bowling business, the Petersen has faced challenging times lately. Entries have declined and the prize list is down from the flush days of the 1980s. The 1645 total rolled by 2009 champ Gregg Zicha earned him a total of $26,600.

Still, the Petersen has its hardy band of loyalists. Year after year, they return. The 99th Classic attracted 4,512 bowlers from forty-two states. When all the optional side events are figured in, the entry total was 12,410.

Typical of the Petersen regular is Don Witt of Oak Park, Illinois. He bowled his first Classic in 1968. He has been a squad sponsor the last thirty-two years, the first sixteen at Archer-35th, and now for sixteen more at Hoffman Lanes. "When they first moved, I wondered if it would be the same," he says. "But they've done a fantastic job making Hoffman look like the old place. It's still the Petersen. They ring the bell, and they open the golden door, and it's like stepping back in time."

But for Witt, like most others, the Petersen is more than just nostalgia. "It's the fairest tournament around—because the conditions are so bad," he laughs. "Nobody has an advantage. I can do just as well as any past winners. That's why I keep coming back. That's why my bowlers keep coming back." Somewhere, Louie Petersen and Mark Collor are smiling.

All Hail, Lady L!

(June 2010)

Who is the greatest bowler of all time? The debate is always going on. Is the answer Don Carter? Dick Weber? Earl Anthony? Walter Ray Williams? Someone else?

Notice that these are male bowlers. If we shift genders and ask, "Who is the greatest female bowler of all time?" the answer is easy. Marion Ladewig.

Lady L died at her home in Grand Rapids on April 16, a few months shy of her ninety-sixth birthday. She hadn't bowled competitively in more than forty years. Yet she still remains the standard by which all others are measured. Let's look at the record.

In 1949 the BPAA added a women's division to its annual All-Star Tournament. The All-Star was a week-long match game event, the most prestigious championship in bowling. Ladewig won the title eight times in fourteen years, including the first five in a row. In 1957 Chicago proprietors launched the World's Invitational Tournament. This event was basically another All-Star, and lasted eight years. Ladewig won the World's five times.

She was Bowler of the Year nine times. In 1961 *Bowlers Journal* began selecting a female All American Team. Ladewig was named to the team four times. But consider this: if *BJ* had started naming a female team when it started naming male All Americans, Ladewig would probably have been honored at least *twenty* times.

Kelly Kulick's victory in the PBA Tournament of Champions is—without a doubt—the greatest single accomplishment by a female bowler. Ladewig never had the chance to compete directly against the men. But in the 1951–52 All-Star, she rang up the highest average among all the bowlers, of whatever gender. Men's champ Junie McMahon won his division with a 209 average. Bowling on the same lanes, Ladewig breezed to her third straight title with a 211 mark. The women did roll against pins that were a few ounces lighter, and you can make of that what you will. It's still a helluva feat.

Ladewig began life in 1914 as Marion Van Oosten, the daughter of a Grand Rapids cop. Armchair psychologists might make something of the fact that her given name was spelled in the male variant, instead of the female "Marian." And the lady always said she was a tomboy growing up. Her favorite sport was baseball.

She went bowling for the first time when she was twenty-two. She bowled badly, but she was hooked. The alleys were called the Fanatorium, the proprietor a man named William Morrissey. He made Marion a bowler. He gave her a job, got her instructions, made sure she practiced every day. By 1941 she was the best female bowler in Grand Rapids, and had won her first tournament.

She had started out taking three steps, swinging the ball over her head and firing it down the lane. Then she added a step and cut the backswing. She concentrated on roll, not bothering to develop a fancy hook. "My rhythm was fairly good, but there was nothing outstanding about my style," Ladewig later recalled. "I threw an angle ball with a slight hook. My biggest asset was my accuracy."

Ladewig was a natural athlete. Whether she had the best temperament for competition was another matter. She was high-strung and nervous. To break the tension, she began chewing gum. Her fingers swelled, and she developed the habit of patting them on the ball as she got set on the approach. "The game never became easy for me," she admitted. "I always had to keep working at it."

Morrissey knew his pupil, and found various ways of keeping her relaxed. During the All-Star, when Ladewig's nerves would start to frazzle, Morrissey and his wife would put her into their car, and the three of them would take long rides together. That would calm Marion down. Other times Morrissey used other tactics. He would call Ladewig lazy and useless, and cuss her out. He'd do it just enough to restore her fighting spirit.

The oldest surviving television bowling show is a half-hour kinescope of the 1950–51 All-Star. As a historic document, it's priceless. The broadcast also opens a window on the emotional rollercoaster Ladewig must have suffered in those marathon events.

The final game is shown. Ladewig has already wrapped up the championship. On the lanes she is relaxed, and even smiling. But then the bowling ends. She comes out of her trance. When announcer Fred Wolf tries to interview her, she breaks down and can't even get out a word.

Ladewig did learn to cope. The next All-Star broadcast we have is the 1952–53 event. Again Ladewig wins. This time the champ has a nice chat with Freddy about the tournament, her plans, and the folks back in Grand Rapids.

The 1950s were the years of the great bowling boom. The sport was being transformed, as the dark and dingy saloon alleys were being replaced with modern, spacious palaces of recreation. Bowling was becoming a family sport, suitable for the wife and kids. And who better to represent the new era than a little lady from the heart of Middle America, who happened to be the world's best woman bowler? Brunswick signed Ladewig to a contract, and she toured the nation giving exhibitions and clinics. When she became a grandmother, that only added to her wholesome appeal.

The women she bowled against knew she was something special. "Marion Ladewig was my idol—she was everyone's idol," Shirley Garms recalled. "She was like a machine. You could put a dime down on the lane, and she'd hit it every time. Her timing was so impeccable, her game so precise, I don't think she had to think about what she was doing."

Besides her bowling skill, Ladewig was also a role model. She

Marion Ladewig addressing her admirers after wrapping up another All-Star Tournament. Generally regarded as the greatest woman bowler of the twentieth century, a 1999 poll ranked her #7 of all the century's bowlers—of either gender.

showed that a woman could remain feminine while rising to the top of her sport. "Marion was always a lady on the lanes and she always dressed neatly," Garms said. "She always came out with a different outfit, in order to look good on the lanes. Everyone copied her [clothing] style."

Ladewig's status separated her from her contemporaries—after all, the press called her The Queen. Most of the women she bowled against were intimidated by her reputation. She never really became "one of the girls," and that led to some resentment. There was jealousy, too. "Marion was a very nice person," Anita Cantaline said. "But you had to get to know her. A lot of people thought she was snobbish, but actually she was timid. She was a very private person."

As bowling's female icon, Ladewig realized she had certain responsibilities. During one All-Star, she was just coming off the lanes at 2 a.m. when publicity director Jim Kearns told her he'd managed to schedule a network radio interview—for 6:45 that morning. Without a second thought, Ladewig agreed to do the gig.

"I groped into the lobby of her hotel at 6:30," Kearns said. "There she was, looking like she had just come out of a band box, groomed, wide awake, happy, and poised. And she turned in a real performance. She was the finest person to handle publicity I've ever encountered."

The ordeal of success got to Ladewig in 1955. "I thought I had to win every year," she later remembered. "The thought of losing made me tense all over. It got to be such a nervous strain that I didn't think I could go on." Morrissey advised her to quit. So she announced her retirement from competitive bowling. *Life* magazine ran a feature story on Ladewig's last All-Star. With her decision made and her mind clear, she went out and finished third. Sylvia Wene won the tournament that year.

But Ladewig came back. With the help of medication, she was able to return to the battle and add to her sterling record. The bowling world got to savor another decade of its Queen. Then, in 1964, she quit for good.

Ladewig returned to Grand Rapids, operated her own bowling center, and bowled in house leagues. She enjoyed her grandchildren, and later her great-grandchildren. While she didn't shun the spotlight, she didn't seek it out, either.

Aside from Gerald Ford, she was the best-known person to come out of Grand Rapids. She didn't put on airs to the hometown folks. She didn't need to. "You couldn't tell from talking to her that she was famous," a friend said. At her bowling center she did the everyday chores along with the hired help, until her final retirement in 1995.

I had two encounters with Marion Ladewig. The first came at the 1962 World's Invitational. A few of us teenagers were watching the tournament from the upper stands when someone noticed The Queen sitting alone a few rows away. We hurried over to ask for an autograph.

Ladewig was gracious and signed our programs. But as more people began to gather, she excused herself and made her way down the steps, all the while smiling, and all the while signing anything that was thrust before her. She never returned to the stands.

In 2002 I began doing a series of oral history interviews for the Bowling Museum. Naturally the Museum wanted to have her interview, and naturally I wanted to talk with her. I phoned Grand Rapids. Marion's daughter answered. I explained why I'd called, and she immediately put me through to her mother.

With Marion on the line, I explained our project. I would need about an hour of her time. I could interview her on the phone at a future date, or I could come to Grand Rapids. Would Mrs. Ladewig like to participate?

"No, I don't think so," she said simply.

I was disappointed, but not really surprised. I asked if there were any particular reason she didn't want to do the interview.

"No, no reason," she replied. "But thank you for thinking of me."

And that was that. Queens don't need to give reasons.

Bowling moves on. Like Kelly Kulick, the women bowlers of today and tomorrow will continue to write fresh headlines, and reach even higher plateaus. But somehow I suspect that, even a century from now, bowlers will still be thinking of Marion Ladewig.

The Bowling Ball That Went Around the World

(August 2010)
The year was 1914, and Brunswick was proud of its Mineralite bowling ball. The vermillion-colored ball was made of hard rubber. The company guaranteed it would not chip or lose its shape for three years.

Still, the $20 price tag was pretty steep for a ball in 1914. Something had to be done to convince bowlers to part with that much cash. That spring a Brunswick manager named Dell Heneman came up with a novel promotion. Why not send a Mineralite around the world?

Travel was hard a century ago. Cars and planes were primitive, and most people spent their entire life within fifty miles of the place where they were born. Go around the world? Now *that* was something to talk about!

The Bowling Ball That Went Around the World

The logistics weren't as difficult as they might seem. This was the heyday of the British Empire, and there were YMCAs in most of the British colonies. Brunswick would simply ship the ball from one YMCA to another, using the Wells Fargo Express Company. Regular reports would be sent back, and bowlers could track the ball as it made its journey.

The saga began on May 28, 1914, when Brunswick Mineralite #391914 left the company offices in Chicago. It arrived in San Francisco two days later. There was a match at the local YMCA, then the ball was sent back across the country to New York. After a match there, the traveling Mineralite was put on a ship and brought to London. Another ceremony, and another match. The next scheduled stop was the International Bowling Tournament in Berlin.

Now things got complicated. While the ball was on its way to Berlin, war broke out between Germany and Britain—a little scrap called World War I. The Mineralite arrived, and German customs was

June 2, 1914: Brunswick officials in San Francisco prepare to send Mineralite bowling ball no. 391914 on its 35,000-mile journey around the world.

suspicious. Nobody had ever seen a big, American-style bowling ball. They thought it might be a bomb. So the Germans sent the ball back. Somehow it wound up in Paris. After sitting around there for a few months, the French returned it to London.

The original plan had been to send the ball from Berlin to Vienna, then to Rome for a hoped-for blessing from the Pope, and from Rome to Bombay. Since that wasn't going to work, the Brits put the ball on a ship and sent it directly to India. It reached Bombay in November.

After yet another YMCA ceremony, the Mineralite was loaded onto a ship headed for Australia. On the way, the ship sank. Oh, well.... But wait! The first reports were wrong! The ball had missed the boat and was still safe in Bombay!

Now the Mineralite was really put on board a ship, and made its way to Sydney without incident. From Sydney it sailed across the Pacific to San Diego, where the ball was exhibited at the California Pacific Exposition. Finally, in June 1915, after thirteen months and 35,000 miles on the road and over the sea, Mineralite #391914 arrived back in San Francisco. There it was proudly displayed at the Brunswick booth of the Panama Pacific World's Fair.

Funny thing. After the fair closed, and all that trouble, Brunswick lost the ball. It was missing for nineteen years. But in 1934, someone found #391914 tucked away in a warehouse. Think of the final scene in *Raiders of the Lost Ark.*

In Chicago, there was another world's fair that year, the Century of Progress Exposition. Brunswick trotted out the lost-and-found Mineralite, and once more put it on display. Stories in the papers related the amazing adventures of the world-touring bowling ball. Then the Chicago fair closed. And once again, the ball disappeared.

Where is it today? Nobody seems to know. But if you're poking around in the attic, and come across Great-grandpa's old Mineralite, and it's marked #391914, hold on to it. You have a piece of history.

Even More Things I Learned While Looking Up Other Things

(March 2011)
- Ernest Fosberg is recognized as the first person to roll a sanctioned 300 game. He turned the trick in 1902 at Rockford,

Illinois, and he did it using a 13-pound wooden house ball. The only reward Fosberg received for this monumental accomplishment came from the proprietor—he gave Fosberg the house ball.

- Harry Dean, St. Louis star of the 1920s, was ahead of his times in one respect. When Dean died in 1951, his obituary noted that he had been "famous for his habit of buying twenty balls a season."
- Sam Reidstra of San Francisco rolled an all-spare game of 179 on November 27, 1937. He followed that with a 300, making him the first person ever to bowl an all-spare game and an all-strike game back-to-back.
- When the 1901–02 season was completed, Johnny Voorhies of New York City was credited with compiling the highest league average in bowling history. The Little Wizard's mark was 199.
- During a 1919 tournament at Des Moines, a cat ambled onto one of the bowling lanes just as Chicago star Joe Fliger delivered his shot. The ball hit the cat, who jumped into the air, then scampered out of the establishment. Meanwhile, the ball continued on and recorded a strike. Fliger could have called "interference" and re-bowled, but accepted the strike.
- George Meier left a 7–10 split during a 1948 league session in Geneseo, Illinois. A second later, the shockwave from an explosion at an army depot rocked the bowling center and knocked over both pins. Since there was no "earthquake" rule in the books, his grumbling opponents were forced to credit George with a strike.
- The ABC Tournament first came to Cincinnati in 1908, when local sportsman Garry Herrmann was president of the ABC. Herrmann was so happy to have the event in his home town that he decided to supplement the prize fund out of his own pocket. During the Team squads, Herrmann walked behind the benches and passed out $5 gold pieces to the high man on each team.
- Jack Larson is best known for playing Jimmy Olson on the classic television series *The Adventures of Superman*. If things had gone differently, we might now be watching him on old videos of *Championship Bowling*. In 1942, at age fourteen, Larson won the California Junior Bowling Championship, and briefly considered a career as a pro bowler.

- In 1860, while visiting the United States, the nineteen-year-old Prince of Wales bowled a few games at the Zimmerman House in Niagara Falls, New York. The event was widely reported as major news, and some papers featured a woodcut drawing of the royal kegler. The prince later became King Edward VII of Great Britain.
- The first inter-city bowling match took place in November 1901, when a team from the New York City Drug League met a team from the Philadelphia Drug League in home-and-home competition. The New Yorkers won.
- During a 1945 Hamilton County League match in Cincinnati, the Pepsi-Cola team went into the tenth frame seven marks ahead, then blew their lead. The conclusion saw anchorman Bill Harris draw a split, and the Pepsis lost by two pins. But they lost more than the game—Harris promptly suffered a heart attack and died.
- In 1911 future Hall of Famer Mort Lindsey staged one of the first marathon exhibitions at New Haven, Connecticut. He rolled for twelve straight hours in the company of local man George Kelsey. To keep cool during the grind, both bowlers wore bathing suits.
- Seven years after Lindsey, Edna Hables became the first woman marathoner at King City, California. Hables rolled seventy-two games in twelve hours against a rotating group of opponents, averaging 158. No report on whether she wore a bathing suit.
- The 1928 ABC Tournament was unique in one respect. The event was staged at the American Royal Building in Kansas City, Missouri. According to contemporary reports, the building straddled the Missouri-Kansas state line. That gave bowlers on the last pair the opportunity to make their approach in Missouri, while knocking down pins in Kansas.

In Search of Johnny King

(May 2011)

Johnny King celebrates his ninetieth birthday this month. In bowling's golden age of the late 1950s, he was a legendary figure. And like most legends, it's sometimes hard to separate the fiction from the fact.

In Search of Johnny King

To begin with, his actual name was Howard King. Growing up in Cleveland during the Depression, he was forced to drop out of school and go to work in a factory. He eventually became a precision grinder.

King didn't make his bowling mark until he was in his thirties. Then he won the Cleveland Match Game Championship twice, and in 1956 posted the city's highest league average, a lofty 223. That same

Johnny King roots home a strike at the World's Invitational Tournament.

year he took home one of bowling's biggest checks in the George London Dream Tournament.

Now he began to appear on TV, and the legend began. In 1957 King was all over the tube. He scored big on two syndicated film series and even rolled a 300 game in front of the cameras. The year ended with King the top television money-winner, with prizes totaling over $25,000—about $200,000 in today's money.

King was fun to watch. He bowled with a long cigar stuck in his mouth, approaching the line slowly and smoothly, sending the ball out onto the lane without a sound. Then he went into action with a dazzling array of body English. A teammate claimed that King used to practice his moves in front of a mirror.

Johnny King was a star. More women were bowling, and they became some of his biggest fans. The ladies liked Johnny. Johnny liked the ladies, too.

He moved to Chicago to bowl with Buddy Bomar's Munsingwear team. That caused a flap, since King had already promised to join the Pfeiffer Beer team of Detroit. Pfeiffer captain Lou Sielaff, ordinarily a soft-spoken gentleman, blasted King all over the bowling press.

If King was bothered, it didn't show. He won the first of two straight Chicago Match Game titles and finished fourth in the World's Invitational. He made exhibition tours for AMF. During an appearance in Indiana, King averaged 277 for seven games.

He was a tough opponent, and looked for very edge. During one match, King flicked some cigar ash onto the side of the approach and started sliding his shoe through it—which made his opponent start worrying about sticking. Another time, on the bench during a television match, King pulled out a mirror to comb his hair. The mirror reflected the glare of the overhead lights onto the other bowler, just as the man was releasing his shot.

King was also known for his prowess at gin rummy. He won so regularly that many people refused to play with him. Others kept coming back for more, trying to figure out how he did it. According one bit of locker-room gossip, King could have won the 1957 World's, but ran out of gas after playing cards all night.

He continued on Bomar's team, then bowled the 1961–62 season with Fresno in the National Bowling League. The NBL folded after one season, but King and some of his ex-teammates won a Classic Division eagle as the California Bombers at the 1963 ABC. That December he won his only PBA title at Hialeah, Florida.

He was living in Florida and selling liquor dispensing equipment when he was tapped for the first Great and Greatest Tournament in 1978. He teamed with Johnny Petraglia and finished in the middle of the pack. It's worth noting that King was the only "Greatest" invitee who is not in the Bowling Hall of Fame.

And that's it. I've talked to dozens of bowlers and writers and bowling officials, and nobody knows what happened to Johnny King. For the last thirty years, he has communicated with the bowling world strictly through rumor.

Happy Birthday, Johnny. And if you get a chance, drop me an e-mail.

Note: Some months after this article was published, I learned that Johnny King had passed away in Florida on March 12, 1998.

A Different Path

(September 2011)
When Ned Day, Jr., was born in 1945, his father was the most famous bowler in the world. Ned Jr., would also become famous, but in a very different way.

The younger Mr. Day—and to keep things straight, we'll simply call him "Ned"—grew up in Milwaukee. From the time he was old enough to walk, his father trained him to be a bowler. In his teens he was averaging over 200, and Brunswick put him on a television special, rolling doubles with Ned Sr., against Buddy Bomar and his son.

Ned entered the University of Wisconsin in 1963. During his freshman year he bowled his first ABC Tournament, teamed with his father's old rival, Connie Schwoegler. The rookie's 1706 All Events just failed to cash. Still, Ned's bowling future looked bright. The *ABC Yearbook* was already referring to the old man as Ned Day, Sr., the same way it was now calling another 1940s star Nelson Burton, Sr.

The bowling dream lasted until 1968. Then Ned quit. "My father did something extraordinary in his field," he said. "Why should I spend my life trying to be just as good as or better than he was?" Ned drifted. He dropped out of school and tended bar. He worked at a racing tout service. For a while he was married to a stripper.

In 1971 Ned Day, Sr., died broke and alone in his shabby used bookstore. Amateur psychologists can speculate whether his sorry end made an impact on his son. But now Ned began to clean up his act. He landed a reporter's job at a community newspaper in Las Vegas. Ned wrote the usual space-filler stuff, but he also began taking on the mob. He was soon hired away by the city's leading paper, the *Review-Journal*. He'd found his niche.

By 1980 Ned was one of Las Vegas's more visible citizens. Reading his column had become the city's morning ritual, and his popularity led to a second job as managing editor of KLAS-TV. He also anchored the station's 5 p.m. newscast.

Ned remained his own man. Yet he didn't let his personality or celebrity get in the way of doing his job. "He was a free spirit, a wild man with bad habits," a colleague said. "But at his core, he was a reporter."

Meanwhile, he renewed his connection with bowling. When Ned, Sr., was honored at the 1985 Brunswick World Open, Ned was on hand with his mother in Chicago. The next year the ABC Tournament came to Las Vegas. Ned didn't bowl, but the program did run an article about his "different path."

He was still battling the mob. Ned received threats and ignored them. In July 1986 his Volvo was torched outside his apartment. With typical bravado, he snorted, "It takes real guts to sneak up on a car like that." What bothered him most was that his golf clubs had burned up in the trunk.

On September 3, 1987, Ned was in Hawaii on vacation. He was engaged to be married and trying to take better care of his health. He went snorkeling and drowned.

Las Vegas was shocked. Though Ned had an enlarged heart and the coroner ruled his death an accident, there were suspicions that his enemies had finally found a way to silence him.

The funeral was held three days later. "The whole town turned out for Ned's service," a reporter wrote. "The rich and powerful, the down and out, colleagues, governors, hookers, you name it. Ned would have loved it."

A quarter-century after his death, Ned Day, Jr., is still fondly remembered in his adopted hometown. A recent article referred to him as "a titan of Nevada journalism." There's even a scholarship in his memory at the University of Nevada–Las Vegas. So maybe the lesson to be learned is this—if your son doesn't want to go bowling with you, it's not the end of the world.

Uncle Joe

(January 2012)

Everybody called him Uncle Joe. He was Joseph Thum of New York City, one of the pioneer builders of American tenpins. As much as anyone, he made bowling respectable.

It all began by happenstance. Born in Bavaria in 1858, Thum came to New York as a teenager and got a job working in a little German café on Greenwich Street. One day in 1880 the owner decided to return to Germany. The man told Joe he could keep the café.

Thum took over the business and prospered. He prospered enough to get married. He prospered so much he couldn't get away from the café for any recreation. So in his spare time he hand-built a pair of bowling lanes in the basement, and he began inviting a few friends over to bowl with him. Then the café customers wanted to get in on the fun. Of course, they were willing to pay for the privilege. Joe Thum had become a bowling proprietor. Within a few years his new business outgrew the café basement. In 1891 Thum built the six-lane Germania Alleys on the Bowery, and later opened a second location in Harlem. He also helped organize the many New York bowling leagues into the United Bowling Clubs, the first successful local association.

Thum may have invented the bowling tournament. He was certainly among the first to stage tournaments. He was a good bowler, and competed in the events himself, and occasionally won the top prize. Even then, Thum was so well-liked that no one seemed to mind.

In 1895 Thum was one of the founders of the American Bowling Congress. He attended the annual convention the next few years, but got into the habit of ducking out the second day to go bowling with some of the other delegates. According to one story, this prompted ABC officials to start their own tournament in 1901.

That same year of 1901 Thum decided to open a swank new bowling center in the heart of Manhattan's shopping district, on Broadway at 31st Street. He planned on putting in twenty-four lanes. Friends told Thum that was too many, that he'd go broke. The place would be a white elephant—the term for any big investment that couldn't earn back its cost. Thum wasn't superstitious, and he had a sense of humor. He named his new pin palace The White Elephant.

From the first day, the money rolled in. People who wouldn't dream of venturing into one of the old dark, dirty bowling cellars tried out this latest entertainment venue on fashionable Broadway, and liked it. The genial proprietor became a celebrity. Whenever the city had a parade, there was sure to be a contingent from the Joseph Thum Bowling Guard.

Having won over New York, Thum set out to conquer the rest of the world for bowling. Beginning in 1921 he sponsored a number of matches between U.S. and European teams. The first events were small, and were more like vacation excursions with a little bowling thrown in. As more countries joined, the International Bowling Association was formed. Who else but Uncle Joe would be the first president?

His great dream was to have bowling recognized as an Olympic sport. When he failed to get bowling on the program for the 1936 games at Berlin, Thum organized an International Tournament in the city, scheduling it for a week before the Olympics. The idea was to showcase American bowling and get it accepted for the 1940 Olympics.

International bowling promoter Uncle Joe Thum in his uniform as Commander of the JTBG—Joseph Thum Bowling Guard.

The 1936 International Tournament attracted 5,000 bowlers from fourteen countries, was widely publicized, and was considered a major success. Thum was confident that bowling had made its case. But World War II cancelled the 1940 Olympics.

Joe Thum was gone by then. He died on January 9, 1937. Eight years later, The White Elephant closed its doors forever.

Bowler's Symphony

(September 2012)
The death of Don Carter brought to mind one of the great bowler's

most unusual performances—his featured solo with the St. Louis Symphony. In the fall of 1955 Andre Kostelanetz was scheduled to guest conduct the symphony at its Kiel Auditorium home. The program included *Hudson River Suite* by the American composer Ferde Grofé. The Third Movement of this piece depicts a group of ghosts bowling ninepins.

Kostelanetz was a showman. For sound effects, he decided to have an actual bowler on stage rolling against actual pins. And since this was St. Louis in 1955, he asked the Budweiser brewery for someone from their famous bowling team. They sent Carter.

The concert took place on November 27. Carter sat on stage to the left, in front of the orchestra. The pins were set up on the right front of the stage, about thirty feet away, with a backstop behind them. For some reason there were ten pins instead of nine. An attendant stood off to the side, acting as a pinboy.

Of course, Carter was used to bowling before an audience. But this time was different. "It was scary," he later recalled. "I sat there for an hour with my palms sweating. The timing had to be perfect—if I missed the pins, it would be really embarrassing."

The big moment arrived. On cue, Carter stood up, grabbed his ball, and shuffled into his familiar approach. He let the ball go, but there was a slight problem. The boards on the stage ran across the direction of Carter's shot, instead of with it as they would on a bowling lane. "The ball gave sort of a rumble as it rolled, but it turned out great," Carter remembered. "I think I got eight pins."

The music score called for the ghosts to bowl twice. The pinboy reset the dead wood, and Carter rolled again. There's no record of how he did. But with his first shot used to find the range, we can assume that the second one was a strike.

The next day the *St. Louis Post-Dispatch* printed a picture of Carter rolling a ball across stage in front of the orchestra. Under the caption "Symphonic Bowler," a short story recounted why the Budweiser star had traded Floriss Lanes for the Kiel Auditorium. The photo was picked up by the wire services and ran in papers throughout the country.

Carter never again performed with a symphony orchestra. But Andre Kostelanetz appreciated the publicity given the stunt. A few years later, he repeated it. The setting was the San Francisco Opera House and the date was February 2, 1958. The bowler this time was local wiz Dick Agee. The staging was the same as it had been in St. Louis.

Like Carter, Agee was tense waiting for his cue. "I was never so nervous in my life," he said afterward. "I've bowled before big crowds, but never anything like this. Just sitting there before my turn raised the tension."

Agee was a fine bowler—he later won the PBA's Showboat Classic—but he was no Don Carter. Still, he rose to the occasion. On his first ball he got a strike, and on his second he counted seven pins. When the concert was over, he took three curtain calls to thunderous applause.

Hudson River Suite was never considered great music, and soon fell out of the standard repertoire. For a half century it was seldom played. But a few years ago, a new performance by William Stromberg and the Bournemouth Symphony was issued on CD. I bought a copy of the CD and I like it. I look forward to the day when my own Chicago Symphony Orchestra will perform *Hudson River Suite.* And if we no longer have Don Carter or Dick Agee, we do have a bowler with a flair for showmanship available to bowl on stage. He also has a suitable operatic first name—"Carmen."

Chief Halftown

(November 2012)
"*Ees Da Sa Sussaway.*" That's Seneca for "Let's get started." It's time to talk about Chief Halftown, the Philadelphia television star who always opened his show with those words—when he wasn't on the road promoting junior bowling.

Traynor Ora Halftown, Jr., was a full-blooded Indian (he preferred that term), born on an upstate New York reservation in 1917. He got into show business in high school, performing in clubs as The Singing Seneca. Then came army service in World War II.

After the war Halftown married and settled in Harrisburg, Pennsylvania. Singing jobs grew scarce. By 1950 he was ready to go to work for the state turnpike commission, when a new Philadelphia television station hired him to host a kids' cartoon show.

The Chief appeared on air in full Indian regalia, but smiled and spoke perfect English. He was determined not to be a stereotype—"Nobody had to teach me how to be an Indian," he said. Along with the cartoons, he soon added lessons on folklore, customs, chants, and crafts. His show became a hit.

He had set pins as a teenager, and done some bowling in Buffalo. Now the sport became his chief off-air exercise. Halftown gradually worked his way up to a 200 average in a couple of Philadelphia leagues. When his team won a local tournament, that caught the eye of Brunswick. The company was looking to expand junior bowling. What better representative than a television entertainer who knew how to work with kids, was an accomplished bowler—and was also an American Indian? In 1959 the Chief joined the Brunswick advisory staff.

His television program was on Saturday mornings. Now, during the nine months of the school calendar, Halftown was on the road, Monday through Friday. During his first year he clocked over 100,000 miles.

A typical day would start with Halftown doing morning assemblies at one or two elementary schools. He'd crack jokes, sing songs, and loosen up his audience—"Most children have never seen a real live Indian laugh," he explained. From there, he would move on to the history of the native peoples, their culture, and the importance of good citizenship. Then it was time to talk bowling.

The Chief would announce he'd be at a particular bowling center after school. With the permission of a parent, the kids were invited to come on down for some free bowling and free instruction. That afternoon, about 4 o'clock, the lucky proprietor would find himself overrun.

A few hours of fun with the kids, then the Chief was off to another town. After he was gone, his new recruits would be given passes to bowl free one night a week for three weeks. Most of them stuck with it, and then became regular league members of the Chief Halftown Junior Bowling Club.

At their peak in the late '60s, the Chief's bowling clubs operated in over 200 cities in the U.S. and Canada. One year he presented his program to 800,000 school children. He received over a hundred fan letters a week.

The travel could get wearing. "Sometimes I wonder why I do it," Halftown said. "But I love kids. I can see the faces of the youngsters I talked to in California, and I can see the kids in Indiana, and Georgia, and Texas. They appreciate what I do for them. I know they think about me, and that makes me feel good."

Halftown left Brunswick in 1998, and retired from his Philadelphia television program the next year. At the time he'd been on the air forty-nine years—a record for a children's show. Chief Halftown died in 2003.

"I know I'm a gimmick," he once said. "Yet I feel my gimmick promotes good. I'm able to make children happy. Isn't that a nice job, making children happy?"

"*Nya-wey*, Chief." Or as we Later Americans would say, "Thank you."

The Schalk Team Tournament

(December 2013)
For thirty years, the finest teams in bowling gathered in Chicago on a single weekend each January. They came to shoot in the Ray Schalk Holiday Team Tournament.

Schalk had been a hall of fame catcher with the Chicago White Sox. In 1928, as his baseball career was winding down, he went into the bowling business on the city's South Side. The grand opening of Stevenson & Schalk Recreation was highlighted by a team tournament that drew 45 entries.

By 1937 Schalk had become proprietor of Beverly Recreation. To promote his new center, he staged a team sweepstakes that January. The event attracted nearly 100 teams, and became an annual affair.

Schalk advertised his tournament as "a fair, neutral test." Instead of the usual three games, his event was four games. The bowlers also switched lanes after each game. To attract out-of-town entries, Schalk was making sure the Chicago teams didn't have a home-house advantage. Sometimes he went overboard. "When I bowled with the [Detroit] Stroh's we always had an easy shot at the Schalk," Joe Norris remembered. "But when I started bowling with Chicago teams, it was like bowling the Petersen." Through the years, most of the Schalk winners came from outside Chicago.

In 1942 the tournament moved to Schalk's newest establishment, Evergreen Towers Bowl. The country had just entered World War II, and the event endured four lean years. But peace brought a rebound. Entries topped 100 teams, with first prize reaching $1,000. With all those topflight bowlers in town for the Schalk, other Chicago proprietors began scheduling singles sweepers on the same January weekend. Two of these classics, the Jerry Peck and the Dom DeVito, both became successful events in their own right.

Michigan teams dominated the immediate postwar Schalk. From 1946 through 1952 the Stroh's and the E&Bs usually took home the top prize. In 1949 a pickup team sponsored by Sharkey Recreation of Battle Creek won the event. They were paced by an eighteen-year-old youngster whom *Bowlers Journal* pegged as a future star—Harry Smith.

The Schalk prosperity was marred by one harrowing incident. In 1948 gunmen invaded Evergreen Towers, locked Schalk and his staff in a storeroom, and stole $2500 from the safe. They then made their escape in Schalk's new Packard.

Still, most of the tales coming out of the Schalk were light-hearted. One incident involved Carmen Salvino and Joe Norris, then teammates. Norris lived near Evergreen Towers, and Salvino dropped in at his home on the way to the tournament. As usual, Salvino grabbed a bottle of 7-Up from Norris's fridge, popped the top, and chugged it. Then he spit it out. The bottle was filled with vinegar.

After he calmed down, Salvino asked how Norris had managed to sabotage the exact bottle that Salvino had picked. "That was easy," Norris replied. "I put the vinegar in all the bottles."

The 1950s are considered bowling's great team era. During this time the Schalk reached its peak. Fans jammed Evergreen Towers to see the world's best bowlers in action. Admission was free, with a collection for charity being taken up. Falstaff Beer of St. Louis won the Schalk four times in five years, beginning in 1957. Though the rival St. Louis Budweisers are generally conceded to be the era's top team, the Buds never won the Schalk.

With the rise of the PBA Tour in the 1960s, high-level team competition declined. Entries to the Schalk fell off, and the tournament became little more than a local Chicago event. The final edition was rolled in 1966. And fittingly, the winner of that last Ray Schalk Holiday Team Tournament was the Tony Piet Pontiac team of Chicago—a team sponsored by a onetime White Sox infielder.

Billy Hardwick, R.I.P.

(January 2014)
The late Billy Hardwick was recognized as one of the greatest bowlers of all time. In 1999 *Bowlers Journal* ranked him #19 on the list of twentieth

century performers. That same year *Bowling* magazine selected him for its twenty-man Millennium team. The 2009 book *50 Greatest Players in PBA History* had Hardwick at #12.

But the historical significance of Hardwick's career is often overlooked. The men who won the early pro events were usually familiar names from the great team era—Dick Weber, Don Carter, Harry Smith, Joe Joseph, and so on. Only rarely would an unknown bowler break through and pick off a tournament. Hardwick was the PBA's first homegrown star.

He won his first title at Mobile in March 1963. In August he won at Phoenix, and two weeks later breezed home at Los Angeles with a record score. He capped the year in November with the PBA National Championship. It was a symbolic changing of the guard. Though nobody realized it at the time, 1962 had been Don Carter's last great year. In 1963 the top man was that new kid on the block, Billy Hardwick.

I was in high school then. My friends and I identified with Hardwick, who'd come from nowhere and reached the pinnacle of bowling. He was only five or six years older than us. He was almost like a big brother. And the wonderful thing about Hardwick was that he didn't bowl the way a pro was supposed to! The bowlers we watched on TV—except for Carter—seemed to radiate power. Their slashing hooks sent the pins flying in five or six directions.

Hardwick was nothing like that. Because of an arthritic condition in his hand, he gripped the ball with his index and middle fingers. Going to the line, he didn't swing the ball as much as he carried it. Then, when he pushed his shot onto the lane, he often fell onto his right hand to regain his balance. His style wasn't pretty. His shot wasn't strong. All Hardwick did was put the ball in the same place, frame after frame, and topple over the pins. That was the lesson he taught.

Hardwick bagged three more PBA titles in 1964, and added two ABC eagles for good measure. He continued to shine through the rest of the 1960s. He won the Tournament of Champions, the All-Star, more PBA events, and was twice elected Bowler of the Year.

Then came a six-year dry spell. By the time Hardwick won at Toledo in 1976, his victory carried an element of nostalgia. The next week he led the Tournament of Champions going into the final match, only to be beaten by a long-haired 21-year-old rookie named Marshall Holman.

Hardwick retired from the tour the following year. He became a bowling proprietor, and was operating Billy Hardwick's All-Star Lanes in Memphis at the time of his death this past November 16.

I finally met Billy Hardwick at Mort Luby's retirement party in 2003. Actually, my wife, Terri, met him first. She had just gotten a glass of wine when Billy walked up to her. He introduced himself and complimented her on the necklace she was wearing. Then he said he'd like to buy it for his wife.

Terri had no idea who Billy Hardwick was. All she knew was that he was very polite, but really wanted to get the necklace. She finally gave in and sold it to him. With that, Billy pulled out his cell phone and called his wife. "Honey," he said into the phone. "You've got to thank this nice lady Terri for the gift I just bought you."

We both spent much of the evening with Billy, and had a wonderful time. Afterward I asked Terri for her impression of Billy Hardwick. "A very charming, funny man," she said. "But very determined." Could any athlete have a better epitaph?

Billy Hardwick in 1963, already a star at 22, contemplating a bright future.

The Longest Longshots

(July 2014)
In 1946, after a four-year intermission for World War II, the ABC Tournament was resuming in Buffalo. Local bowlers filled the first few weeks. The early morning Doubles squad on the tournament's seventh day—Wednesday, March 20—featured lower-average Boosters. Though the Boosters had a special prize list for the Team event, in the Doubles they were competing against everyone else, a record 12,780 duos.

Henry Kmidowski was scheduled on that squad. He was forty-two years old and carried a 173 average. He'd made his ABC debut with a Booster team the night before. His scores hadn't been anything special. Now Henry was waiting for his partner, John Gworek. John was a year older and a pin higher in average than Henry. This was John's second ABC. Both men had jobs at the General Mills plant, though John was on the night shift and coming directly from work.

John finally arrived. The partners changed shoes, grabbed their balls, and walked out onto the lanes with the rest of the bowlers. They were relaxed, and their opening scores showed it—198 for John, 199 for Henry. Not bad for a couple of Boosters.

John tailed off to 185 the second game. But Henry rolled 234. So for two games they had more than 800 pins. All they had to do was bowl average the last game, and they'd probably cash.

Leading off the third game, John left the 5–7 split. Well, reality was setting in. Without much bother he ran up to the line, tossed his ball out—and picked up the split! Henry followed with a strike. Now the boys were charged up. They both struck in the second frame. And in the third. And in the fourth. John, the ABC "veteran," kept encouraging his partner. "Let's get some more," he said. "We've got it going, let's see what we can do."

Fifth frame, and again they both struck. John struck in the sixth. After his opening conversion, he now had a five-bagger. Henry already had five strikes. His legs were shaking as he went for six. His ball skidded down the lane, and he left the 5–7.

How many times has a bowler left a split that a teammate converted earlier in the game? And doesn't the teammate say "I showed you how to do it, pick it up"? But does it ever really work out that way? Today it did. Henry smartly slid the 5-pin into the 7-pin for the spare.

Seventh frame. Another strike for John. Henry left a 10-pin, his toughest spare. Still shaking, he converted it. Just like that the tension broke, and he was calm again. Both men struck in the eighth and ninth. John opened the tenth with a strike, running his string to nine in a row. He then left a 10-pin and picked it up for 279. Henry closed with a double and eight pins for 265. Only when they'd finished did John and Henry learn they had set a tournament record with a 544 Doubles game. Their score would remain on the books for thirty years, until topped by pros Tommy Hudson and Les Zikes.

Both Gworek and Kmidowski had rolled their personal-best series, 662 and 698 respectively. Their 1360 put them on top of the Doubles.

Still, the tournament had two months to go, and they'd surely be knocked down a few rungs. Who ever heard of a couple of 170-average Boosters winning an ABC championship?

But the magic held. When the tournament ended on May 14, John and Henry had their eagles. "We never figured we were anything more than a couple of mediocre bowlers," John later said. "[But] it gives you a warm feeling when you're lucky enough to do something outstanding."

Henry Kmidowski died in 1979, John Gworek in 1992. Their legacy is simple, yet profound—in a bowling tournament, anything can happen.

The Man in the Picture

(August 2014)
More than forty years afterward, Don Johnson is most famous for one picture. The setting is the final ball of the final match at the 1970 Firestone Tournament of Champions. Johnson has just left a 10-pin after stringing the first eleven strikes, costing him a $10,000 bonus for a televised perfect game. Now he lies face down and dejected on the approach.

It's a helluva way to remember Don Johnson. Because he was one helluva bowler.

Indiana-born in the town of Kokomo in 1940, he would become known as The Kokomo Kid, or simply Koko. But that was in the future. Johnson went out on tour in 1962, when he wasn't yet ready, and cashed for all of $900.

In those early years he was best-known for his shaggy Beatles hair style. This ran counter to the button-down corporate look the PBA wished to project. Johnson was threatened with suspension, so he grudgingly got a crew cut. To avoid future flaps, tour chief Eddie Elias decided to form a new PBA Image Committee—and put Johnson in charge.

Johnson won his first title at the 1964 Denver Open. His second victory came at Portland in 1966. That began a string of twelve straight years in which he'd capture at least one event. In an era when 300 games were rare, he also ran off a streak of eleven years with at least one perfect game.

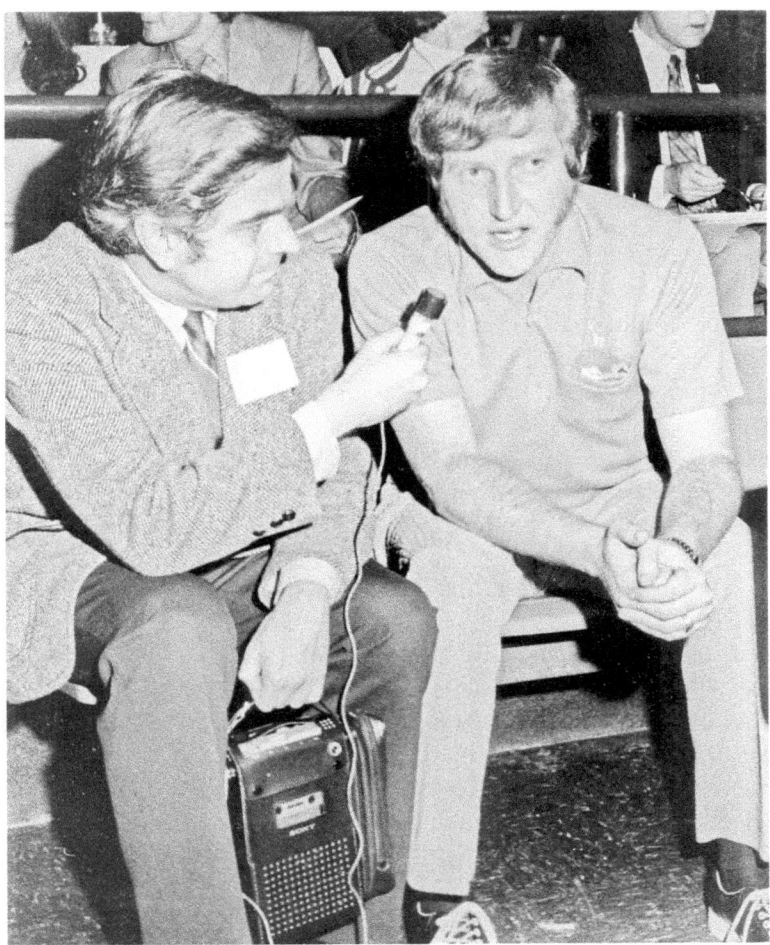

Don Johnson sits for an interview during his early, days on the Tour. Photographs like this—featuring Johnson's shaggy haircut—prompted PBA chief Eddie Elias to form an Image Committee.

The Firestone was then the richest event on tour, climaxing thirteen weeks of nationally televised finals. Maybe Johnson got geared up for the big event. Maybe Riviera Lanes simply matched his game. For five years Koko was as regular a presence on the Firestone telecast as Chris Schenkel and Billy Welu, the television announcers—1967—qualified second, tied Jim Stefanich in title match, lost roll-off. In 1968—qualified fifth, advanced to title match, lost to Dave Davis. 1969—qualified fifth, lost to Wayne Zahn in opening match. In 1970—led qualifying and defeated Dick Ritger for championship, 299–268. In 1971—qualified third, advanced to title match, lost to Johnny Petraglia.

Johnson was at his peak. He was named an All American five times. He was elected Bowler of the Year two seasons in a row. He won a second major, the 1972 U.S. Open. He won three ABC championships.

He was changing the way the game was played, too. Bowlers had been using black, hard rubber balls since the days of the gas-lit saloon alleys. Johnson's weapon of choice was a caramel-colored plastic ball. Seeing this week after week on TV made an impression on the 150-shooters. If the best bowler in the world had ditched the old hockey puck, why shouldn't I do the same?

Competition got stronger as the 1970s rolled on. Now Johnson was winning less often. In 1976 he teamed with Paul Colwell to take the PBA Doubles Classic, and tie Dick Weber's record of 25 career titles. He bagged #26 the following year in grand fashion, advancing from fifth place through the television finals to beat Earl Anthony in the championship match.

Johnson would win no more titles. Experimenting with a longer grip led to a pinched nerve in his thumb, resulting in unpredictable, excruciating pain. His game became "embarrassing," to use his own word. "It's tough to climb to the top of the mountain," he told an interviewer in 1981. "However, once you've been there, it's tougher coming down the other side."

He had retired from the Tour by then. Settling in Las Vegas, he worked as an instructor. He bowled a few senior events, without much success. When he died of a heart attack in 2003, to many younger bowlers Don Johnson was only a name in the record book.

Or more accurately, an iconic picture. "I would have liked that $10,000," he once mused. "But that 10-pin made me famous." Perhaps so. But to repeat the simple truth—Don Johnson was one helluva bowler.

Allie and Orf and Allison and Some Others

(January 2015)
Many of us have signed the petition asking that Glenn Allison's 900

series be given official recognition. For perspective, let's look at the history of high-series records.

In 1908 A.C. Jellison of St. Louis became the first person to win an American Bowling Congress award for a 300 game. Jellison's 826 series was also the highest reported three-game set that year. However, ABC did not give out high series awards yet. Though many leagues rolled three-game matches in 1908, many did not. In fact, most record books of the era listed the best series as the 1628 six-game total rolled by Lee Johns in 1910.

As the three-game league match became standard, Jellison's 826 gradually gained recognition as the highest-ever series. In 1930 it was topped by another St. Louis bowler, future Hall of Famer Otto Stein, with 844. Shortly afterward, ABC issued a statement saying Stein's score was the "real record" for a three-game set.

Yet there were still no high-series awards. Stein's 844 earned him nothing more than whatever he made in pot-games that night. Finally, in 1933, ABC began giving out an annual gold medal for the highest three-game series, and two bowlers—Virgil Gibbs of Kansas City and Mitzi Weinstein of St. Louis—set a new record, each with 847.

The next year Ray Holmes pushed the mark up to 853. Holmes was yet another St. Louis bowler, and there was muttering about the easy conditions in that city. Of course, with the Depression in its depth and many proprietors using cracked and light-weight pins, scores were up all over. In 1937 a Cleveland bowler broke the Missouri monopoly, when Harvey Braatz shot 864. Then came the big one.

The date was October 25, 1939. The place was Lockport, New York. The bowler was Allie Brandt. The scores were 297–289–300–886.

Brandt's 886 was a public relations bonanza for bowling. He was a small man, 5-foot-5 and 125 pounds. His size made the point that you didn't have to be a muscle-bound giant to succeed on the lanes. For years, nearly every book about bowling featured a picture of the all-time record holder, "Little Allie Brandt."

Brandt's 886 was also a personal bonanza. In 1960 he was elected to the Bowling Hall of Fame. Brandt won a few tournaments, finished second in the All-Star, and had a second-place at the ABC. It's a fine resume, but no better than Bob Chase—except for that 886.

As the decades passed, 886 became bowling's magic number, the record that might never be broken. I even used 8–8–6 as the combination lock on my first briefcase. The closest anyone came was 876, rolled by Carl Wilsing in 1966.

The biggest threat to Brandt's record came from Ray Orf of St. Louis. In fact, Orf actually topped the score with an 890 series on February 6, 1972. ABC rejected the 890, Orf went to court, and eventually received a settlement. Meanwhile, later in 1972, John Wilcox, Jr., rolled an 885 series—which ABC certified. Allie Brandt remained atop the heap, though scores in the 870s were starting to go up on the board. Allison's 900, in July 1982, was the culmination of this upward trend. Sooner or later, someone was going to displace Little Allie.

Allie Brandt died on April 17, 1982. His 886 was tied by Pat Landry in 1988. In 1989 Tom Jordan rolled an 899 series, and was recognized as a new record by ABC. In more recent times, of course, there has been something like two dozen sanctioned 900 series.

I don't know how thorough the lane inspection was in 1939, when Brandt's 886 was certified. I don't know whether the inspection of Allison's lanes was more stringent—or, for that matter, the inspection of Orf's lanes. I don't know whether sentiment for Little Allie affected the rejection of their scores. But I do know it's time to give Ray Orf and Glenn Allison their due.

The National Bowling League

(May-June-July-August 2015)
Almost anyone with an interest in bowling history has heard of the National Bowling League. The NBL was an intercity league of five-man teams, based on the model of major league baseball, playing in purpose-built arenas on a six-month-long schedule. Today the whole concept seems outlandish. But to understand how the idea seemed plausible, you have to understand the temper of the times, more than a half-century ago.

In 1961 bowling was booming. In the past five years, the number of bowling centers had grown 25 percent. Brunswick and AMF were the hot stocks on the New York exchange. All-star athletic banquets always featured at least one bowler. During the bowling season, most metropolitan newspapers ran bowling news several times a week. Some of the larger dailies even had a bowling editor.

Two statistics sum up bowling's prosperity. In 1961 Therm Gibson won $76,000 for rolling six straight strikes on the *Jackpot Bowling* television show, making more money in four minutes than Mickey Mantle earned playing an entire season in the Yankee outfield. And also in 1961, out of an adult population of 110 million Americans, 6.5 million bowled in sanctioned leagues—*1 out of every 17* men and women. So in 1961, the idea of a National Bowling League was not so outlandish at all.

Plans for an intercity bowling league had been floated as early as 1904, and there'd already been a few such leagues on a limited, regional basis. But the man who succeeded in making the old dream a reality—at least for a while—was a Los Angeles proprietor named Leonard Homel. In 1959 Homel put together a 54-page prospectus detailing plans for a national pro league, then ran a blind ad in *The Wall Street Journal* seeking investors for "a new and unusual bowling promotion." He received more than 100 replies, most of them enthusiastic. Yet nobody was ready to put up any money.

Then, in January 1960, *Bowlers Journal* ran a story by Don Snyder about the proposed league. That got the bowling world talking. The next month Homel held an organizational meeting in Chicago. After listening to Homel's presentation and grilling him on details, seven investors forked over $5,000 each for NBL franchises. The initial roster of cities was Chicago, Los Angeles, Dallas, Fort Worth, San Antonio, Omaha, and Raleigh, North Carolina. Homel was elected league president.

The NBL planned to launch in September 1961. The next eighteen months were a busy time. More meetings were held. New investors bought in, and some of the original members dropped out. Dick Charles, an Omaha sportscaster, was hired as league commissioner. As interest in the venture grew, the price of a franchise rose to $50,000.

The league held a player draft at Omaha in July 1960. By now there were twelve franchises. Miami went first, and picked Billy Welu. The process continued through thirty rounds. With 360 slots available, nearly every bowler of some reputation was selected. The draft closed with New York picking a bowling proprietor, Yankee catcher Yogi Berra.

The #1 pick—Billy Welu—surprised many people. In 1960 Don Carter was the most famous bowler in the world. Why wasn't he picked first? This highlights one of the main problems facing the NBL

In 1960 the Professional Bowlers Association was brand new, and operating a limited schedule of tournaments. Carter and the other elite bowlers had salaried positions on locally sponsored five-man teams. Many had exhibition contracts with equipment manufacturers as well.

Though the NBL had advertised a minimum player salary of $6,000, Carter already had security, and one writer speculated it would take at least $40,000 for the bowler to join the new league. Still, the Carter-name had magic, and Fort Worth made him the #2 pick.

The league signed its first player on September 5. Fred Riccilli was a 39-year-old Californian whose main claim to fame was winning the 1952 Petersen Classic. He'd also spent a year with the Stroh's Beer team in Detroit, capturing the Michigan Match Game championship during his hitch. His contract with Los Angeles was for $10,000.

The NBL had a year to go until its planned September 1961 opener. Once Riccilli's name was on a contract, other bowlers began to sign on. Steve Nagy became the first "name" star to join the league, securing a $20,000 pact as captain of the L.A. team. Nagy's crony Buzz Fazio did even better. Omaha gave Fazio $24,000 and a rent-free luxury apartment.

Bowler of the Year Ed Lubanski signed up for the league when Pfeiffer Beer dropped sponsorship of his team. Lubanski and Pfeiffer teammate Billy Golembiewski would now bowl for Detroit in the NBL. The other Pfeiffers—Joe Joseph, Bob Hitt, and Bob Kwolek—quickly caught on with other NBL teams.

Still, Don Carter and most of the St. Louis stars remained outside the fold. They preferred to watch and wait. Fort Worth offered Carter a contract for $1,000 a week, a piece of ownership, a cut of the gate, and half-interest in a goat farm. Carter turned down the deal.

The NBL wanted to advertise its status as "big-league." Nothing could do that better than purpose-built arenas with ample spectator seating. In November Commissioner Dick Charles announced that the twelve franchise-holders would have sites ready and construction underway by the following March.

Different cities came up with different types of facilities. Kansas City and Omaha installed four lanes in shuttered theaters. Fort Worth and Fresno built stand-alone arenas. Dallas and Detroit constructed large commercial bowling centers, with the intimate NBL stadium as an annex. League president Leonard Homel tacked an arena onto his existing L.A. establishment. A plan to put New York's lanes in Grand Central Terminal was vetoed by the city, and the team built in New Jersey instead.

The seating capacity of the arenas ranged from 1,800 to 3,200. The All-Star Tournament had attracted crowds of over 5,000 spectators, so the NBL had reason to believe they might fill their stands. However,

A typical crowd at a late-season National Bowling League match. The site is New York Gladiator Arena in Totowa, New Jersey.

no matter how large the live gate, the new league was counting on the power of television.

Bowling was all over the tube in 1960. *Championship Bowling* was the most prominent of several syndicated series, and there was that prime-time, national network program, *Jackpot Bowling*. In addition, every "bowling city" had its own local show. The NBL hired a consultant to secure a television contract. League officials talked of having a nationally televised Game of the Week, similar to baseball. The season would climax with the NBL World Series between the two divisional champions, followed by an individual tournament paying $100,000 to the winner.

But the NBL wasn't the only one going after television dollars. PBA chief Eddie Elias had initially welcomed the new league. Now there were reports that Elias was advising his members to steer clear of the NBL. In the end, the PBA got the vital network contract, and the NBL didn't.

Meanwhile, the league came up with an innovative way of deciding matches. Traditional scoring was retained. However, teams would be awarded points based on individual matches, as well as five-man game totals. There would also be bonus points for high individual scores. At the end of the night, the team with the most points would get a "Win" in the league standings.

In March 1961 the NBL dropped two franchises for failing to meet deadlines. There were now ten teams—Dallas Broncos, Detroit Thunderbirds, Fort Worth Panthers, Fresno Bombers, Kansas City Stars, Los Angeles Toros, New York Gladiators, Omaha Packers, San Antonio Cavaliers, and Twin Cities Skippers.

Finally, it was time to bowl. The National Bowling League staged its first exhibition match at Meadowbrook Lanes in Fort Worth on May 22, 1961. About 500 people turned out to watch Dallas beat Fort Worth. The three-game format seemed to drag, so all future matches would be two games.

A second exhibition was held at Kansas City on July 24. Rolling in their home arena at the Midland Theatre, the Kansas City Stars defeated an all-star squad drawn from the other nine teams. A pilot video was made, to help sell the league.

The NBL also issued its final schedule. Opening Day was pushed back to October 13. After that the teams bowled five nights a week through the end of April, with breaks for the World's Invitational and All-Star tournaments. The season concluded with the Eastern and Western division winners meeting in the World Series.

Now the league faced a major crisis. The San Antonio franchise lost its backer, leaving the team without a stadium. The rest of the owners chipped in to cover the players' salaries, and all San Antonio matches were rescheduled as away games.

Bowlers Journal devoted thirty-six pages of its October 1961 issue to the NBL, with founder/president Leonard Homel on the cover. Mort Luby, Jr.'s lead editorial was titled, "The NBL Can Succeed, So Give It a Chance!" Don Snyder wrote an article on the league's "day of reckoning," and Fresno captain Bill Bunetta sat for an interview. Dallas owner Curtis Sanford was profiled in a major feature. There were rosters, schedules, a primer on NBL scoring, and numerous photos. The magazine also polled eleven bowling experts about the NBL's chances. They hoped that the league would be a success—but most thought it would fail.

As it happened, the regular NBL season opened with a single match at Dallas on October 12. The hometown Broncos trounced the visiting New York Gladiators 22–3, before an announced crowd of 2,200. The rest of the league began play the following night. Rather ominously, that was Friday the Thirteenth.

While fans had trouble getting used to the NBL's point system, the league's "wild card" proved popular. Under that rule, a team could bring in a sub to make a single shot—for instance, a lefty who might have a better chance at converting a particular split. When the sub came through in the clutch, there was no more dramatic moment.

The NBL said it was selling fun, so fans were encouraged to be lively, and heckle visiting teams. The bowlers didn't appreciate that. Working on a string of strikes, Ed Lubanski refused to continue until some loudmouths were silenced. The men shut up, and Lubanski went on to roll a perfect game. In a famous incident, Carmen Salvino climbed into the stands to reason with an obnoxious spectator.

By mid–November NBL officials knew they were in trouble. With construction costs, player salaries, travel expenses, and other incidentals, the investors had sunk close to $14 million into the venture. They still had no television contract. And after the initial euphoria, attendance was way down. Detroit had the top turnout, with an average attendance of 1,221. Yet most teams were attracting less than a 1,000 fans for a match. Fresno had the lowest attendance, with an average gate of only 404.

High ticket prices were partly to blame. The best NBL seats went for $3.00, about the same as a box seat at a major league baseball game. But bowling fans had never paid that much to watch their sport. For that matter, even the cheaper seats at NBL matches weren't being filled.

Publicity was lacking, too. On the way in from an airport, Commissioner Dick Charles routinely asked his cab driver about the local NBL team. None of the cabbies had even heard of the league. Barely two months into the schedule, a number of teams were ready to fold.

The owners met to discuss the future of the struggling circuit on December 9, 1961. Afterward, Commissioner Charles denied the Fresno team would be dropped. "We think we're trudging along merrily," he said. "We have every confidence we ultimately will be successful."

Brave words. Just a week later, the NBL announced that the Omaha and San Antonio teams were being cut loose. Then Kansas City quit. But perhaps the biggest blow came on January 15 of the new year, when Los Angeles surrendered.

L.A. was Leonard Homel's team—Leonard Homel, founder and president of the league. His Toros were drawing less than 500 people a match, not nearly enough to sustain the franchise. There were tears in Homel's eyes as he made his farewell.

Now there were six. Still, the remaining owners were determined to see things through to the finish of the season. Perhaps then a television contract would pump in fresh cash.

With only six teams left, the league's two divisions were consolidated into one. The NBL also adopted a split-season schedule. The Detroit team had the best won-lost record, so they were declared winners of the first half. At the end of the season, they'd meet the winners of the second half in the World Series. The schedule was also streamlined. League play was cut to three matches over two nights—a doubleheader on Sunday, and a single match on Monday. Commissioner Charles said that the change would allow more PBA bowlers to join the NBL.

And the belt-tightening went on. Player salaries were trimmed to $100 a week, causing Johnny King of Fresno and other stars to quit. Some teams had to bring in local bowlers to fill out their roster. On March 3 Charles himself was axed, with the league's attorney taking on the dual job of commissioner.

Ticket prices had already been slashed. By now the league was giving away free tickets on the slightest pretext—anything to fill the empty seats. Some teams tried staging half-time shows between games. Dallas brought in a seven-piece jazz band. Another team featured a bowling chimp.

Nothing worked. Attendance continued to slide. At one match, Mort Luby, Jr., counted "ten lonely fans" in the entire arena. In those final weeks, many of the bowlers seemed to give up, too. The matches had the intensity of a pre-teen birthday party.

The NBL staggered on to the finish line. The Twin Cities Skippers won the second half-season, and faced off against the Detroit Thunderbirds on May 5–6. The entire best-of-five series was rolled in Detroit's home arena. It was cheaper that way.

The Thunderbirds made quick work of the Skippers. They swept the first three two-game matches to become the 1961–62 NBL champions. The winners split a purse of $2,500, while the losers took home $1,500. A Detroit station televised the final match.

You may have noticed that bowling scores haven't been mentioned much in this story. That's because NBL statistics have been difficult to find—for one thing, Detroit newspapers were on strike during the league's World Series—and different sources give different information. So the following stats are not necessarily the final word. Three NBL bowlers rolled perfect games—Ed Lubanski (Detroit), Dale Seavoy (Detroit), Jim St. John (Twin Cities). Highest two-game series was 276–290–566, registered by Earl Johnson (Twin Cities). Most sources credit St. John with the high individual average, 221 over 132 games.

In the aftermath of the World Series, league owners said they'd be back for a second season. The elusive television contract would be signed any day now. But on July 9, the NBL officially gave up the ghost.

Fifty-some years later, the most prominent relic of the National Bowling League is Thunderbowl Lanes and its arena, in the Detroit suburb of Allen Park. Drop in some time—and then consider what might have been.

Billy Durant's Bowling Fling

(November 2015)
William Crapo Durant earned his place in history as the founder of General Motors. What's less well-known is his bowling connection.

Born into a wealthy New England family in 1861, Billy Durant was a visionary. He got into the infant auto business in 1904. Convinced of the industry's future, in 1908 he put together a collection of small companies to form GM. But as it turned out, Durant was more promoter than administrator. He was twice forced out of the GM presidency, and lost his fortune in the 1929 stock market crash. By the 1930s he was getting by on a small pension from the giant corporation he'd founded.

Quiet retirement didn't appeal to Billy Durant. He had built GM into an industrial powerhouse in Flint, Michigan. In 1940 he returned there to launch a new business—a bowling alley. After scouting out a number of properties, Durant settled on an abandoned garage on North Saginaw Street, not far from the Buick plant he'd once bossed. He began converting it into an eighteen-lane bowling center. No one knew where he'd gotten the money for the venture.

Durant supervised the smallest construction details. He measured the location of lockers and spectator seats, swept the floors, and took a hammer or saw in hand when necessary. He personally hired each employee, down to the lowliest pinboy. He wanted his staff to feel they were a vital part of the business.

North Flint Recreation opened that spring. The thousands of people who turned out for the festivities found a bowling alley different from any they'd seen before. The place was air-conditioned, and it was spotless. The walls were cream-colored, with deep blue and red appointments. And there was no bar! After the amazed public finally left, Durant threw a party for the pinboys.

The "bowling without beer" angle captivated the news media. In the succeeding months reporters journeyed to Flint to sound out the old wizard on his latest plans to recoup his fortune. They were not disappointed.

"Bowling has a noble tradition," Durant told them, "requiring a delicate coordination of brain and muscle." The sport's problem was its disreputable image. Correct this condition, and the opportunities were boundless. "Clean recreation for the ladies, for their daughters, for the whole family will attract greater and greater crowds," he said. "I'd like to see [bowling] in an entirely different atmosphere and on a higher plane than it has always been considered." And North Flint Recreation was only the first step.

Durant had confounded skeptics who'd said the automobile would always remain an expensive curiosity. He saw no reason why bowling should be satisfied with a limited market. He envisioned "a chain of recreation centers for clean sports in cities throughout the United States." He'd put fifty bowling palaces in operation. Reflecting his family friendly principle, some of them would be managed by women. Reflecting his automotive background, each of them would have a parking lot.

Meanwhile, he continued to spruce up North Flint Recreation. A few months after the bowling center launched, he opened a lunchroom next door. Besides the counter service, there was another innovation—a drive-through window. Durant himself often took turns at the grill, preparing his special hamburger recipe.

Durant was pushing eighty when got into the bowling business. Though his bold talk may have been simply an old man's dreams, his past record showed that he could never be counted out. This time, it wasn't to be. The U.S. entered World War II in December 1941, and any business expansion was halted for the duration. The next year Durant suffered a stroke. He remained a semi-invalid until his death in 1947.

North Flint Recreation closed its doors many years ago. Yet Billy Durant is still remembered fondly in Flint. In 2013 the city unveiled a statue of its favorite adopted son in a downtown plaza. Has any other bowling proprietor been so honored?

The Shanghai Bowling Congress

(December 2015)
In 1936 bowling was rebounding from the Depression. The American Bowling Congress was expanding into the Pacific Coast states, the Territory of Hawaii, and Quebec province in Canada. That September ABC received another request to affiliate—from the bowlers of Shanghai, China.

Though Shanghai had no commercial bowling centers, a number of private clubs had their own lanes. A local league had been running since 1929. After reading about the recent International Tournament in Germany, the Shanghai bowlers had decided to join ABC.

A packet of materials was immediately sent from ABC headquarters in Milwaukee to George Friedgen, the American businessman who served as president of the Shanghai Bowling Congress and its Shanghai Ten Pin League. Mail traveled slowly in 1936, especially when it was going halfway around the world. It wasn't until November that the completed sanction forms made it back to Milwaukee.

There'd been suspicion that the Shanghai Bowling Congress was an elaborate prank—who'd ever heard of bowling alleys in China? So Friedgen made sure that the documents he returned carried the seal and signature of the U.S. Consul General. That convinced ABC this really was a serious application. The official sanction was granted in January 1937.

Shanghai bowlers normally rolled a three-month season, from January through early April. There were five venues with a combined total of twenty-one lanes. Columbia Country Club was the largest, with six lanes. The American Club, the Foreign Y.M.C.A., and the Shanghai Race Club each had four lanes. The three lanes at the International Club accounted for the rest.

The Shanghai Ten Pin League was actually two leagues—the A-Division for the better bowlers, and the B-Division for the rest. In 1937 thirteen teams bowled. Each of the five venues fielded one A-team and one B-team. The remaining three teams were made up of men from the nearby U.S. Marine installation. Within a division, a pair of teams faced off against each other twice, once in each house.

Because the competition was conducted in private clubs, only members of those clubs—and the invited Marines—bowled in the league. Most of the bowlers were American. Still, in a letter to ABC,

Friedgen noted that "seven different nationalities" were represented in the league. He also said that the younger Chinese men were showing an aptitude for the game.

The league season ended in April, and was immediately followed by a tournament. Fifty men rolled in the Team, Doubles, and Singles events. A women's tournament was held at the same time.

The scoring of the Shanghai bowlers was modest. C.C. Squires of the A-Division champ Columbia Country Club team posted the top league average, 180. The league high game and high series were 248 and 686. However, in the post-season tournament, G.K. Kleffel rolled a 279, a new "all-China" record.

The Shanghai Bowling Congress concluded its first ABC-sanctioned season with a banquet at the Columbia Country Club on April 16. One-hundred-twenty people attended. The guest of honor was Colonel Charles Price, commander of the U.S. Marine battalions, who passed out the awards. One of the bowlers honored was Elsie Soong, who shared the women's Doubles championship. The *ABC Bulletin* reported that this was "probably the first time in bowling history that a Chinese lady has won an award in tenpin competition." Though it wasn't mentioned in the story, Elsie Soong was the sister of Madame Chiang Kai-shek, China's "First Lady."

Pleased with the results of their successful season, the Shanghai bowlers planned to expand, adding a team of sailors from the U.S.S. *Augusta*. However, outside events intervened. In August the Japanese army attacked Shanghai. After three months of fighting Chinese forces withdrew, abandoning the city to the invader. Though the Shanghai Bowling Congress announced it would continue operations during the occupation, it soon disbanded. For the time being, tenpin bowling was dead in China.

The Pleasure of His Company

(January 2016)
Tom Hennessey was the kind of guy you'd want to have on your bowling team. "He was a comic, he defused the tension, he was just fun to bowl with," said Tony Lindemann, his Stroh's teammate. "Tommy was one

of a kind, he kept you loose," said Dick Weber, his Budweiser teammate. Besides that, Hennessey was a great bowler. "He had a tremendous amount of talent," said Don Carter. "I think he was one of the most underrated players in the game."

Born in St. Louis in 1925, Hennessey grew up on the Illinois side of the Mississippi, in Granite City, where his father was a steelworker. He bowled his first game wearing a tuxedo after a high school dance. Soon afterward, he dropped out of school and went to work.

He also worked on his bowling. By 1948 Hennessey was back across the river and leading the St. Louis Classic League in average. That led to a spot on the Hermann Undertakers team, and the start of a lifelong friendship with Carter, another Hermann recruit.

Hennessey spent three seasons with the Hermanns, and another with the Ziern Antiques. He began getting some national notice, winning the Petersen Classic, finish fifth in the All-Star Tournament, then nearly winning the Petersen a second time. In 1952 he was recruited by the Stroh's Beer team of Detroit.

The Detroit years were good. The Stroh's were the best team in bowling, the BPAA Team Match Game champions. Hennessey himself was named King of Detroit Bowlers in 1956. But that same summer, when he was offered a contract with the Budweiser Beer team in St. Louis, he returned home.

On the Buds he joined his old teammates Carter, Ray Bluth, Pat Patterson, and Whitey Harris, and the new kid from Indiana, Dick Weber. With the addition of Hennessey (and later Bill Lillard), the Buds assumed the status of bowling's top team—then and forever.

While they were winning championships and setting scoring records, the Buds had fun. Hennessey was the chief agitator. There are dozens of stories, ranging from spontaneous shaving-cream battles to elaborately staged pranks. To select just one tale, there was the time Hennessey began receiving secret rings, model airplane kits, treasure maps, and other toys in the mail. He soon determined Weber was the man behind the gag. So Hennessey went to the local newsstand, pulled out subscription cards from a couple dozen magazines, and mailed them in with Weber's name. When the magazines started arriving, that caused some excitement in the Weber home—since some of them were "men's magazines."

Beginning with his move to the Buds, Hennessey was named an All American four straight times. He won the BPAA Doubles with Carter twice, and took three Southern Match Game titles, a semi-major championship in pre–PBA days. After he won the 1958 Masters, Mort Luby, Jr., wrote that Hennessey was "the second-best bowler in the world," second only to Carter.

Then, in 1961, Budweiser dropped its sponsorship. The team stayed together a few more years as the Don Carter Bowling Gloves, but big-time bowling was transitioning into an individual sport. Though

"The second-best bowler in the world": Tom Hennessey in 1958, with the second of his three Southern Match Game Championship trophies.

Hennessey won three PBA titles during the Tour's first few years, his game was going into a long decline.

He missed the camaraderie of five-man play. Concentrating on the team had kept him relaxed and made him a better bowler. And as he later admitted, he began drinking too much. "I'd start out with a bad block in a PBA tournament and I'd go to the bar," he said. "I had opportunities. I drank them away."

There's not much to be said about Tom Hennessey's later years. When he died in 2001, his passing brought forth memories of his glory days, when the stocky little guy with the crew cut was blasting the pins, and had the smoothest style and biggest smile in bowling. So let's leave it with that.

Undefeated Champion

(May 2016)
When cancer killed Joe Falcaro in 1951, he had been calling himself Bowling's Undefeated Match Game Champion for twenty-two years. That billing was open to dispute, but Chesty Joe did have a point. No one ever took away his title on the lanes. A gun did that.

He'd won the championship from Joe Scribner in a 60-game set in 1929. Falcaro was a New Yorker, knew about publicity, and knew that being the champ was worth much more than being an ex-champ. So after beating Scribner in a rematch, he concentrated on socking away the dollars from endorsements and exhibitions, while refusing all challenges. "Go get a reputation first," he'd snarl at would-be opponents.

Early in 1933, a group of Eastern proprietors decided to blast Falcaro into action. They announced a series of elimination tournaments to provide a challenger for the champion. With the Depression getting deeper and money getting scarcer, Falcaro agreed to the plan.

Joe Miller of Buffalo won the eliminations. On February 23 the contract for the championship match was finalized. Falcaro and Miller would bowl 80 games, spread over eight 10-game blocks, at eight different houses in six cities. The opening block was set for the evening of March 31, in Philadelphia.

What happened next was reported on the front page of the *Brooklyn Daily Eagle*. On the afternoon of March 30, the day before the big match, Falcaro emerged from a house on 31st Drive in the Astoria section of Queens, to be confronted by a man named Frank Mazzola. With hardly a preamble, Mazzola pulled a pistol and shot Falcaro in the groin.

The street was crowded with children from a nearby school. Amid the screams and chaos Mazzola tried to get away, but was tackled by a passerby. Police arrived and placed Mazzola under arrest for felonious assault. Falcaro was taken to St. John's Hospital.

The reason for Mazzola's attack came out in court two weeks later. Mazzola had been serving a prison stretch, and thought Falcaro had been paying too much attention to the estranged Mrs. Mazzola. According to Mazzola, Falcaro had reached for a gun when they'd met in front of the wife's home on 31st Drive. Mazzola claimed he'd shot Falcaro in self-defense.

By then Falcaro was out of the hospital and declined to pursue the case. Mazzola was sent to the Welfare Island jail after pleading guilty to a reduced charge of illegal firearm possession. The reports about him end there.

Meanwhile, the bowling promoters were doing some hasty improvising. Instead of waiting for Falcaro to recover, they matched Miller against Stewart Watson, who'd won a Chicago elimination and was scheduled to meet the winner of the Falcaro-Miller match. When Miller defeated Watson in May, the promoters proclaimed Miller the new match game champion. That didn't set well with Falcaro. He sent a press release to forty-one newspapers that he was still the champion, and that the Miller-Watson match was nothing more than a "pot game."

Now things get fuzzy. One report said that the promoters got Falcaro to sign a statement surrendering his title. There was also a story that Miller would bowl Falcaro to settle the matter. The match didn't come off, and Falcaro was soon reasserting his claim. In February 1934 the Bowling Proprietors Association of America assumed control of the match game championship, recognizing Miller as champ. If Falcaro wanted a crack at the title, he'd have to enter future eliminations, like any other bowler.

He never did. And to the chagrin of the BPAA, Falcaro continued to cash in as the Undefeated Match Game Champion. He branched out into magazine articles, an instruction book, movie shorts, and the first-ever bowling television program. He was the subject of feature stories in *The New Yorker* and *The Saturday Evening Post*.

Joe Falcaro became the highest-paid bowler in the world. So in the end, did it really matter whether his title was official or bogus?

Index

Page numbers in ***bold italics*** indicate pages with illustrations.

ABC 1, 3, 4, 8, 9, 12, 13, 14, 40, 53, 54, 56, 68, 69, 92, 118, 124–130, 140, 141, 142, 154, 161, 166, 168, 174, 177, 198, 211, 212, 221
ABC Bulletin 222
ABC Tournament 5, 6, 7, 8, 9, 10, 11, 13, 16, 17, 18, 19, 20, 22, 23, 24, 30, 31, 33, 34, 36, 37, 41, 42, 45, 48, 49, 56, 60, 63, 68, 70, 77, 78, 79, 81, 82, 83, 84, 91, 92, 93, 95–97, 98, 101, 102, 104, 105, 125, 131, 133, 137, 142, 144, 151, 152, 153, 154, 156–157, 158, 162, 164, 165, 166, 167, 173, 174, 178, 192, 193, 195, 197, 198, 205, 206–208, 211
Adamek, Donna 151
The Adventures of Robin Hood 81
The Adventures of Superman 192
Agee, Dick 200–201
Airport Bowl 118
Alger, Horatio 159
All-American Trio (team) 79
Allen, Bill 155
Allen's Bowling Alleys 60
Allison, Glenn 61, 85, 210–212
All-Sports Hand Conditioner 100, 138
All-Star Tournament 6, 18, 34, 37, 47, 48, 49, 53, 58, 60, 62, 64, 68, 69, 70, 100, 105, 115, 130, 131, 139, 140, 149, 160, 162, 164, 167, 172, 173, 175, 178, 179, 185, 186, 188, 205, 211, 215, 216, 223
American Bowling Congress *see* ABC
American Royal Building 193
AMF 86, 102, 103–104, 139, 146, 154, 155, 175, 195
The Andy Griffith Show 40
Andy Rock Lanes 74
Angel, Harry 165
Animal House 110
Anson, Cap 82, 96, 144
Anthony, Earl 63, 75, 131, 141, 147, 178–180, ***180***, 184, 210
Arcade Lanes 60, 69
Archer, Jimmy 145
Archer-35th Recreation 60, 181, 183
Arledge, Roone 132

Armitage Recreation 31
Asher, Barry 18
Asplund, Harold 72
Astroth, Joe 145
Atlantic Coast Tournament 115
Aulby, Mike 75
Avenue Recreation 44, 60
Avondale Arcade 31

BaseBowl Championship 146
Baumgarten, Elmer 32, 56, 93
Bedford Rest 94
Beethoven Hall 60, 124, 125, 127, 136
Belushi, John 110
Bender, Paul 94
Benkovic, Frank 9
Benny, Jack 91, 173
Bensinger, Benjamin 56
Bensinger, Moses 125
Bensinger's Randolph Recreation 26, 57, 60
Berle, Milton 121–123, ***123***
Berlin, Mike 183
Berra, Yogi 122, 145, 213
Better Bowling: How It's Done 46
Beverly Recreation 203
Biasetti Steak House (team) 170
The Big Lebowski 61
The Big Three (team) 82–84
Billick, George 40, 70
Bill's Junior All-Stars (team) 156, 157
Billy Hardwick's All-Star Lanes 206
Biondolillo, Jack 86
Blackstone, James T. 13
Blakely, Susan 111, 112
Blong Classic 100
Blouin, Ed "Pop" 22, 115
Blouin, Jimmy 5, 21–29, ***23***, 31, 32, 115, 159
Bluth, Ray 47, 84, 117–119, ***119***, 140, 177, 223
Bodis, Joe 158
Bomar, Buddy 14, 40–43, ***41***, 46–48, ***48***, 55, 74, 78, 84, 86, 87, 99, 100, 103, 140, 162, 167, 173, 177, 182, 183, 195, 196

227

Bonds, Barry 146
Boudreau, Lou 146
Bowl Haven Lanes 60, 111
Bowl the Professor 33, 107–109
Bowl to Win 152
Bowler's Handbook 100
Bowlers Journal 1, 2, 4, 9, 10, 19, 21, 24, 31, 32, 37, 49, 50, 56, 57, 86, 89, 93, 102, 105, 114, 116, 145, 146, 150, 160, 165, 167, 174, 181, 185, 204, 213, 216
The Bowler's Journal (New York) 79, 81, 94, 127, 134, 136
Bowlers Journal All-Stars (team) 31, 32
Bowlers Journal Tournament 6, 19
Bowling 205
Bowling Alone: America's Declining Social Capital 4
Bowling Hall of Fame 1, 6, 8, 10, 19, 21, 31, 34, 37, 48, 70, 74, 83, 91, 102, 105, 131, 147, 154, 155, 196, 211
Bowling Museum 1, 189
Bowling Palace 175
Bowling Proprietors Association of America *see* BPAA
Bowling Stars 77
Bowling Writers Association of America 167
The Bowlium 76
Bowl-O-Drome Recreation 60
BPAA 31, 47, 146, 173, 226
BPAA Doubles Match Game Championship 18, 34, 149, 152, 164, 173, 177, 178, 223
BPAA Individual Match Game Championship *see* Match Game Championship (Individual)
BPAA Team Match Game Championship 7, 20, 34, 42, 57–59, 62, 99, 117, 152, 160, 223
Braatz, Harvey 211
Branca, Ralph 146
Brandt, Allie 60, 210–212
Brill, Frank 23, 72, 96, 137, 147
Bronx Central Recreation 7, 8
Brooklyn Daily Eagle 225
Brosius, Ed 58
Bruck, Nick 22–23, 25, 27, 31, 56, 150
Brunswick 25, 48, 81, 83, 95, 97, 103–104, 125, 159, 171, 173, 174, 186, 189–191, 202
Brunswick All-Stars (team) 7
Brunswick Mineralites (team) 15
Brunswick: The Story of an American Company from 1845 to 1985 125
Brunswick World Open 197
Bryson, Robert H. 128
Budweiser Beer (Chicago team) 163
Budweiser Beer (St. Louis team) 41, 42, 43, 61, 64, 116–120, *119*, 131, 140, 200, 204, 223, 224

Buffalo Evening News 38, 39
Bujack, Fred 58, 59
Bunetta, Bill *41*, 42, 47, 58, 83, 84, 216
Burkett, John 147
Burton, Nelson, Jr. "Bo" 112, 158
Burton, Nelson, Sr. 62, 89, 158–159, *158*, 182, 196

Cain, C.J. 114
Calder, Ace 53–55, 72, 91
California Bombers (team) 195
California Junior Bowling Championship 192
Campi, Lou 72, 83
Candiotti, Tom 146
Cantaline, Anita 161, 175, 188
Capitol Recreation 60
Capone, Al 43, 44
Carlson, Adolph 74, 170, 171, 182
Carter, Don 4, 10, 63–65, *65*, 69, 77, 78, 83, 94, 100, 103, 105, 106, 117–119, *119*, 131, 139, 140, 141, 147, 175, 184, 199–201, 205, 213–214, 223, 224
Carter, LaVerne 100
Carter, Pete 152
Caruana, Frank 116
Cassio, Marty 171
Castellano, Graz 62, 91, 162
Central Alleys 82
Central States Tournament 27
Cermak, A.J. 50
Chamberlain, Wilt 122
Chambers-Detroit (team) 115
Champion of Champions Tournament 105
Championship Bowling 14, 55, 63, 68, 76, 77, 90, 94, 103, 104, 133, 147, 155, 160, 161, 162, 174, 192, 215
Chaplin, Charlie 166
Charles, Dick 213–218
Chase, Bob 211
Chene-Trombly Recreation 68
Chiang Kai-shek, Madame 222
Chicago Bowling Association Tournament 30–31, 144, 165
Chicago Classic League 16, 19, 33, 40, 42, 50, 84, 100, 165, 169–170
Chicago Coliseum 25, 26, 60
Chicago Heights Recreation 60
Chicago Herald 115
Chicago Herald-Examiner Women's Bowling Tournament 32
Chicago Inter-Ocean 95
Chicago Match Game Championship 87, 195
Chicago Post 95
Chicago Sports Hall of Fame 178
Chicago Sun-Times 133
Chicago Tribune 32, 95
The Cincinnati Kid 158

Index 229

Cioffi, Lou 170
Claro 138
Clause, Frank 40, 74, 121
Clemente, Roberto 130
Cleveland Kegler 76
Cleveland Match Game Championship 194
Cleveland Public Auditorium 60
Clingen, John J. 23
Cobb, Ty 148, 149
Collier, Chuck 14–15
Collor, Mark 183–184
The Color of Money 113
Colwell, Paul 210
Comiskey, Charles 144
Conti, Bill 112
Coy, Eddie 51
Crest Lanes 60
Crimmins, Johnny 74, 76, 172

Dallas Broncos (team) 86, 214, 216, 218
Daumit, Harry 47, 99
Davis, Dave 179, 209
Daw, Charley 70, 182
Day, Ned 14, 33, 34, 40, 42, 47, 49, 61, 63, 74, 84, 89, 93, 102, 103, 131, 138, 167, 170–174, *172*, 182, 196–197
Day, Ned, Jr. 196–197
Dean, Harry 192
Del-Mar Recreation 61
DeLuca, Buddy 183
Dempsey, Gladys 52
Dempsey, Jack 121
Denver Bowling Company 61
Denver Open 208
Desperate Characters 145
Detroit Recreation 61, *66*, 66–68
Detroit Thunderbirds (team) 214, 216, 217, 218
DeVito, Dom 32, 182
Dewey, George 134, 136
Diamond Café 61, 144
DiCaprio, Leonardo 82
DiMaggio, Joe 63, 140
Dom DeVito Classic 17, 203
Don Carter Bowling Gloves (team) 120, 224
Don Carter 300 Bowling Slacks 139
Dreamer 45, 60, 111–113
Du-Bowl Tournament 100
Dugay, Al 76
Dunn, Larry 181
Durant, William C. 219–220
Durham Open 87
Dykes, Jimmy 145

E&B Beer (team) 34, 57–59, 62, 204
Earp, Wyatt 6, 92
Easter, Sarge 17–19, 74
Ebbets, Charles H. 129, 144

Eberl, Don 170
Ebonite 16, 45, 46
Edward, Prince of Wales 193
Eisenhower, Mamie 93
Elias, Eddie 155, 209, 210, 215
Elkins, Red 74
Ellis, Don *41*, 42, 47, 102, 121–122
Ennis, Del 145
Esposito, Frank 62
Evergreen Towers Bowl 145, 203, 204

Faetz, Leo 165
Faetz, Matt, Jr. 165
Faetz, Matt, Sr. 77, 115
Faetz-Niesen Recreation 61, 77–78, 100, 177
Falcaro, Joe *11*, 45, 61, 72, 151, 158, 225–226
Falcaro Recreation 61
Falkenberg, Cy 144
Falstaff Beer (team) 20, 40–43, *41*, 47, 131, 149, 162, 204
Fanatorium 61, 185
Faragalli, Lindy 74, 78
Fazio, Buzz 14, 43, 65, 74, 101, 147–150, *148*, 151, 152, 153, 214
Feller, Bob 100
Fidelias (team) 7
Fifty Greatest Players in PBA History 205
FIQ Tournament 130
Firestone, Harvey 155
Firestone Tournament of Champions *see* PBA Tournament of Champions
Fitzsimmons, Freddie 145
Flesch, Bill 47, 165
Fliger, Joe 192
Floriss Lanes 42, 61, 117–118, 200
Flynn, Errol 81
Ford, Gerald 188
Ford, Henry 66
Foremsky, Skee 179
Fort Lewis 70–72
Fort Worth Panthers (team) 214, 216
Fosberg, Ernest 61, 191–192
Fourth of July Singles Tournament 152
Fox, Nellie 145
Fraenkle, George 79
Freddie Fitzsimmons Recreation 145
Fresno Bombers (team) 195, 216, 217, 218
Friedgen, George 221–222

Gabby Hartnett Recreation 145
Garagiola, Joe 145
Garms, Shirley 176, 186–187
Gazzolo, Larry 99
General Motors 219
Genesee Arcade 38, 39, 61
Gengler, Count 13, 60, 67, 72, *73*, 113–116

George London Dream Tournament 195
Germania Alleys 198
Gersonde, Russ 182
Gibbs, Virgil 211
Gibson, Therm 58, 59, 61, 84, 91, 92, 121–123, *123*, 212–213
Gifford, Stan "Mighty Mouse" *41*, 42, 75
Gil Hodges Lanes 145
Gleason, Jackie 113
Globe Bowl 61
Glover, Howard 50
Golembiewski, Billy 74, 104–106, *153*, 214
Grange, Red 130
Grant, Cary 171
Great and Greatest Tournament 48, 196
Great Lakes Naval Training Camp 57
Greater New York Individual Tournament 7
Greene, Ethel 67–68
Grofe, Ferde 200
Grzelak, Vince 170
Gworek, John 207–208

Habetler, Rudy 15, 74, 100, 169, 170
Habetler Bowl 16, 103, 169, 170
Hables, Edna 193
Haefner, Ray 117
Hagerty, Jack 61
Hagerty's Interurban 61
Halftown, Chief 201–203
Hamilton County League 193
Hamm's Beer (team) 16, 19
Hardwick, Billy 204–206, *206*
Harold Lloyds (team) 167
Harrelson, Woody 150
Harris, Bill 193
Harris, Sydney J. 49
Harris, Whitey 74, 91, 117–119, *119*, 223
Hartnett, Gabby 145
Harvey, Paul 125
Hawks, Howard 43, 44
Hearn, Chick 121–122
Hecht, Ben 43, 44
Heerman, Bill 13
Heil, Julius 171
Heil Products (team) 9, 171
Heneman, Dell 189
Hennessey, Tom 83, 91, 117–120, *119*, 222–225, *224*
Hermann, Cone 116, 117, 120
Hermann Undertakers (team) 61, 116–120, 223
Herrmann, Garry 127–129, 144, 192
Hitler, Adolf 44, 74
Hitt, Bob 214
Hodges, Gil 145
Hoffman Lanes 183
Hogan, Ben 63
Hollywood Star Lanes 61

Holman, Marshall 205
Holmes, Ray 211
Homel, Leonard 213–217
Hoover, Dick 91
Hoppe, Willie 96
How to Be a Better Bowler 104, 106
Howard, George *153*, 155
Howard, Judge 57
Howley, Peter 25
Hrbek, Kent 146
Hudson, Tommy 207
Hudson Recreation 61, 68
Hudson River Suite 200–201
The Hustler 111, 113, 150
Hustlers Tournament 70
Huston, Irvin 66–68

Illinois Bowling Association 126, 134
International Bowling Association Tournament (Minnesota group) 32, 165
International Bowling Tournament (1900) 62, 133–137
International Tournament (Thum group) 9, 45, 171, 199
Interstates (team) 95
Irwin, Red 74

Jackpot Bowling 37, 63, 120–123, 212–213, 215
Jackson, Lowell 49
Jellison, A.C. 13, 211
Jerry Peck Classic 203
Jockey Cooper (team) 47
Joe Wilman Timer 139
Johari, Azizi 111, 113
Johnny-Behind-the-Deuce 92
Johns, Lee 211
Johnson, Don 112, 179, 208–210, *209*
Johnson, Earl 42, 47, 83, 219
Johnson, Walter "Red" 74
Johnson's Alleys 61
Jones, Bobby 130
Jones, R.D. 96
Jordan, Tom 212
Joseph, Joe 74, 91, 105, *153*, 205
Jouglard, Lee 152, 176
Junker, Dave 156–157

Kaadland Recreation 54, 55
Kaelin, Houdini 74–75
Kafora, Frank 29–33, 73, 91, 144, 145, 150
Kansas City Stars (team) 216, 217
Karlicek, Tony 72, 90
Karloff, Boris 43, 44
Karpf, Samuel 81, 127, 128, 134, 137
Kartheiser, Frank 28
Kathryn Products (team) 47
Kawolics, Eddie 15–17, 47, 58, 91, 169, 170

Index

Kearns, Jim 188
Keaton, Buster 166
Keeley's Half-and-Half (team) 54, 55
Kelsey, George 193
Kennedy, John F. 132
Kiel Auditorium 200
King, Johnny 86, 103, 193–196, *194*, 218
King Louie Bowling Shirts (team) 16, 57–59, 62
Kingpin 150
Kissoff, Joe 74, 91
Klares, Johnny 73, 162
Kleffel, G.K. 222
Kmidowski, Henry 207–208
Knox, Billy 13, 31, 91, 150
Knueppel, Henry 110
Kogan, Rick 125
Koralewski, Barney 38–40, 61
Kostelanetz, Andre 200
Koster, John 6–8, *7*, 72, 79, 96
Kouros, Tom 97
Kovacs, Ernie 162
Kreunz & Quer (team) 90
Kristof, Joe 47, 54, 98–102, *101*, 138, 149
Kristof, June 100, 102
Kristof, Karl 100, 102
Krumske, Paul 33–34, 37, 51, 58, 59, 62, 84, 99, 107–108, *108*, 169, 173
Kulick, Kelly 185, 189
Kwiecien, Bob *153*
Kwolek, Bob 121, 214

Ladewig, Marion 53, 61, 103, 131, 184–189, *187*
LaHabra "300" Bowl 61
Landrum, Don 146
Landry, Pat 212
Langhenry, Godfred 96
Langtry, A.L. 24, 62, 115, 128, 129
Langtry-McBride Bowling Café 113, 114
Larsen, Don 122
Larson, Jack 192
Las Vegas Review-Journal 197
Laudner, Tim 146
Lausche, Charley 49
Lenzen, William "Jake" 164–166
Levine, Louis 32
Levine, Sam 76
Lewis, Jerry 62, 106–108, *108*
Lichthemeyer & Green's Alleys 22
Life 188
Lillard, Bill *41*, 42, 47, 65, 103, 177–178, 223
Limmer, Punk 74
Lindemann, Tony 149, 151–154, *153*, 222–223
Lindsey, Mort 5–6, 24, 25, 26, 62, 74, 91, *91*, 158–159, 182, 193
Lindsey, William J. 50
Linsz Recreation 68

Lippe, Harry 58, 169
Live Stock Press Building 61
Llo-Da-Mar Bowl 61, 167, 168
Lloyd, Harold 61, 130–131, 166–168, *168*
Loch, Larry 76
Lollar, Sherman 145
Lombardi, Vince 106
Long Distance Bowling Championship 94
Los Angeles Toros (team) 162, 214, 216, 217
Lown, Roy "Bing Bong" 75
Lubanski, Ed 18, 76, 147, 149, 151, 152, 162, 174–176, 214, 217, 218
Luby, Dave 4, 24, 114, 116, 181
Luby, Mort, Jr. 1, 97–98, 112, 141, 206, 216, 218, 224
Luby, Mort, Sr. 49, *65*, 99, 116, 171
Luby, Pat 98
Lustre Crème Shampoo (team) 99
Luther, Martin 110
Lutz, Dick 156–157

Mady, Ed 74
Mamie's CATS (team) 93
Mantle, Mickey 121, 122, 146, 213
Marigold Arcade 33
Marino, Hank 8, 10–12, *11*, 25, 28, 31, 32, 37, 57, 61, 62, 131, 145, 150, 167, 171, 182
Marino Open 17
Marino Recreation 62
Martin Kern Missouri Big Three (team) 82
Marx, Groucho 121
Masters Tournament 64, 101, 105, 133, 147, 149, 178, 224
Match Game Championship (Individual) 10, 11, 23, 24–28, 34, 60, 70, 79–81, 171–173, 225–226
Matheson, Tim 110–112
Mazzola, Frank 226
McClaren, Don 117
McCune, Don 163, 170
McCutcheon, Floretta 45, 53, 61, 91, 131
McDowell, Marion 13
McGrath, Mike 179
McGraw, John 61, 144
McGurn, Jack 44, 60
McKeever, Frank 141–143, *143*
McMahon, Helen 36
McMahon, Junie 34–38, *35*, 58, 63, 74, 90, 99, 109, 140, 185
McQueen, Steve 158
Meadowbrook Lanes 216
Meier, George 192
Meister Brau Beer (team) 16, 33, 34, 37, 58
MEK 163
Mercurio, Skang 63, 74

Mesger, Elvin 62, 68–70
Metcalf, Billy 22
Metcalf's Recreation 93
Michaels, Cass 145
Midland Theatre 216
Midwest Singles Tournament 100
Mikiel, Val 50–53, *52*
Mikiel, Vince 51, 99
Miller, Joe 225–226
Miller Lite Beer 65
Milwaukee Journal 93, 114
Monarch Beer (team) 36, 37, 47, 165
Monarch Recreation 82
Monday Night Football 132
Montana, Joe 21
Montauk Alleys 79
Moore, Terry 145
Morningstar, Ora 67
Morrissey, William 185–188
Mueller, Jake 56
Mullen, Edward 93
Muni, Paul 43
Munsingwear (team) 47, 86, 195
Muscular Dystrophy Telethon 106
Musial, Stan 140–141, 145
Mussey's Alleys 96
Mystery Science Theater 3000 131

Nagurski, Bronko 130
Nagy, Steve 50, 78, 86, 91, 103, 105, 149, 161–163, 214
National Bowling Association 126–130
The National Bowling Association (TNBA) 154
National Bowling Association Tournament 5
National Bowling League 19, 64, 86, 149, 153, 162, 195, 212–219, *215*
National Women's Bowling Tournament 96
Nelson, Ray 41
New Jersey State Tournament 36
New York City Drug League 193
New York Gladiator Arena 214, *215*
New York Gladiators (team) 214, 216
New York State Tournament 8
New York Times 19
The New Yorker 226
Newark Recreation Center 62
Newman, Paul 113, 150
Nichols, Kid 145
Nickel, Bob *153*
Niesen, Chet 77
Niesen, Matt 77–78
Noren, Irv 146
Norris, Joe 1, 54, *65*, 67, 70, 74, 96–98, 131–132, 139, 148–149, 160, 169, 170, 176–177, 203, 204
North End Traveling League 54
North Flint Recreation 219–220

Nosseck, Noel 111
Nyack Roofing (team) 8

O'Farrell, Bob 145
Old Fitzgerald (team) 16
Olsens (team) 57
Olympic Alleys 62
Omaha Packers (team) 149, 214, 216, 217
Oppenheim, Morrie 83–88, *85*
Orf, Ray 68, 210–212
Oswald, Lee Harvey 132, 133
Overland Alleys 82

Pabst Blue Ribbon Beer (team) 100
Palace Recreation 62, 68
Palm Beach Recreation 58, 62
Palmer, Arnold 50, 122
Parade 146
Paramus Lanes 62
Pasdeloup, Frank 56, 126
Patriotic Bowling Tournament 55–57, 181
Patterson, Floyd 122
Patterson, Pat 100, 117–119, *119*, 223
PBA 3, 4, 6, 16, 18, 19, 20, 21, 23, 28, 49, 54, 62, 64, 69, 75, 83, 87, 90, 91, 92, 101, 102, 105, 111, 112, 120, 131, 140, 146, 147, 149, 151, 154, 155, 163, 164, 169, 170, 178–180, 195, 201, 204, 205, 208, 210, 213, 215, 218, 224, 225
PBA Doubles Classic 210
PBA National Championship 64, 86–87, 154, 205
PBA Tournament of Champions 62, 111, 179, 185, 205, 208, 209, 210
Peace Evangelical Lutheran Church 109
Pennino, Jim 76
Peoria Auto Parts Recreation 62, 158
Pepsi-Cola (Cincinnati team) 193
Pepsi-Cola (Detroit team) 18
Peters, Carl *153*
Petersen, Louis 25–26, 181–184
Petersen Classic 6, 8, 10, 23, 48, 70, 89, 99, 158, 165, 181–184, 203, 214, 223
Petersen 2-in-1 Tournament 100
Petraglia, Johnny 196, 210
Pfeiffer Beer (team) 105, 121, 162, 175, 195, 214
Phelps, Robert 57
Philadelphia Drug League 193
Pierce, Billy 146
Piet, Tony 204
Pit-Catcher Lanes 145
Pla-Mor Lanes 165
Plankinton Arcade 66
Playboy 111
Playdium 145
Pluckhahn, Bruce 1
Police Gazette 7
Polk City South 62

Index

Potter, Nelson 146
Powell, Junior 91
Presley, Elvis 131–132
Price, Charles 222
Prima Recreation 56
Pritchett, Jess 49
Pro Bowlers Tour 68, 132, 178
Professional Bowlers Association *see* PBA
Pulaski Savings (team) 42, 117, 119
Putnam, Robert D. 4

Quinzi, John 182

Raiders of the Lost Ark 191
Rautenberg, G.H. 128
Ray Schalk's Holiday Team Tournament 145, 201–204
Raybestos-Manhattan Company 163–164
Red Bird Lanes 145
Reidstra, Sam 192
Reycraft, John J. 94
Riccilli, Fred 91, 214
Richard, Carl 42, 43, 91
Ridge Bowl 78; *see also* Faetz-Niesen Recreation
The Right Stuff 112
Ripley's Believe It or Not 13
Ritger, Dick 210
Riviera Lanes 62, 210
Rizzuto, Phil 145
Robertson, Lorne 38, 39
Robinson, Edward G. 158
Robinson, Wilbert 61, 144
Rochez Brothers (team) 117–118
Rocky 112
Rodriguez, Alex "A-Rod" 146
Rogoznica, Andy 74, 170
Rolfe, Bob 57, 115
Roosevelt, Franklin D. 44
Ross, John 94
Rossen, Robert 113
Roth, Mark 89–90
Ruby, Jack 133
Ruth, Babe 130, 146

St. Francis de Sales Rec Center 109
St. John, Jim 19–21, *20*, 218–219
St. John's Evangelical Lutheran Church 109–110
St. Louis Classic League 223
St. Louis Masters League 41, 42, 117
St. Louis Post-Dispatch 128, 200
Salvino, Carmen 38, 83, 86, 87, 151, 155, 175, *177*, 178, 201, 204, 217
San Antonio Cavaliers (team) 153, 216, 217
San Francisco Opera House 200
Sanders, Homer 13

Sandford, Curtis 216
The Saturday Evening Post 226
Sauer, Hank 146
Scarface (1932 film) 43, 44
Schade's Academy 62
Schalk, Ray 145, 203–204
Schanen, Ray 73
Schenkel, Chris 112, 132–133, 209
Schmidt, Gene 78
Schuenemann, Leo 56
Schuetzen Park 62, 134, 136
Schultz, Peter 7
Schutte, Louis F. 134, 136
Schwoegler, Connie 18, 40, *52*, 54, 91, 99, 196
Schwoegler Lanes 17
Scott, Don 154–156
Scott, Everett 144–145, 147
Scott, George C. 113
Scribner, Joe 28, 225
Seavoy, Dale 218
Selbach, Kip 144
77 Sunset Strip 103
Shanghai Bowling Congress 221–222
Shantz, Bobby 145
Shaul, Bill 45–46, 89
Sherman, Sid 14
Showboat Classic 201
Sielaff, Lou 58, 195
Sims, J. Wilbert 155
Sinke, Joe 34
Sixty, Billy 10, 93, 113–114, 150
Sixty, Billy, Jr. 93
Small, Johnny 163–164
Smith, Crook 22
Smith, Harry 72, 149, 204, 205
Smith, Jimmy 8, 24–25, 26–27, 28, 45, 60, 61, 67, 79–81, *80*, 89, 115, 116, 131, 158, 182
Snead, Sam 100
Snell, Bob 109–110
Snyder, Don 213, 216
Soong, Elsie 222
Soutar, Dave 87, 88
Southern California Open 83, 85
Southern California Team Tournament 167
Southern Match Game Championship 223–224
Spalding, Al 125, 144
Spalding, Jim 151
Spalding's Official Bowling Guide 89
Sparando, Tony 171, 182
Spinella, Barney 6
Sport 93
The Sporting News 146
Sports Illustrated 162
Sprague, Howard 38
Squires, C.C. 222
Stafford, Bill 146

Index

Standard (team) 95
Starr, C.K. 96
Stassen, Harold 49
State Fair Recreation 68
Steele, Gus 171
Steers, Harry 81–83, 181, 182
Stefanich, Jim 16, 170, 209
Stein, Louis 125
Stein, Otto 25, 32, 62, 89, 90, 150, 211
Stein Brothers Recreation 62
Stevenson & Schalk Recreation 203
Strike 'n' Spare Lanes 62, 107
Stroh's Beer (team) 60, 105, 149, 152, 153, *153*, 160, 162, 204, 214, 222, 223
Stromberg, William 201
Strong, Fred 81–83
Sullivan Bowl 62, 69, 70
Superba Recreation 79
Sweeney, Dennis 63, 128, 129
Sweeney, Irvin 66–68

Tavern Pale Beer (team) 16, 47
T-Bowl 63
Thoma, Sykes 31, 182
Thompson, W.V. 81–83, 128
Thompson Restaurant (team) 165
Thorpe, Jim 130
Thorson, Bill 96
Thum, Joe 63, 198–199, *199*
Thunderbowl Lanes 219
Timm, Henry 95, 96
TNBA (The National Bowling Association) 154
Tomasch Recreation 63
Tountas, Pete 21
Truman, Harry 173
Twin Cities Skippers (team) 19, 216, 218, 219

Unitas, Johnny 122
United Bowling Clubs 134, 198
U.S. Open Tournament 210
Universal Bowling Academy 79
Universal Bowling Stores 107
Universal Recreation 30, 31
University Lanes 63
Uptown Melody Lanes 58
USBC 1, 4

Varipapa, Andy *11*, 14, 37, 47, 54, 131, 158, 170, 176–178, *177*
Voorhies, Johnny 72, 79–81, 96, 192

Wabash Recreation 56
The Wall Street Journal 213
Ward, Walter 74
Warden, Jack 110
Washington Alleys 63
Watson, Stewart 226
Waukegan Open 21
Wayne, John 46, 47
Weber, Dick 42, 63, 69, 75, 83, 91–92, 100, 104, 105, 106, 112, 117–119, *119*, 131, 139–141, 179, 182, 184, 205, 210, 223
Weinstein, Mitzi 211
Weinstein, Sam 106–108, 163–164
Welsbach Building 63, 95
Welu, Billy 65, 117, 132–133, *135*, 175, 209, 213
Wene, Sylvia 188
Wernicke, Bill 29, 32
Weston, Cowboy 30
White, Sammy 145
White Elephant Bowling Academy 63, 198, 199
White House Bowling Lanes 173
WIBC 3, 4, 63, 129
WIBC Tournament 51, 68
Wilcox, John, Jr. 212
Williams, Bill 58
Williams, Matty 181
Williams, Mitch 146
Williams, Walter Ray 141, 178, 184
Willow Grove Park Lanes 63
Wilman, Joe 7, 36, 37, 50, 70–72, 78, 139, 147, 163, 171
Wilsing, Carl 211
Wilson, "Whispering Joe" 61, 78, 100, 147
Winsberg, Dick 165
Witt, Don 184
Wolf, Fred 104, 147, 159–161, *160*, 174, 186
Wolf, Phil 23, 25, 26, 74
Women's International Bowling Congress *see* WIBC
Worden, Fred 81–83
World Classic Tournament 5, 25–27, 31–32, 60
World's Invitational Tournament 19, 20, 21, 53, 60, 61, 64, 68, 105, 131, 175, 185, 188, 195, 216
Wronski, C.J.B. 30–31
Wurm's Recreation 52

Young, George 58

Zaharias, Babe 130
Zahn, Wayne 209
Zicha, Gregg 184
Ziern Antiques (team) 223
Zikes, Les, Jr. 16, 170, 207
Zikes, Les, Sr. 170
Zimmerman House Alleys 193
Zunker, Gil 8–10, 90–91

www.ingramcontent.com/pod-product-compliance
Ingram Content Group UK Ltd.
Pitfield, Milton Keynes, MK11 3LW, UK
UKHW041941140426
5217IPUK00014B/599